Calling Out Liberty

★ ★ ★

Calling Out Liberty

★ ★ ★ ★ ★ ★ ★ ★ ★ ★ ★

THE STONO SLAVE REBELLION AND THE
UNIVERSAL STRUGGLE FOR HUMAN RIGHTS

Jack Shuler

University Press of Mississippi
Jackson

www.upress.state.ms.us

The University Press of Mississippi is a member of the Association of American University Presses.

Copyright © 2009 by University Press of Mississippi
All rights reserved
Manufactured in the United States of America

∞

Library of Congress Cataloging-in-Publication Data

Shuler, Jack.
Calling out liberty : the Stono slave rebellion and the universal struggle for human rights / Jack Shuler.
p. cm.
Includes bibliographical references and index.
ISBN 978-1-60473-273-3 (cloth : alk. paper) 1. Slave insurrections—South Carolina—Stono—History—18th century. 2. Stono (S.C.)—Race relations—History—18th century. 3. South Carolina—Race relations—History—18th century. 4. Slaves—South Carolina—Social conditions—18th century. 5. African Americans—Civil rights—History—18th century. 6. Slavery—South Carolina—History—18th century. I. Title.
F279.S84S48 2009
975.7'02—dc22   2009001937

British Library Cataloging-in-Publication Data available

For Mary Louise Fairey,
who taught me to be patient, listen, and always ask good questions.
I miss you.

PROSPERO: How now? Moody? What is 't thou canst demand?
ARIEL: My liberty.

—William Shakespeare, *The Tempest*

CONTENTS

★ ★ ★

Acknowledgments - xi -

Introduction - 3 -

Chapter 1. Carolina's Colonial Architecture and the Age of Rights - 11 -

Chapter 2. Dissension in the Ranks
Regarding, Evaluating, and Revealing Slavery in Eighteenth-Century America - 35 -

Chapter 3. Claiming Rights
The Stono Rebels Strike for Liberty - 66 -

Chapter 4. Negro Acts
Communication and African American Declarations of Independence
- 96 -

Chapter 5. The Heirs of Jemmy
Slave Rebels in Nineteenth-Century African American Fiction
- 116 -

Chapter 6. Plantation Traditions
Racism and the Transformation of the Stono Narrative - 141 -

Chapter 7. Doin' de Right
The Persistence of the Stono Narrative - 167 -

CONTENTS

Notes - 184 -

Bibliography - 195 -

Index - 211 -

ACKNOWLEDGMENTS

★ ★ ★

W. E. B. DU BOIS WROTE *The Souls of Black Folk*, that seminal work in American literature, while teaching at Atlanta University and working, I'm quite sure, under difficult circumstances. I note this in order to recognize all of those who toiled before me; without the determination, intelligence, and perseverance of thousands of scholars, artists, and other advocates for human rights, I wouldn't have a story to tell. I honor and respect those human rights researchers who are doing that work right now.

I must begin by acknowledging those historians whose work on Stono and early American history and culture has inspired me and shaped this book, in particular, Peter Wood, Mark M. Smith, and John K. Thornton.

Thank you to my friends at the University Press of Mississippi. Thank you, Seetha. And thanks to Karen Johnson.

I owe special thanks to those who read this work as it took shape. Thank you to my colleague Katherine Jager. Thank you, Mark Noonan, for your many insights into American literature and culture. Thank you, Fred Porcheddu, for reading and cheering me on. And, of course, thanks to all of my friends in the English Department at Denison University.

Robert Reid-Pharr, Jon-Christian Suggs, and David Reynolds helped me get the ball rolling and connect the dots. I count myself lucky to have worked with y'all while studying at the Graduate Center of the City University of New York. Finally, thanks to the students at Brooklyn College and Denison University who have been my most thorough and honest "readers."

Many thanks to those who helped me find what I was looking for: Craig Keeney, Chuck Lesser, Mike Coker, Jane Aldrich, and all of the librarians

ACKNOWLEDGMENTS

at Denison University. Special thanks to Heather Lyle and Pam Magelaner for last-minute assists.

Thank you to the folks in the Stono and Charleston area who blessed me with their time, energy, and knowledge: Shawn Halifax, Rep. Robert Brown, Curtis Inabinett, Marvin Dulaney, Obi Kalu, Desinique Robinson, and John Boineau.

Finally, many thanks to my family and friends. Y'all form the community that shaped the thinking behind this book and taught me to do unto others as I would have others do unto me. Jane and John Shuler, thank you for constantly reinforcing that golden rule. And Ceciel, you have inspired me and supported me throughout this process. Thank you.

Calling Out Liberty

★ ★ ★

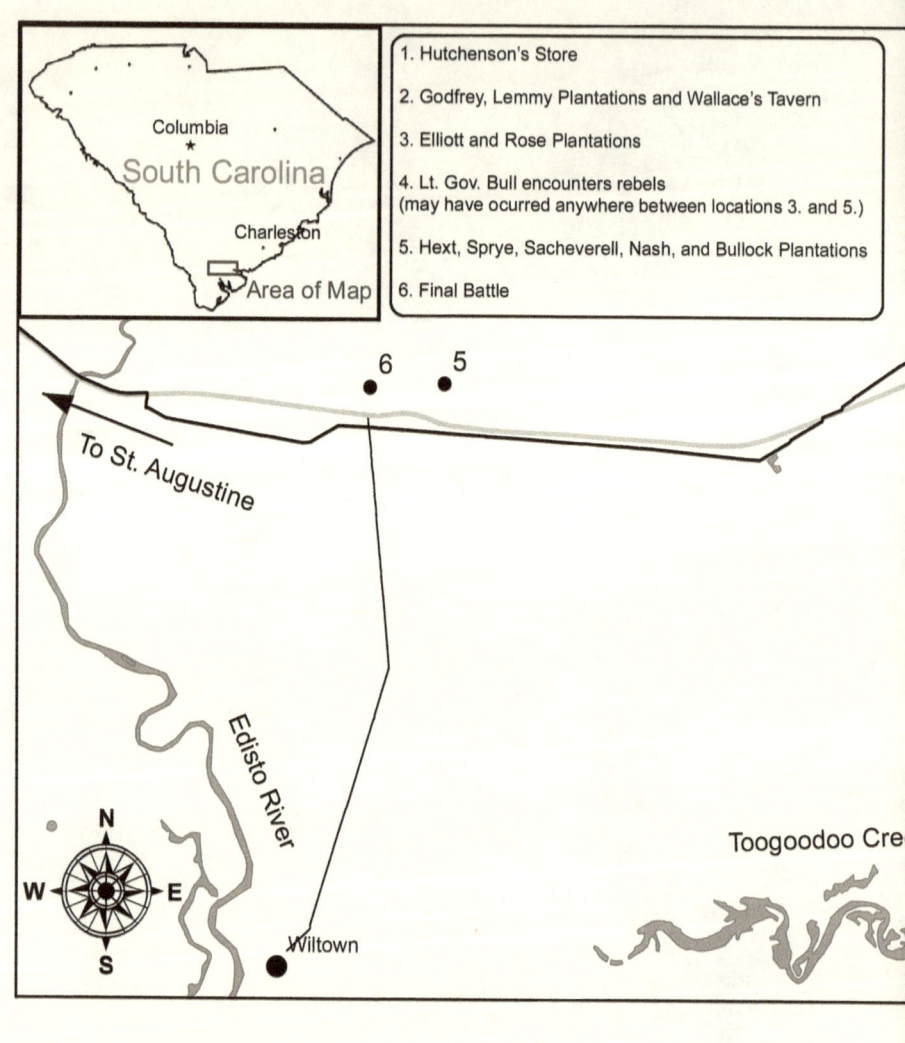

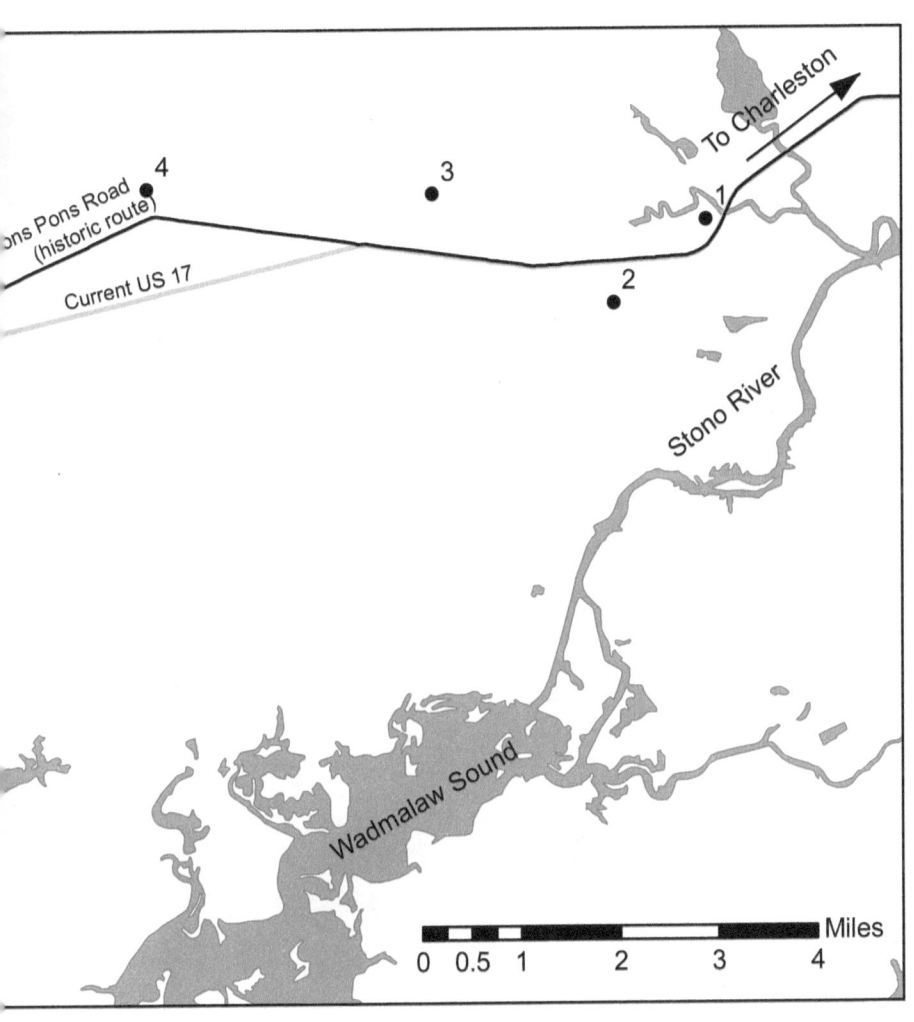

STONO REBELLION ROUTE, SEPTEMBER 9, 1739

Map by Brian Heagney
Sources: Tiger (2000); Shawn Halifax

INTRODUCTION

★ ★ ★

STORIES SHAPE LIVES AND PERSPECTIVES. Thus, how history is told generation after generation is crucial. I am reminded of an event from my own childhood in South Carolina. I cannot recall the exact circumstances, but on one occasion a friend's father told me that, in fact, African Americans had it easy during slavery. When I told my father about this conversation, he was apparently disturbed and decided this was a teachable moment. He took me to the county courthouse and showed me a list etched into a wall of all the men from Orangeburg County who had died fighting in the Civil War.

"Son," he said, "do you see how many Shulers are up on that wall?"

"Yes," I said, "almost more than any other last name."

"That's right. And do you know why?"

I thought for a moment but could not figure it out.

"I'll tell you," my father said. "They were either bad shots, or they were fighting for the wrong cause. I reckon it's the latter."

But there are other stories about slavery. One goes like this: on Sunday, September 9, 1739, a group of Kongolese slaves broke into a storehouse about fifteen miles south of Charles Town in the colony of South Carolina. The slaves, now rebels, killed the two storekeepers and took all the guns and powder they could carry. Led by a man named either Jemmy or Cato, the rebels moved southward and killed about twenty-three white colonists, destroyed property, recruited other slaves to join them, and marched toward Spanish Florida, where they expected to find freedom. Before the day ended, they encountered, of all people, South Carolina's Lieutenant Governor William Bull, who hastened away to alert the local militia. In the meantime, the rebels were spotted in an open field dancing and playing drums—a call to arms, a preparation for battle. They were soon surrounded by the militia, and in the battle that ensued militia members noted that many among the rebels fought like well-trained soldiers, using flags and fighting in formation. And yet they were outnumbered. The rebellion was put down and many slaves were executed. Some of the rebels escaped into the woods; one was not captured for several years.

Soon after the Stono Rebellion, the South Carolina government passed a comprehensive legal code called the Negro Act that helped to re-enforce white power in the colony. This act placed strict controls over the ability of slaves to communicate with one another: the pass system was codified; literacy and drums were outlawed; and blacks could no longer congregate in public. The only positive provisions for slaves were limits on workloads and a ban on the most severe punishments. But the institution of slavery was not abandoned by any means. This legal code, a result of the rebellion, would become a model for slave codes in the American colonies and in the United States for years to come, providing another pillar of support for the plantation regime.

Few primary sources on the Stono Rebellion survive, but those that do reveal it to have been an event of some significance for South Carolina and the slave trade—a moment of uncertainty and of choices made that caused widespread reverberations in the Atlantic world. This rebellion had international political implications: white colonists believed that the Spanish, foes of the British, were offering slaves their freedom in Florida if they rebelled. However, displacing the blame for rebellion may also have been a way for South Carolina's colonial government to assuage fears of future rebellion and negate perceived risk factors of trading with the colony. Disease was taking a toll on South Carolina's population, and the colony needed to attract new residents; frequent slave rebellions would not serve as an enticing selling point. After the rebellion was put down, the Benjamin Franklin–supported *South Carolina Gazette* chose to ignore the event, despite the fact that it was one of the largest slave rebellions in North America to date.

But word of the rebellion leaked. Correspondence from colonists before and after the rebellion depicts the shaky social and political climate of South Carolina and, in essence, of the European colonial design in general. Letters by Robert Pringle and Andrew Leslie, a minister for the Society for Propagation of the Gospel in Foreign Parts, cross the ocean and reveal heightened colonial anxieties and desires for swift retribution. Reports of the event from the South Carolina Commons House of Assembly are

INTRODUCTION

dramatic, taking a step beyond simple reportage: "On this occasion every breast was filled with concern. Evil brought home to us within our very doors awakened the attention of the most unthinking.... With regret we bewailed our peculiar case, that we could not enjoy the benefits of peace like the rest of mankind and that our own industry should be the means of taking from us all the sweets of life and of rendering us liable to the loss of our lives and fortune" ("Report" 84). The writer, of course, implies that "mankind" is white. Such biases pose a problem for any analysis of this rebellion because in most reports the white author and white human are privileged as both subject and actor. This raises questions about the presence of human rights in a colony that would, thirty-seven years later, declare itself part of a project to secure the inalienable rights of all human beings.

What then are human rights? In short, human rights are those rights or entitlements one has simply by virtue of being human.[1] Human rights are prior and above civil rights, which are contingent on one being a citizen of a country. They are moral claims, ultimate protections of human dignity. Discussions of contemporary human rights issues often begin with the Universal Declaration of Human Rights adopted by the United Nations on December 10, 1948. I wish to analyze the ways in which this concept of human rights develops in the eighteenth century—in particular, the patterns and ways in which individuals talk about and describe human rights. Who can claim human rights? Who is considered "human"? And where did the idea come from originally? More often than not, human rights scholars and policy makers offer the writings of figures of the European Enlightenment as default sources for contemporary human rights discourse. In a telling transcript from the 1965 Second International Conference on the European Convention on Human Rights in Vienna, Ulrich Scheuner notes that human rights did not emerge first from international law but "within constitutional law of individual States" (214). He notes that the emergence of these laws—which were, first of all, protections of property and self and, later, protections of religious practices—is directly linked to the "natural rights" traditions of the seventeenth and eighteenth centuries. Scheuner adds that these protections were enhanced by the work of Locke and Rousseau and through the constitutions of the United States and the French national assembly.

More recently, in 2007, historian Lynn Hunt's *Inventing Human Rights: A History* explores the development of empathy or sentiment in the Western world and its relationship to the "invention" of human rights in the eighteenth century. Hunt argues that as Europeans and U.S. Americans became enamored with art and literature that manipulated the sentiments of readers and viewers, they armed themselves with the philosophies of John Locke and Cesare Beccaria to denounce acts of violence and abuse committed against human beings. It was then that our modern concept of human rights was born. Certainly, the Enlightenment fostered a kind of liberal democracy, but the abuse of the rights of women, children, and indigenous peoples, not to mention the Atlantic slave trade, was still painfully apparent during and after the Enlightenment's heyday. Micheline Ishay notes that "the Enlightenment legacy represents little more than an imperialist masquerade aimed at subduing the rest of the world under the pretense of promoting universality" (8). I hope to suggest ways we might alter and enrich our understanding of the origins of contemporary human rights. The belief that all humans have rights and an inherent dignity that must be respected is not a concept that originated only in the writings of Locke or Rousseau. Human rights discourse has many and varied roots. The plethora of cultures and nations that have signed on to contemporary human rights conventions is just one indication of this.

However, the history of the development of human rights in the eighteenth century too often excludes the contributions of poor people, women, and slaves—especially slaves. Indeed, in the eighteenth century black slaves were not often considered participants in or contributors to the developing human rights conversation. Laurence Mordekhai Thomas acknowledges the difficulty that eighteenth-century whites may have had imagining blacks as speaking subjects because, "at the time of American Slavery, Africa was not thought to have had a central role in the history of moral and intellectual Western thought—not even, in fact, the role of a substantial footnote" (122). Perhaps this was once the case, but this does not excuse contemporary erasures of the role slaves played in shaping human rights discourse. It is not that they could not speak; it is that popular history has written them out of the rights discussion. Can we learn anything about human rights through an examination of the Stono Rebellion? Could it serve as a possible source for human rights discourse? If so, how do we "read" this eighteenth-century event?

Contemporary scholarship on Stono by Peter Wood, John K. Thornton, Edward Pearson, Donald Wax, and Mark M. Smith is rooted in the discipline of history and focuses on the possible connections of agriculture, language, religion, Spanish Florida, colonial newspapers, and gender roles to the rebellion and its aftermath. This book, however, is not that of an historian per se, though it owes much to the exceptional work of the above-mentioned scholars. As someone rooted in literary and cultural studies, I have, I believe, examined the Stono Rebellion from a different angle. While keeping a close eye on the historical record, I have also been open to the evidence of Stono Rebellion resonances that surface in creative literature and oral narratives. Thus, the questions I wish to answer are rooted in the work of many academic disciplines: How did the rebels communicate among themselves and decide to act? What was their intent? Where does this event fit into what we traditionally think of as a "century of revolutions"? How does it connect with the broader Atlantic world? And what does Stono say about how we imagine human rights?

I respond to these questions from a literary studies perspective by exploring the Stono Rebellion's relationship to the *discourse* of natural or human rights in the eighteenth, nineteenth, and twentieth centuries as well as in the present moment. As I interrogate the intersections of theory and intellectual history, I will make much use of this term "discourse." My understanding of the word comes from Michel Foucault as filtered through the work of Edward Said. Said describes "discourse" as a method or "style for domination, restructuring, and having authority over" another (3). As he demonstrates in *Orientalism*, a discourse can shape material realities by connecting institutions of power to language. It is a textual practice that becomes a political and social reality, a method of domination practiced with "enormously systematic discipline." In this manner, Said cogently demonstrates how an intellectual concept—the way something is written about and discussed—can affect the lives of human beings in often negative ways. John Storey clarifies this point, noting that "the 'truth' of a discourse depends less on what is said and more on who is saying it and when and where it is said" (98). Language is never neutral; it has the ability to define as well as to exclude (96–97).

In this manner, a discourse *controls* the ways in which something is described, distinguished, and discussed. "Control" in this sense "means, rather, control by the power of positive production: that is, a kind of power that generates certain kinds of questions, placed within systems that legitimate, support, and answer those questions; a kind of power that, in the process, includes within its systems all those it produces as agents capable of acting within them" (Bove 54). This is a significant point: a discourse, an exchange of experiences of power, does not have to be negative. Foucault speaks to this problem, acknowledging that too often we describe power in negative terms; power is more ambiguous than that (*Discipline* 194). On the surface the idea of human rights appears to be a positive and progressive one; but, as we shall see, it has always been a site of contest. In "The Discourse on Language," Foucault claims that discourse will often disguise reality, writing, "I am supposing that in every society the production of discourse is at once controlled, selected, organised and redistributed according to a certain number of procedures, whose role is to avert its powers and its dangers, to cope with chance events, and to evade its ponderous, awesome materiality" (216). The "powers" and "dangers" of human rights discourse are that it might get out of hand or out of the hands of those controlling the discourse. All discourses are open to transformation, resistance, or actualization. As "enlightened" intellectuals theorized concepts of human rights in the seventeenth and eighteenth centuries, could they have imagined that African slaves had similar ideas? Could they have imagined slaves as shapers of the discourse of human rights?

Events often take place that are jarring and cause discursive formations to shift and momentarily transform. Is such a moment when a group of enslaved human beings kill their masters and fight for their freedom? Are they asserting their right to shape discursive practices in the public sphere? I believe so. Human rights discourse is often shaped by the actions of human beings, actions that seep into the collective cultural conscious, raising questions and asking the public to seek redress, to seek solutions. Why would a young man stand in the way of a tank at Tiananmen Square? Why would he do that if he knew the ramifications of such actions? Why would thousands of African Americans risk clubs, water hoses, and German shepherds? Why do human beings, often amidst repressive and violent circumstances, put their bodies, their lives, on the line? Human rights have been articulated in numerous ways throughout history, but it will require some creativity to tease out these moments of articulation from the bins of history and place them within the context of the cultural and literary canon.

I believe the Stono Rebellion is one such moment of articulation. Despite the lack of a central "text," this rebellion offers an entry point for the exploration of eighteenth-century human rights discourse and communication rights. One report of the incident alleges that the rebels were overheard shouting "Liberty," a word intimately connected to the rights discourse of the European and American Enlightenment and often used by the patriots of the American Revolution. Another report claims the rebels were fighting for their "Liberty," and the colonists for "every thing that was dear to them." The rebels may have had some understanding of their rights as human beings, but with limited access to the sophisticated communication technologies of the day, they were prevented from effective organization or avenues of protest or redress. This raises questions about the human right to communicate as defined today by Article 19 of the Universal Declaration of Human Rights. The existence of this article, while limited in scope, has fostered a discussion among scholars and activists about the need for a broader and more comprehensive right to communicate. From a comprehensive standpoint, the right to communicate is a civil and political right encapsulating many human rights, including the right to assembly, to move freely, to send and receive information, to associate, to express, to practice cultures, and to receive an education. The ability to communicate makes us human and strengthens our dignity and potential to speak in the public sphere. And in this contemporary globalized moment, the right to communicate freely has enormous consequences. If we cannot communicate freely, we cannot claim our human rights or call foul when they have been violated. Through Stono I will explore one early manifestation of the struggle to achieve this particular right while acknowledging that this struggle has been relevant for quite some time.

I invite readers to view the Stono Rebellion as a "literary act," by which I mean a public event or action that seeks to shape a particular discourse or narrative and that has a relationship with a variety of texts, printed or otherwise. Clearly, the Stono Rebellion falls into this category. The event may have been precipitated by a variety of texts, and it resulted in a variety of texts—laws, letters, reports, newspaper articles, and oral histories. In such a manner this literary act fostered a kind of human rights discourse. Stono serves as an exemplum, in the medieval sense of the word—it illustrates a moral truth as it participates in the project to extend human rights to all human beings. To be sure, this is a complicated moral truth; the Stono rebels committed acts of horrific violence. And yet there are countless examples in American letters of such acts of violence being approved and praised. We enshrine some violent acts within American mythology as daring assertions of human rights, but not others like Stono. American history, though, is quite complex, and the too-often linear and triumphant narrative of it discounts this complexity. There have always been multiple voices challenging powerful forces and offering significant counter-narratives. Ultimately, by naming and claiming this event in such a fashion, I am acknowledging the performative nature of such overt acts of subaltern rebellion and the ways in which such acts resonate across cultures and time. It is my wish to demonstrate the ways in which the Stono rebels are not anonymous rebels but humans participating in a grand public debate. Centering the Stono Rebellion within the context of these larger questions pushes us to consider the relationship of local struggles to global ones and to witness the operation of a "master narrative" outside the direct control of the masters.

I begin with an analysis of John Locke's philosophy of natural rights and his ambiguous political and economic ties to the colony of South Carolina (chapter 1).[2] How does this rights discourse emerge in the writing of Quaker abolitionists, Thomas Jefferson, Thomas Paine, and others (chapter 2)? I then offer a close reading of the rebellion (chapter 3), its legal repercussions (chapter 4), and the resonances of the Stono rebels' calls of liberty in African American literature (chapters 4 and 5). How do we understand the human rights claims made by early African American writers like Olaudah Equiano, Prince Hall, Phillis Wheatley, David Walker, Omar ibn Said, Frederick Douglass, or Martin Delany? Do these claims take part in that same struggle for liberty and dignity? I then assess the intertextual challenge to universal human rights offered by writers of the Charleston School and the competing "plantation traditions" of Henry Timrod, William Gilmore Simms, Angelina Grimké, and Edmund Quincy (chapter 6). In the final chapter, I explore the presence and persistence of the Stono narrative today.

Chapter 1

★

CAROLINA'S COLONIAL ARCHITECTURE AND THE AGE OF RIGHTS

The natural liberty of man is to be free from any superior power on earth.
—John Locke, *Second Treatise on Civil Government*

ONE ACCOUNT OF THE STONO REBELLION describes the scene, early on the morning of September 9, 1739, as a group of slaves made its way down the Pon Pon Road in the direction of Florida. The writer, who may or may not have been James Oglethorpe, claims, "Several Negroes joined them, they calling out liberty, marched on with colours displayed, and two drums beating, pursuing all white people they met with, and killing man, woman, and child when they could come up to them" ("Account" 234). That these slaves were shouting "liberty" may simply have been in the author's imagination. But if it did happen, if the Stono rebels did shout "liberty," it would encourage us to frame or re-frame how we view the enlightenment and the eighteenth century—the age of revolutions. What would it say about the slaves' ideals, their humanity? What would it say about the range of contemporary criticisms of slavery? One interpretation of this moment is that the slaves were repeating something overheard, perhaps from a master, a preacher, or on board a ship. Another interpretation is that the slaves knew exactly what they were saying. Either way, they were participating in a powerful discourse that was sweeping through Europe and North America during the time, a discourse rooted in the belief of natural or human rights, human freedom, and human liberty.

That these ideas could travel from Europe to South Carolina (or to wherever the Stono revolutionaries picked up the term "liberty") should come as little surprise. Colonial America was a node in a growing network of communication and commerce that crisscrossed the Atlantic and supported economies in both the New World and Old World. Innovations in governance, navigation, and communication technologies enhanced this network and heightened the interconnectedness of previously disparate cultures and economies. A similar language of globalization is in vogue today: part and parcel to this language is the recognition that new media are changing our lives, our culture, and our ideas. New media and the virtual world of cyberspace and its attendant information and communication technologies have increased our ability to share ideas and information with ease and often with people we may have never connected with otherwise. We talk on phones that fit in our pockets; we check our "electronic mail" on machines the size of small books; we browse through information in a virtual agora; we send and receive instant messages online. We are, for better or worse, *interconnected*.

This new media bonanza with its dizzying transformation of both human communication and human culture is not the first. Beginning with Johann Gutenberg's printing innovations around 1439 and, in 1517, when Martin Luther tacked his "95 Theses" to the chapel doors in Wittenberg, a perfect storm of technology and capitalism was developing in Western Europe. By the late seventeenth and eighteenth centuries, this storm propelled the printing industry beyond its function as a new method for copying and sharing information into a mechanism for promoting ideas (Starr 26). Publishing (or making something known via a technological intermediary) connected human beings in ways that before had only been possible through the church or the royal court. Most importantly, the publishing industry fomented public conversations about what had been printed—about what it had produced. Such "public conversations," according to Jürgen Habermas in his famous critique of this period, not only brought political debate to a larger audience but transformed systems of governance. Habermas argues that in eighteenth-century Europe, a literal and figurative space began to develop in which people—specifically, the growing bourgeoisie—could discuss the pressing issues of the day in an open and public manner apart from the government. This bourgeois public sphere was "the sphere of private people coming together as a public" and a place for "debate over the general rules governing relations in the basically privatized but publicly relevant sphere of commodity exchange and social labor" (27). It manifested on the streets and through the growing number of coffee shops, salons, voluntary associations, newspapers, and journals as a growing reading public began to consider and realize new concepts for political formations. The "representative publicness" of the king or priest was being replaced by public debate and public decisions, leading eventually to legislative governments (9, 52). Michael Warner writes that at this time Western Europe transformed "from a world in which power embodied in special persons is represented before the people to one in which power is constituted by a discourse in which the people are represented" (*Letters* 39).

Women, servants, and other property-less people, however, were more marginal participants in this decision-making process. Habermas notes that *in theory* there was "universal access" to the public sphere (85). Practice was another matter. Natalie Zemon Davis suggests that even though subaltern groups (for her purposes, peasants in sixteenth-century France) lacked the privilege of participating in this public sphere on the same level as propertied literate men, they did participate in print culture (66). Rural peasants often experienced the new media by hearing books read aloud, for example, during a winter evening gathering, called the *veillée*, or through the public pontifications of itinerant preachers (71). However, print culture had a greater influence among *urban* merchants, craftsmen, and even semiskilled workers like gardeners and fishermen and those in their circles—domestic servants and wives. Books were, of course, cheaper than manuscripts, though still too expensive for many; book sharing, lending, trading and group reading were popular practices. The group reading was an important holdover from a completely oral culture and was directly connected to the spread of Protestantism and its adherence to close biblical study.

In describing these phenomena, Davis writes that we should "consider a book not merely as a source for ideas but as a *carrier of relationships*" (66). Indeed, from its inception, the printing press transformed communications and carried relationships throughout Western Europe. As this print culture developed, economies transformed from those based on feudal monopolies to those based on free market principles, a transformation that would have serious political implications. Benedict Anderson acknowledges this burgeoning symbiotic relationship when describing the period's new political formations. He argues that publishing—the rise of the daily newspaper, in particular—began to shape political formations around national identities. The advent of newspapers in England (1621), France (1631), and Holland (1632), for example, gave anyone with access to them access to ideas about business and government that pertained, more or less, to their daily lives. The ability to buy a newspaper was not always a prerequisite, as papers, as they often do today, passed through many hands on the streets and in bars and coffee shops. Newspapers offered readers a sense of community in part because of their use of vernaculars and because mastheads displayed the paper's point of origin and current date. In addition, newspapers often reported the news about a particular place and were read and shared by those in that place. Anderson writes that, like taking communion, reading the newspaper became a daily and "extraordinary mass ceremony" (34). Publishing was a transformative technology "which made it possible for rapidly growing numbers of people to think about themselves, and to relate themselves to others, in profoundly new ways" (36).

The rise of the printing press coincided with the development of another significant technology—governments appointed by "the people." In Western Europe, the right to rule became the "divine right" not of kings but of human beings. This right, though, was mostly limited to property-owning human beings. Still, this was a major step in human governance; and it led to much tension and revolutions—most notably the English, American, French, and Haitian. Human beings, now citizens of nation-states fueled by booming economies and burgeoning print cultures, began to express their natural or human right to property, to liberty, and to life itself in the public sphere; rights were not solely the domain of royalty but of the public. During this moment, "a secularized version of Judeo-Christian ethics lent itself to the development of a broad liberal discourse on human rights, a discourse that has shaped contemporary thinking" (Ishay 64). Human rights were by no means universally practiced in the late seventeenth century or throughout the eighteenth century, but these rights and their practical applications became an important part of a revolutionary discourse.

One could argue not only that human rights are based on legal precedent, but that the Zeitgeist, the spirit of the age, also plays a role in establishing who has rights and what those rights are. In this and the following chapters, I will discuss some of the written and cultural underpinnings for human rights discourse in the seventeenth and eighteenth centuries, paying close attention to what might have been in the air (other than yellow fever) in the Americas and in South Carolina before and after the Stono Rebellion. Had discussions of human rights crossed the Atlantic? What did the public sphere look like in colonial South Carolina? The colony was not isolated from the currents of contemporary political thought; it was becoming quite a cosmopolitan outpost. Whites and blacks commingled with peers from all parts of the Atlantic world. In fact, John K. Thornton suggests that the slaves that rebelled at Stono were, at the very least, bilingual, and perhaps even Catholic ("African" 1113). They, too, had been touched by the wider world. And chattel slavery did not exist in a vacuum either before or after Stono. Slavery persisted, despite calls for human rights, despite the Zeitgeist, despite what was in the air.

What was in the air was spurred on by what was on the page, and that, of course, was connected to and supported by an economy built on the backs of African slaves—so much so that even some of the era's most ardent supporters of the rights of human beings, writers whose work helped lay the theoretical foundations for the eighteenth century's revolutions, played significant roles in the slave trade. Writers, for example, like John Locke.

AUTHOR OF LIBERTY AND ARCHITECT OF SLAVERY?

John Locke's late-seventeenth-century writings are significant to any discussion of the development of human rights discourse—especially given the part he played in the realization of slave labor in the colony of Carolina. His commentaries about the nature of human liberties, with a particular focus on the right to private property, the right to religious worship, and the right to legislative governance, were significant to the development of political thought among the growing bourgeoisie. Though these *specific* rights are crucial, I am most interested in the ways in which Locke's work shapes a discourse for framing human rights and, ultimately, how each specific right becomes interconnected. When initially produced, this framework was meant to have practical implications: Locke's interpretation of natural rights was a challenge to absolute monarchies because it rested on the idea that rights belong to each individual human. Central to his concept of individual rights is the notion that governments are created via a "contract" among individuals, to which each individual may or may not give consent. Any other regime, Locke asserted, is contrary to natural or human rights and is, therefore, oppressive. In the opening line of his *First Treatise on Civil Government*, Locke reacts to Sir Robert Filmer's support of absolute monarchs, writing, "Slavery is so vile and miserable an estate of man, and so directly opposite to the generous Temper and Courage of our Nation; that 'tis hardly to be conceived, that an Englishman, much less a Gentleman, should plead for't" (7). Locke refers here to the English government, though one could imagine a connection to the absolute authority promoted by the flourishing Atlantic slave trade. Human beings, according to Locke, should be allowed to exist free from absolute control and with the ability to make decisions regarding how they are to be governed. This argument against the tyranny of absolute monarchies would surface again in the eighteenth century and form, to a great extent, the bedrock of American revolutionary thought and, to a lesser extent, that of the French.[1]

The traditional primary source for Locke's argument for a system of governance determined by the people as opposed to tradition or the divine right of kings is his *Second Treatise on Civil Government*, published in 1690. In the *Second Treatise*, Locke asserts that authority can only be constituted in the people through a government founded on legislative rule. If power is created by the people and if they have the right to create legal authority, then they also have the right to discern what that authority should constitute. In other words, human beings have the right to communicate among themselves, to deliberate, to pass into and out of the public sphere—to establish governments as they see fit. Locke claims that the road to the establishment of governments began in a primeval state of nature where humans existed equally with no one having authority over another (2.4).[2] During this "Golden Age" humans were governed by the law of nature. This law, predicated on reason, asserted "that being all equal and independent, no one ought to harm another in his life, health, liberty, or possessions" (2.6). If one lives contrary to this law, then one "declares himself to live by another rule than that of reason and common equity" (2.8). Locke means that we all have ultimate possession of our bodies—this being *the* fundamental human rights protection. Those who do not respect this fundamental right violate the laws of nature. Unfortunately, those who live by rules other than "reason and common equity" do exist; and because protection is therefore necessary, Locke claims that "God hath certainly appointed government to restrain the partiality and violence of men" (2.13). To be clear, though, he does not say that absolute monarchs are a part of this equation; he was specifically making a case against Filmer's "Natural Power of Kings," or the idea that the right to rule had been given to Adam by God and thus to the monarch. For Locke, the only legitimate government is one established when people consent to come together to protect themselves and their property.

The roots of this property are clearly defined. Locke writes that God made the earth to be used by humans for their comfort and subsistence (5.26). "Though the earth and all inferior creatures be common to all men, yet every man has a property in his own person. This nobody has any right to but himself. The labor of his body and the work of his hands, we may say, are properly his" (5.27). Again, each person's body belongs to his or herself, and this is the ultimate right to property—the right to security as an individual human being. Property outside of one's self comes from one's own labor: "As much land as a man tills, plants, improves, cultivates, and can use the product of, so much is his property" (5.32). Donald Greene finds this assertion problematic, noting that it can lead to "laissez-fare thinking," and claims that "God's in his heaven, all's right with the world, and if other people remain poor, it is the result of their own willful folly and laziness" (117). This is an argument some on the Right wing of liberalism find quite appealing.

But later Locke writes that because man is born free, he or she "hath by nature a power not only to preserve his property, that is, his life, liberty, and estate, against the injuries and attempts of other men, but to judge of and punish the breaches of that law in others, as he is persuaded the offence deserves, even with death itself" (7.87). Estates, or property, are included in this list, but only alongside "life" and "liberty." Defending these rights that are so crucial to a dignified existence are often difficult to do alone. And so people band together to form governments, to form the "body politic" (8.95). Locke claims such cooperation is part of a greater divine plan. He makes the claim that God thought man should live in community and not alone because God "fitted him with understanding and language" (7.77). These communities, then, agree upon the right to protect personal property together by agreeing to give their collective authority to a government.

This act of forming a government is an act of trust. Humans may "give up the equality, liberty, and executive power they had in the state of nature into the hands of the society," but they do this trusting that the government will do all things with the "public good" in mind (9.132). Locke clarifies this, noting that when the legislative or "supreme executor" goes against the public good or goes beyond the limits of authority, the people have "a right to resume their original liberty" (12.222). So this act of trust has an escape clause—a right to revolution. The people reserve this right to re-establish a government because "the end of government is the good of mankind" and not tyranny (12.229). Those who argue against rebellions in opposition of governments that invade, destroy, or thieve the property of those who have placed their trust in them "may as well say, upon, the same ground, that honest men may not oppose robbers or pirates, because this may occasion disorder or bloodshed" (12.228).

But who holds this right to revolt? Who participates in the social contract? Who is privileged in Locke's equation? And, by extension, who does he consider human? In his *Second Treatise,* Locke raises a number of questions about the general equality of human beings and states, "Though I have said above ... *That all men by nature are equal,* I cannot be supposed to understand all sorts of equality: Age or virtue may give men a just precedency" (6.54). In other words, the equality that Locke describes is somewhat limited. In order to partake in this equality, one must have "reason, which is able to instruct him in that law he is to govern himself by, and make him known how far he is left to the freedom of his own will" (6.63). Accordingly, this rule limits children, "lunatics and idiots" from having complete freedom.

While Locke is no egalitarian in the strictest sense, at times he exhibits a belief in an inherently limited equality that could foster a limited tolerance of others and promote the ideas that all humans deserve the right to exist and believe as they wish. Such a case is made in his "Letter Concerning Toleration," Locke's argument against the persecution of religious sects, in particular those being persecuted in France. As with his *Second Treatise,* this is a response to real-world events as Locke must have been privy to the stories told by persecuted French Huguenots while he was living in Holland. The treatment they received must have disturbed him, for he writes that a true Christian must "make war upon his own lusts and vices" and not torment others for the sake of religious belief ("Letter" 6). The Gospel of Jesus Christ teaches love and tolerance, not the right to physically torture those who do not believe as you do (8). "That the Church of Christ should persecute others, and force others by fire and sword to embrace her faith and doctrine," Locke writes, "I could never yet find in any of the books of the New Testament" (16). Such intolerant behavior would qualify as a "civil injury," an infringement on one's personal liberty or property, because these actions would, inevitably, require the consent of governments. The church must be concerned only with "the salvation of souls" and should have nothing to do with influencing governance (30). We should be wary, he writes, of church leaders who use their power to make "use of the immoderate ambition of magistrates, and the credulous superstition of the giddy multitude" to attack dissenters (58). Faith can be a useful tool for those seeking political and economic gain.

Locke's "Letter Concerning Toleration" exposes his belief in the separation of church and state and is, thus, an important source for understanding the relationship of his theory of government to human rights (9). He believes that church and state should have little to do with one another. Civil magistrates must be mindful of this separation when executing and enforcing laws; their power is limited to "outward force"; therefore, they can debate the issue but cannot force someone to believe in one thing or another (11). Locke makes it clear that government toleration of religious beliefs is a matter of rights: "Nobody, therefore, in fine, neither single persons nor churches, nay, nor even commonwealths, have any just title to invade the civil rights and worldly goods of each other upon pretence of religion. Those that are of another opinion would do well to consider with themselves how pernicious a seed of discord and war, how powerful a provocation to endless hatreds, rapines, and slaughters they thereby furnish unto mankind. No peace and security, no, not so much as common friendship, can ever be established or preserved amongst men so long as this opinion prevails, that dominion is founded in grace and that religion is to be propagated by force of arms" (20). True religious belief comes from an internal transformation, not from having it imposed upon you by the church or by the magistrate. But magistrates do have the authority to intervene with religious assemblies in order to prevent actions that are typically unlawful, though they cannot use their power "to the oppression of any Church, under pretence of public good" (35). They may also be *intolerant* on behalf of the public good and with those who do not believe in God at all.

Until Locke makes this last claim, his "Letter" appears to be a recipe for the establishment of a quite tolerant society, as he explains, "Neither pagan nor mahometan, nor jew, ought to be excluded from the civil rights of the common-wealth because of his religion" (52). But those who do not believe in God at all should be excluded because their promises or oaths cannot be trusted (47). Locke further disqualifies those sects that seek to disrupt civil authority and argues that in such circumstances the magistrate has every right to intervene (46). Alex Tuckness notes, "Locke would claim that there are some beliefs that we can clearly foresee would have devastating effects if widely held and that if we wait until they are widely held before moving against them our actions may be futile" (297). In other words, he adds, "If the danger is really clear, we need not wait until it is present."

However, it is in the interest of governments to be tolerant of religious differences: "Just and moderate governments are everywhere quiet, everywhere safe; but oppression raises ferments and makes men struggle to cast off an uneasy and tyrannical yoke" (Locke, "Letter" 49). Oppression will breed rebellion, and toleration peace: "Some enter into company for trade and profit, others for want of business have their clubs for claret.

Neighborhood joins some and religion others. But there is only one thing which gathers people into seditious commotions, and this is oppression.... The sum of all we drive at is that every man may enjoy the same rights that are granted to others" (50). Whatever his reasons for writing this, be they religious or political, such a pronouncement is a decidedly pragmatic and somewhat secular-leaning argument for human rights.[3] It is a warning to governments regarding the perils of oppression. But Locke's brand of toleration, while pioneering in some ways, does not necessarily assert a positive social justice agenda. He simply wishes to end arbitrary and discriminatory practices in a narrowly defined set of issues, asking for "negative" rights not "positive" ones. But limited interpretations can and do create evolutionary discourses that foment change in language and social views. Locke's limited interpretation of toleration here speaks to the strict, calculating motives of contemporary human rights law. Such protections are not always positive measures that breed happiness and goodwill to all; they often only seek an immediate end to ongoing discrimination, abuse, or violence, arbitrary or otherwise.

Despite Locke's writings, which seek to protect property (life, liberty, estates), his life and his body of work are full of contradictions that still raise concern given his supposed influence on the development of political thought in the United States and on contemporary human rights discourse. The most glaring problem with any analysis of John Locke and his relationship to human rights discourse is that he invested six hundred pounds in the Royal African Company, which, among other things, traded in African slaves. In addition, he gave of his time serving as secretary to the Council of Trade and Foreign Plantations from 1673 to 1674 and as commissioner on the Board of Trade from 1696 to 1700, bodies that played significant roles in the colonial project as advisors and policy scribes. Most significantly, while working as secretary for Lord Anthony Ashley Cooper, Locke played a part in the development of the Fundamental Constitutions of Carolina, which, among other things, cleared a path for establishing a slave regime in South Carolina. Slavery was by no means an abstract concept in Locke's world. Thus, determining the true nature of the great philosopher's relationship to slavery in theory and in practice has always stirred up controversy with regards to his theory of rights. Slavery is the enormous elephant in the room of Locke.

Dated March 1, 1669, and thus written prior to the *Second Treatise* and "Letter Concerning Toleration," the Fundamental Constitutions of Carolina provides some insight into Locke's textual connections to slavery and, perhaps, to the development of plantation culture and legal codes in the future colony and state of South Carolina.[4] Despite numerous revisions, the Fundamental Constitutions was never actually approved by the colonists, though the document lent an air of authenticity to the project and served as a social blueprint and advertisement for potential participants. Locke's connection to this text and to the Carolina project began in 1668, when he saved the life of Lord Anthony Ashley Cooper, soon to become the First Earl of Shaftesbury, by the successful performance of a dangerous medical procedure. Lord Ashley was the leading figure in the project to settle Carolina, and Locke was his dutiful secretary when the future earl initiated an effort to write the Fundamental Constitutions. There is much debate as to whether or not Locke actually crafted the document by himself. We know that Locke was the official secretary to the eight Lords Proprietors, the group spearheading and funding the colonization of Carolina, but was he more than a copyist? In a compendium of foundational texts for North Carolina, Mattie Erma Edwards Parker writes in an introduction to the Fundamental Constitutions that, at the very least, the document crossed his path and he did write some of it down (128). One scholar is more specific and notes that of the first of the four versions of the document, "the main text is in an unknown hand, but the first two paragraphs and first sentence of the third, and most of the large number of amendments, are in Locke's hand" (Goldie 160). Peter Laslett believes that the Fundamental Constitutions may have been "the result of literary co-operation" between Ashley and Locke (29). Walter Edgar, citing others, including M. Eugene Sirmans, Robert M. Weir, and Barbara Arneil, agrees, "The final document ... was as much Locke's work as Lord Ashley's" (42). But Sirmans himself argues that there must have been collaboration, "but the weight of the argument indicates that the ideas were mainly Ashley's" (9). Whatever the precise degree of his participation in its authorship, John Locke was certainly deeply connected to this document and to this particular colonial project throughout his life. Arneil claims that Locke had more than a passing interest in colonialism and trade and that, at the very least, "colonial policy dominated Locke's life from 1668 to 1675," during which time "The Fundamental Constitutions" was first penned (592). Besides his connections to colonial policy, Locke carried on a personal correspondence with Sir Peter Colleton, a wealthy Carolina planter, and eventually had an island off the coast of South Carolina named for him.[5]

Maurice Cranston writes that Lord Ashley also convinced Locke to apply his writing talents in helping him with the Carolina project by drafting other legal documents as well as advertisements to promote this business venture (*John Locke* 119). Like these advertisements, the Fundamental Constitutions was a document meant to lure settlers and establish legitimacy for the project through its plan for governance "because the King had entrusted the Lords Proprietors with full responsibility for its government." It should also be noted that because the document was used to attract customers, a.k.a. colonists, it provided a legal framework for a society in which they might be interested in living. In this sense, it can be viewed as foundational. Some of the Fundamental Constitutions' articles, for example, those protecting religious freedom, are more palatable than others. Perhaps because of his Presbyterian roots, Lord Ashley supported religious toleration and made certain that such tolerance would be written into the document. Article 102 claims, "No person of any other church or profession shall disturb or molest any religious assembly." Similarly, Article 109 states, "No person whatsoever shall disturb, molest, or persecute another for his speculative opinions in religion or his way of worship." Article 97 advises that "Jews, heathens, and other dissenters" will be allowed to live in this colony, at the very least, so they may experience "the purity of Christian religion, may not be scared and kept at a distance from it, but, by having an opportunity of acquainting themselves with the truth and reasonableness of its doctrines." This, according to the Fundamental Constitutions, will hopefully lead to their eventual conversion. Cranston believes Lord Ashley's tolerant beliefs and his influence on this document were motivated by his economic interests. He writes, "Ashley opposed religious persecution because religious persecution divided a nation, drove many of its most industrious citizens to emigrate, and generally impeded commercial development" (107). In essence, Lord Ashley "was the complete progressive capitalist in politics."

But as with Locke's "Letter Concerning Toleration," there are limits to the toleration espoused by the Fundamental Constitutions. Article 95 states that there is no place in this colony for atheists: "No man shall be permitted to be a freeman of Carolina, or to have any estate or habitation within it, that doth not acknowledge a God, and that God is publicly and solemnly to be worshipped." There is also a clause in Article 103 which prohibits the use of religious meetings to defy authority. Surprisingly, though, a limited freedom of religion is established in the Fundamental Constitutions for slaves in Article 107: "Since charity obliges us to wish well to the souls of all men, and religion ought to alter nothing in any man's civil estate or right, it shall be lawful for slaves, as well as others, to enter themselves, and be of what church or profession any of them shall think best, and thereof be as fully members as any freeman. But yet no slave shall hereby be exempted from that civil dominion his master hath over him, but be in all other things in the same state and condition he was in before." What "civil dominion" means is established in Article 110: "Every freeman of Carolina shall have absolute power and authority over his negro slaves, of what opinion or religion soever." The authors of the Fundamental Constitutions authorize slavery while ensuring for the religious instruction of slaves. However, they make it very clear that they do not wish those slaves who become Christian to equate baptism or Christian worship with notions of liberty.

In addition to limited religious toleration and slavery, the Fundamental Constitutions of Carolina establishes a landed gentry complete with a servant class, here called "slaves." Essentially, the Lords Proprietors were establishing the framework for a splendid aristocratic, merchant-friendly society in the New World. Sirmans writes that the "Grand Model," as it was often referred to, was akin to "the manorial system.... [T]he Constitutions provided for manors, manorial courts, and the equivalent of serfs" (9). The people who would buy into this model were people who were interested in holding human beings in bondage in order to maximize profits. In this light, whether or not John Locke, the great theorist of human rights, had a hand in writing the Fundamental Constitutions becomes a significant question. Locke's labor, time, and money went into the production of a document which, by hook or by crook, assisted in the development of two colonies—North and South Carolina—that supported and were supported by slavery. South Carolina was at the forefront of establishing chattel slavery on mainland North America, a system that created divisions among groups of human beings to such a degree that one group was considered more human than the other. Did the Fundamental Constitutions have a hand in establishing this precedent in South Carolina?

There is no definitive answer, but the belief that Locke had a hand in its creation was and is a part of American popular culture. In bits and pieces, claims for Locke's role as author of this document are scattered throughout American letters. In 1847, a short story by Edmund Quincy appeared in the abolitionist journal *Liberty Bell* describing the colony of South Carolina decades after the Stono Rebellion. The narrator summarizes one view of the role Locke and the Lords Proprietors played in the development of the colony: "The noble proprietaries were endeavoring to revive on those distant shores the decaying feudality of the Old World. They had called philosophy to their aid, and in making John Locke the Lycurgus of their infant realm, the fantastic spirit of Shaftesbury thought they had imitated the wisdom of the ancients who made their philosophers their law-givers. But the experiment redounded as little to the credit of philosophy, as the incorporations of Negro slavery with the institutions he ordained, did the honor of the philosopher. But at the first establishment of the Constitutions of Carolina, their defects were not developed, and their fanciful structure attracted more general attention, doubtless, than a more rational plan would have done" (43–44). Even if Locke did not write the Fundamental Constitutions of Carolina, many believed (and still believe) that he did. Several significant examples of this phenomenon completely erase Lord Ashley's role in writing the Fundamental Constitutions.[6]

From the outset, the Locke "contribution" was widely recognized. In 1673 Sir Peter Colleton wrote Locke glowingly, hoping that soon in Carolina "that excellent form of Government in the composure of which you had so great a hand may speedily come to be put in practice" (395). A century later, when the first histories of South Carolina were published, Locke would, once again, receive all the credit. Alexander Hewatt's 1779 *An Historical Account of the Rise and Progress of the Colonies of South Carolina and Georgia* includes an appendix with "the First Set of the Fundamental Constitutions of South Carolina as Compiled by Mr. John Locke." A year later Captain Johann Hinrichs, fighting for the British, wrote in his diary, "These colonists took as their lawgiver the great Locke, whose basic principle was complete, unlimited freedom of conscience for every religion and creed" (147). Did Locke do all that? Such a fiction may have had more influence on popular discourse than the actual ambiguous truth. Ultimately, what we do know is that the Fundamental Constitutions opened the door for slavery, and this is what matters most. Locke himself seems to have been aware of that fact. Writing of Carolina in 1671, he notes, "Sir Jo Yeamans intends to stay all the winter. . . . [He] brought negroes and expects more" (qtd. in Wood 23). Locke knew that this illicit trade was flourishing.[7]

Peter Laslett attempts to rescue Locke from complete implication with the Lords Proprietors, writing that as Locke matured as a philosopher "his views on people, who they were and how they related to government" as well as his relationship to the practice of slavery changed over time (30). While escaping potential persecution for his association with the Earl of Shaftesbury, Locke lived for a time with a Quaker named Benjamin Furly, who was adamantly opposed to the slave trade (Farr 268). By 1677 Locke had sold off his interests in the Royal African Company (Glausser 201). And most critics tend to agree that Locke's most mature theoretical view of slavery is clearly established in the *Second Treatise*. This theory is closely linked to his theory of just wars and follows a strict line of reasoning. First of all, humans cannot be governed by any other authority except that which is "established by consent in the commonwealth" (Locke, *Second Treatise* 4.22). Humans must be free "from absolute, arbitrary power" because that freedom is tied to their right to live (4.23). Therefore, no one can be a slave except in the case of a just war: "This is the perfect condition of slavery, which is nothing else but the state of war continued between a lawful conqueror and a captive" (4.24). A just war occurs when one group is not allowed the right to live—when they are subject to "absolute, arbitrary power." Those who cause such wars to take place exclude themselves from civil society and, thus, from their right to liberty, their right to life (7.85). Only under such conditions is slavery to be permitted. James Farr agrees that "Locke's just-war theory of slavery *is* consistent with his account of natural rights"; he argues that Locke was silent on the issue of African slavery but was not, necessarily, "a racist in the strong sense to justify slavery" (264). The slave captured in a just war had made a choice—and was apparently rational enough before the war—to violate the property and rights of another (271). David Brion Davis appears to offer a similar argument that Locke's theory of the origins of slavery begins within the context of a just war. "For Locke," he writes, "original sin had been replaced by a supposedly willful act which required that the slave be forever excluded from the paradisial compact and worked, in the sweat of his brow, for the benefit of others. And from this secular hell there was apparently no redemption" (*Problem of Slavery in Western Culture* 121). In this sense, according to Locke, Davis writes that "slavery was in conformity with natural law and was as universally valid as private property. And since slaves were private property, and the titles of owners was based on natural right, it would presumably be the duty of any state to protect the rights of slaveholders" (120).

In the end, all we really know about Locke's view on slavery is that at one point he actively supported the trade. Perhaps there are flaws in Locke's character, but we must respect the fact that he was astutely legal and that his focus was on a strict interpretation of natural law in order to protect the fundamental rights of at least some human beings. Such strict interpretations create a precedent in which language works in favor of groups that would otherwise be denied their natural rights—Christian dissidents and prisoners of unjust wars, for example. The problem, though, is that we cannot always be sure of whom or for whom Locke writes. And in the case of the Fundamental Constitutions, his words cracked the door open for slavery in the colony of South Carolina.

OTHER ARCHITECTS OF RIGHTS DISCOURSE

The work of Jean-Jacques Rousseau provides a contrast to Locke's conception of individual rights, his focus on the protection of private property, and what one could argue is essentially a road map for social inequality and chattel slavery. His argument emerged as disputes between the American colonies and the British crown were increasing, and his ideas influenced many writers of the American Revolution—and perhaps the leader of another important revolution, Toussaint L'Overture. In 1762, Rousseau's *Du contrat social* or *The Social Contract* proposed a political framework that served also as a plea for fundamental human rights. Unlike Locke, Rousseau saw power as ultimately resting within the collective, not the individual. He claimed that this true authority represented "the legitimate powers of the State" and that these "legitimate powers" only come about through collective social agreement, through a social contract (173). Through this contract, the individual recognizes the rights of the whole community. This contract requires that individuals lose "natural liberty" but gain a more collective "civil liberty" and are bound by a mutual "identity of interests" (185, 190).

In some senses utopian and in some senses rational, Rousseau imagines these changes as steps toward the creation of a more civilized and just world, suppressing base instincts and elevating social justice. Reason and a sense of collective duty guide actions and, ultimately, how laws are established and observed. When forming society, humans give up some personal freedoms but gain equality before the law. In order to maintain this equality before the law, Rousseau opposes the use of legislative governments; states should be kept small so that everyone can have an equal voice and participate ("Social Contract" 259). In this way, a government can be directed by what he calls the *volanté general* (the general will) of the people, the citizens. This is the crucial difference between Rousseau's vision of governance and Locke's. "The essence of Lockean democracy is an impulse toward liberty. . . . The essence of Rousseauean democracy is an impulse toward equality" (May et al. 2). From the most radical perspective, Rousseau is a communist; and Locke, a libertarian. These opposing impulses filter into their visions of human rights as well. A Lockean theory of rights begins with the individual and negative rights, and a Rousseauean theory of rights begins with the group and positive rights. Locke says, "You can't do these things to me!" Rousseau says, "I have a right to these things!" In this way, equality is guaranteed collectively because if *I* do not have rights, then *you* do not have rights. An "impulse toward equality" is what should protect everyone from slavery to a state or to a person. But if a society is property-focused—as Rousseau warns against in his *Discourse on Inequality*—it would be capable of legitimizing chattel slavery. If a society consists of people who can own things, then it would not be a stretch for that society to have individuals lay claim to those humans considered "things" and thus deny them of their liberty. This was the case in colonial South Carolina, where by 1740 approximately forty thousand black human beings were held in bondage.

But the egregious wrongs of the African slave trade were not passing unnoticed in the eighteenth century; slavery was beginning to shape rights discourse among some noted public intellectuals. Samuel Johnson famously toasted a group of "very grave men at Oxford" by saying, "Here's to the next insurrection of the Negroes in the West Indies" (qtd. in Boswell 876).[8] And Voltaire's 1759 satire *Candide* offers a scathing critique of the faith in rationalism pervasive among Enlightenment philosophies by noting the ways in which humanity chooses to rationalize certain practices as natural and right despite daily evidence of the contrary. He exposes the limits of Optimism, a philosophy that protagonist Candide's "wise" teacher Pangloss summarizes in the phrase "all is for the best in the best of all worlds." This view is an absurdity in a world of warfare, intolerance, and slavery. Acknowledging connections between new economic patterns and the intellectual flowering of the Enlightenment, Voltaire displays the source of the coffee in the coffee shop and the sugar used to sweeten it:

> As they drew near the town they came upon a Negro lying on the ground wearing only half his clothes, that is to say, a pair of blue cotton drawers; this poor man had no left leg and no right hand. "Good heavens!" said Candide to him in Dutch, "what are you doing there my friend, in that horrible state?" "I am waiting for my master, the famous merchant Monsieur Vanderdendur." "Was it Monsieur Vanderdendur," said Candide, "who treated

> *you in that way?" "Yes, sir," said the Negro, "it is the custom. We are given a pair of cotton drawers twice a year as clothing. When we work in the sugar mills and the grindstone catches our fingers, they cut off the hand; when we try to run away, they cut off a leg. Both these things happened to me. This is the price paid for the sugar you eat in Europe. (282)*

Voltaire's "Negro" reveals the glaring contradictions of the Enlightenment and the horrors of the slave trade. This statement of fact by an unnamed African slave is clearly aimed at "caffeinated" Europeans. What this man says is the literal and bloody truth; he has the wounds to prove it. He says, in effect, "You can't have cheap sugar without cheap labor." Through Voltaire's pen, this slave enters the public sphere; he is given access to the debate and is allowed to acknowledge his human dignity if only for this brief yet horrifying moment. Such violent juxtapositions—a quiet road and a tortured slave—are the bread and butter of enlightened satirists. Voltaire effectively scorns humankind through his literary production, yet the Negro is still on the side of the road, half naked, "with no left leg and no right hand," as Candide saunters off to cultivate his garden.

Even in this era when there was an "upwelling of ideas about human rights . . . surprisingly few people saw a contradiction between freedom for whites and bondage for slaves" (Hochschild, *Bury the Chains* 87). Writers making "enlightened" and rational arguments for human liberty were confronted with serious empirical evidence that the world was far from being equal, that deep poverty and inequality persisted. Peter Gay points out the fact that in this age of Enlightenment not everyone was the recipient of human rights; not everyone could afford it: "Progress itself called for new victims, and the very improvements that lightened the burdens of many intensified the sufferings of others: for the majority . . . the eighteenth century remained a time in which there was little to be enjoyed and much to be endured. The new style of thought was in the main reserved to the well-born, the articulate, and the lucky: the rural and the urban masses had little share in the new dispensation" (4). Philosophic and scientific explorations were not a part of the day-to-day routines of the poor in Western Europe, nor did they have time to participate in the rational-critical debate of the coffee houses and salons. And despite their calls for human liberty, Locke and Rousseau did not launch campaigns to end slavery. Other Enlightenment figures like Adam Smith made claims that slavery was natural and there was no hope of abolishing the practice (Hochschild 86–87). Even Voltaire was involved—a slave ship with his name roamed the seas. Many of the great theorists of the day, it seems, had trouble putting theory into practice. Thus, many human beings were on the outside of the developing public sphere and, by default, were robbed of their humanity.

That Enlightenment-era rights discourse is built on shaky ground does not bode well for the humanist tradition in general. Rights discourse as expressed by Locke, Rousseau, and their peers comes into question. Locke adequately describes the rights of "man," on one hand, while supporting slavery through both action and inaction, on the other. We can decipher, therefore, what he meant by "man," who he considered to be fully human. And the laws and constitutions of this period reflect these implied distinctions by restricting participation in the public sphere. One cannot communicate effectively if one is not a human being—does not own property, including one's self.

Alternative opinions, emanating from the poor and from women, *were* expressed in seventeenth- and eighteenth-century Western Europe. These "voices" comprise what Nancy Fraser calls "subaltern counterpublic spheres"—"parallel discursive arenas where members of subordinated social groups invent and circulate counter-discourses, which in turn permit them to formulate oppositional interpretations of their identities, interests, and needs" (81). The "counterpublics" of the seventeenth and eighteenth centuries acknowledged the contradictions within the burgeoning capitalist economy and the public ideas that developed alongside it. Significant changes had taken place and, in some ways, more human freedoms were protected. Indeed, the representative public sphere, as Habermas describes it, can best be exemplified by Louis XIV's declaration, "L'état, c'est moi" (I am the state). He embodied state power and acted on it accordingly; he was power in a body. But this absolutist form of governance was transformed through the rise of a public sphere whose motto could have been "L'état, c'est nous." But who was this "we"? It is this question that arises when, as Gay describes it, "new victims" suffer on behalf of progress. Counterpublics are "by definition, formed by their conflict with the norms and contexts of their cultural environment" (Warner, *Publics* 63). Counterpublics are made up of these new victims who recognize their rights and wish to realize them.

One counterpublic leader, a religious dissident named Gerrard Winstanley, exemplifies the counterpublic's potential to offer the subaltern a space in the public sphere, especially in moments of cultural and social conflict. To say that there were conflicts within English society throughout the seventeenth century is to put it mildly—the events that took place on St. George's Hill on April 1, 1649, were the tip of a rather large iceberg. On that day, Winstanley and other hungry, destitute, and property-less people dug up the commons at St. George's Hill, just outside of London, in order to plant crops. In a very public way, the Diggers, as they were called, put theories of natural rights into practice long before Locke wrote about them. Fittingly, Winstanley writes, in "The True Levellers Standard Advanced," "The common people are filled with good words from pulpits and council tables, but no good deeds" (263). Winstanley identifies himself as part of a revolutionary alternative seeking change through deeds, through rebellious action. His goal was to demolish the notion of private property, thus giving all people the ability to feed themselves, which he claimed was a fundamental positive human right. Winstanley attacked the landed gentry and mercantile classes of early modern England and posited a radical counter-narrative to property rights. By digging and planting, exhorting for the rights of the poor, and claiming that the earth belonged to all, he extolled the fundamental belief that private property was a slippery slope that led only to greed and selfishness. Servitude and misery, he asserted, were the bastard children of private property.

The ideology that framed the Fundamental Constitutions of Carolina, with its rigid class system and emphasis on personal property, was the very ideology Winstanley railed against. His view of a just society, and most importantly of property, was quite different than that of John Locke or of mainstream protestant mercantilists. Sounding more like Rousseau, Winstanley wrote that the idea that property should be protected above all is the primary motivator for violence and the root of all inequality.[9] He argued that if England placed private property rights above the rights of humans to feed themselves, many would suffer and all discussions of human rights would be null and void. The lives of most people within such an economy would never change. Winstanley was aware of this conundrum from his own experiences with poverty and hunger, acute problems in seventeenth-century England as land formally deemed "common" and free for all to use was enclosed or fenced in. The situation was made more dire by several years of poor harvests coupled with the repercussions of the civil war and widespread unemployment.[10]

James Holstun notes that rich people rarely want to experience the agony of those who are starving. When they record the voices of the poor, "they usually want to hear their legal testimony, their religious confessions, and their deferential greetings—not stark embarrassing cries like 'We want to eat!'" (Holstun 368). Winstanley's manifestoes are quite direct and intended to embarrass the rich; hunger can be a rather sharp and precise literary device. On June 1, 1649, he wrote "A Declaration from the Poor Oppressed People of England" on behalf of all those starving in England. This document, a poor people's Bill of Rights, addresses the positive right to have food, heat, and shelter. Winstanley declares, "Lords of manors, lords of the land . . . the earth was not made purposely for you, to be lords of it, and we to be your slaves, servants, and beggars; but it was made to be a common livelihood to all, without respect of persons: and that your buying and selling of land and the fruits of it . . . was brought in by war" (269). Anyone in power, he argues, established that power and their ownership of land through violence and theft and is thus undeserving of it. God's law, he writes, "hath made us sensible of our burdens"—we are aware of the injustices inflicted upon us; we are aware that current conditions are immoral and wrong (269). He alerts the "lords of the land" that he and his comrades will be digging up the commons in England and laws cannot prevent their actions. The poor, he notes, are guided by "the inward law of love" and "have an equal right to the land. . . . For the Earth, with all her fruits of corn, cattle, and such like, was made to be a common storehouse of livelihood to all mankind, friend and foe, without exception" (269–270). Winstanley claims that "everyone is to have the benefit and freedom of [God's] creation without respect of persons" (274). He reminds wealthy members of Parliament that this covenant requires them to protect the liberties of all, including the poor: "England, the land of our nativity, is to be a common treasury of livelihood to all, without respect of persons" (273). Yet Winstanley takes his plea a step further, noting that his demands are not only made on behalf of the poor of England, but "of all the nations of the world" (274). The right to eat, really, the right to live in dignity, is established as a *universal* human right.

In "The True Levellers Standard Advanced" (April 26, 1649), Winstanley writes that private property was the first sin and cause of the Fall of Man and the expulsion from the Garden of Eden (256–257). England, indeed, the Earth, will never regain paradise until all property is held in common.

Winstanley insists that landlords will face dire consequences if they do not heed his words. God, he claims, has told him, "[I will] multiply my plagues upon thee . . . and I will bring out my people with a strong hand, and stretched out arm" (266). Despite the implicit religious implications of calling on "God's wrath," and the real threat of mobs of angry poor people, Winstanley's exhortations are imbued with the moral imperatives of universal human rights claims. He sees human rights as residing within "the people" because he believes that all are created by the same god and that all are the same in the eyes of that god. The Earth belongs to everyone, and everyone, no matter their station in life, should share in its wealth. Only in states that respect the common dignity of all humans can common dignity exist.

While Winstanley's analysis of private property is useful, in some ways he is most significant for this discussion of human rights discourse simply because he wrote. Winstanley's narrative can be placed within a more inclusive history of communication pioneers who sought access to the public sphere. And like the slaves at Stono, he belonged to a group that was for all intents and purposes outside of the public discussion. His essays are some of the few remnants of a period of dramatic outbursts in pamphleteering among poor people. Winstanley directly and indirectly argued for the right to free speech, to assemble, to organize, and to communicate. These rights were tested by the Diggers and by the author himself in an England whose nobility was growing increasingly tired of religious radicals. Remember, Locke was essentially asking for toleration of those like Winstanley in his "Letter Concerning Toleration." By virtue of his writing and publishing, Winstanley practiced the right to communicate freely. He used the printing press to his advantage during a short window of unparalleled press freedom. Christopher Hill notes that "before 1641, and after 1660, there was a strict censorship" (*World* 17). Winstanley and other religious radicals of the period, like Abiezer Coppe and Laurence Clarkson, pushed the envelope by modeling what free thought and free transmission of ideas, what greater democracy might look like if it could take hold of England. But perhaps the great hero of this period was Winstanley's printer, Giles Calvert, who through his London print shop fostered a network of religious radicals (Hill, *World* 373).[11] Or, as Hill suggests, he was simply interested in printing works that gave him a unique niche in a literary market bursting at the seams (17). Whatever the case, the lords of the manor clearly had no desire for such literature or for this kind of democracy to take hold and pushed for wider printing regulations and, thus, control of the transmission of ideas.

In 1662, Parliament enacted laws that limited the number of printers and required strict licensing.[12]

Despite the fact that Winstanley's argument for human rights was rooted in a legitimate and personal quest for human dignity, we should not throw out Locke and the popular European roots of rights discourse completely. Because Locke's conception of liberty was so important to the revolutionary projects of the eighteenth century, we must address his work cautiously and, perhaps, alongside the work of more inclusive theorists like Winstanley and Mary Wollstonecraft. From such a reading, a richer, more critical history of rights discourse in Western Europe might emerge. On the other hand, human rights theorist and historian Jack Donnelly warns that we should not be misled by the tendency of some to focus solely on Locke's interest in the protection of property and, ultimately, self-preservation in his *Second Treatise*. He offers a more radical interpretation in an effort to overturn the notion that Locke is simply the founder of a conservative form of liberalism.

In fact, Locke's theory of rights may form the bedrock for a theory of social justice. Donnelly contends that in Locke, "*self-*preservation typically appears not alone but in conjunction with the right and duty to preserve *all mankind*" (91). Self-preservation and the protection of one's self as property means that one has the fundamental right to safety and security. In order to maintain everyone's right to self-preservation, we are obliged to protect one another because we have entered into a social contract. In turn, we are obliged to support practices that foster social justice and human dignity for all. These would include the obligation to allow others to communicate their needs and desires, for example, to seek redress for grievances. We have a duty to let others speak for themselves when their right to self-preservation is violated. Following this argument, rights are interdependent; you cannot have one without the other. You cannot own yourself if you cannot cry foul. You cannot cry foul if you cannot own yourself. Such a reading could lead to openings in the public sphere for the subaltern. In "Letter Concerning Toleration" Locke is interested in protecting (mostly) everyone's right to religious freedom—he is at the very least concerned with protecting everyone from physical harm. However, in his own life, his interests were less than positive as his scandalous ties to the advent of the Carolina slave regime suggests.

So it goes that in fits and starts, rights discourse progresses toward claims of greater rights for all human beings, including the right to communicate freely. When *La Déclaration des droits de l'Homme et du citoyen* or the *Declaration of the Rights of Man and of the Citizen* was published in 1789, it, more than any document produced in Western Europe up until that time, synthesized the most egalitarian and democrat arguments for human rights in the eighteenth century. Most importantly, for this discussion, it declares in Article 11: "La libre communication des pensées et des opinions est un des droits les plus précieux de l'homme; tout citoyen peut donc parler, écrire, imprimer librement" or "Free communication of ideas and opinions is one of the most precious of the rights of man. Consequently, every citizen may speak, write, and print freely." This is, perhaps, the first clear articulation of the human right to communicate freely in a broad sense. The *Declaration of the Rights of Man and of the Citizen* places this right within a pantheon of other rights, claiming the general importance and significance of human communication—sharing information, ideas, and needs. Though the authors discussed above did not necessarily establish the "right to communicate freely" specifically, they lay the groundwork for this right by establishing or seeking to establish other rights: to movement, to assembly (especially for religious purposes), to the press, to representation, and to speaking freely.

These communication rights are especially significant because, ultimately, human rights in the seventeenth and eighteenth centuries are limited to those who can define themselves in the public sphere. To be able to define one's self and to have access to mechanisms for doing this, not just to print technology, but to literacy, education, culture, and community, is absolutely important. Humans of all shapes, sizes, abilities, classes, colors, and sexes must have the ability to communicate freely within the public sphere and, in doing so, represent themselves, their ideas, and their human rights. If they do not, that space must be redefined. In the seventeenth and eighteenth centuries, it is the exception, not the rule, that we hear the voices of the subaltern. But the African slave—the bearer of the economic burdens propelling Western Europe at a blinding pace into the nineteenth century, on the cusp of the modern age—is still without a voice in the public sphere. The slave is still spoken of and for by those with means, by those sipping on coffee sweetened by a dollop of sugar and sweat.

Chapter 2

* *

DISSENSION IN THE RANKS
Regarding, Evaluating, and Revealing Slavery in Eighteenth-Century America

> Come, join hand in hand, brave Americans all,
> And rouse your bold hearts at fair liberty's call;
> No tyrannous acts shall suppress your just claim,
> Or stain with dishonor America's name.
> —John Dickinson, "The Liberty Song"

IN THE FALL OF 1774 Englishman Thomas Paine arrived in Philadelphia carrying with him an introductory note from Benjamin Franklin, one of America's first media moguls. At that time, Philadelphia was the center of colonial communications, displacing Boston in no small part due to Franklin's press. Having achieved much since his humble beginnings working for his abusive brother in Boston, Franklin was connected to printing presses throughout the Americas. This network included partnerships in Philadelphia, New York, Lancaster, New Haven, and Antigua. In 1731, after the South Carolina government offered a reward of 175 pounds sterling to any printer willing to set up shop in the colony, Franklin dispatched one of his own printers, Thomas Whitemarsh, to accept the position. However, Whitemarsh passed away shortly after arriving. His replacement, and the first successful printer in South Carolina (meaning that he did not die shortly upon arrival into the colony's disease-inducing climate), was Lewis Timothy. Timothy, of French Huguenot origins, lived in Philadelphia after first immigrating to the colonies and soon became one of Franklin's trusted employees. Apparently, though, Timothy was a better printer than accountant. Franklin writes in his *Autobiography*, "He was a man of learning and honest, but ignorant in matters of account" (166). Despite his financial ineptness, Lewis Timothy's publications were widely disseminated. One of his greatest successes was the *South Carolina Gazette*, controlled by his wife, Elizabeth, and his son, Peter, after his death. In its heyday it was one of the most popular publications in the Southern colonies. It was so widely read that information contained in the *Gazette* could have crossed the paths of literate or attentive slaves. Some historians speculate that a notice printed in the newspaper may have influenced the planning of the Stono Rebellion. Peter Wood asserts that the rebels may have "been influenced by the newspaper publication, in mid-August [1739], of the Security Act which required all white men to carry firearms to church on Sunday or submit to a stiff fine, beginning on September 29" (313). Knowing that "all white men" would soon be armed on Sundays, a day when they may have gone otherwise, the plotters perhaps felt the need to act quickly.

The hypothesis that Timothy and Franklin's *South Carolina Gazette* stood in some causal relationship to the Stono Rebellion underscores the growing importance of print technology in the colonies. In eighteenth-century America, and in the greater Atlantic world, print communications connected disparate ports and nations and fostered a substantial trade in ideas. While publications were closely censored in the early years of the colonies, this regulation slowly relaxed, allowing colonial writers to speak more freely, in some cases, than their European counterparts. The Massachusetts Assembly took a major step in the direction of free and open debate by publishing its minutes in 1715. And by 1730 colonial governors were no longer mandated to control and license the press—thus opening the door for even more liberated publishing. But the 1765 Stamp Act was the great tipping point as it forced newspapers into a focused political engagement.[1] Printers were hit hard by this act and seized the opportunity to organize the public via their newspapers and pamphlets. This opposition to the Stamp Act dramatically increased communications among the colonies, spreading ideas through newspapers, broadsides, and pamphlets in an effort to promote a unified front against the British. Paul Starr believes the critical role of publishing in this revolutionary moment established free and open communication as a foundational principle of the new nation. He notes, "The pre-Revolutionary crisis in America established the press as the central venue of public discussion independent of government, and the conflict and its immediate aftermath consolidated the status and rights of the press and the priority of open debate as a means of conducting politics in the new republic" (70).

Therefore, of all the rights Revolutionary writers argued for, the most significant were those that supported free communication—the right to a free press, free speech, and free assembly. They knew that without access to these rights, they could not represent themselves and their ideas in the public sphere. The framers of the United States Constitution remembered the importance of these communication rights because the practice of free speech, press, and assembly allowed the colonies to unify so rapidly, and they enshrined them as civil rights in the first amendment: "Congress shall make no law respecting an establishment of religion, or prohibiting the free exercise thereof, or abridging the freedom of speech, or of the press, or the right of the people peaceably to assemble, and to petition their government for a redress of grievances." While Starr agrees that such protections in the Bill of Rights and in the courts helped establish the right to communicate, "the traditional basis of a free press lay not in courts, but in politics and in the fragmented and decentralized structure of American institutions" (81). In other words, communication rights are defined by and because of rational, critical debate in the public sphere. During the Revolutionary period, rights discourse with its European Enlightenment roots fanned the flames of political and social agitation and helped define these specific rights. It was the theory behind the practice. Without the ability to publish, the argument would go nowhere. In fact, because so many exercised their right to communicate, the argument was everywhere.

Colonial printers were capable of publishing materials that could respond rapidly to the latest crisis and be placed into the hands of an eager and consuming public. Pamphlets were produced often and served as excellent vehicles for the spread of ideas, both popular and unpopular. Most importantly, they were inexpensive and could be published anonymously. Beginning as a trickle and developing into a waterfall, pamphlets were an incessant part of the colonists' rights campaign. "Over and over, the pamphlets of the period rehearse[d] the essential connections between legal philosophy, social contract theory, and the American situation in a step-by-step presentation of the truth and its sources from the beginning of history down to the present moment" (Ferguson 87). This repetition of "evidence" produced a uniquely American rights discourse that, even though it was anchored in the secular Enlightenment's idealization of reason, did not deny the religious roots of most colonists. This brand of rights discourse wed reason and religion in pamphlet after pamphlet in an effort to create a unified public.

John Locke was one important influence on writers of this period. The force of his political theories, in particular, his description of the social contract and natural rights in his *Second Treatise*, compelled many to seek independence from England on the basis of the right to just governance and the right to revolution. John Hope Franklin notes that Locke's ruminations on government were "political gospel" (127). Samuel Adams, a vocal member of this "Church of Locke," championed Lockean political theory in his pamphlet *The Rights of the Colonists* (1772). His argument owes much to the author of the Fundamental Constitutions of Carolina. Adams claims, "Among the natural rights of the colonists are these: first, a right to life; secondly, to liberty; thirdly, to property; together with the right to support and defend them in the best manner they can. These are evident branches of, rather than deductions from, the duty of self-preservation, commonly called the first law of nature" (417). Adams summarizes the Lockean description of the evolution of the social contract and the necessity of human rights. Governments exist, he asserts, to protect life, liberty, and property. If governments are based on protecting these human rights, then the American colonists, because they have consented to this government through the social contract, should have them too. Adams writes that colonists must assert these rights through this revolutionary struggle. He cites Locke directly: "'Just and true liberty, equal and impartial liberty,' in matters spiritual and temporal, is a thing that all men are clearly entitled to by the eternal and immutable laws of God and nature" (417). Like many writers before and after him, Adams rests his argument on human rights claims as a last resort because no civil redress, in his view, has been afforded the colonists. Living within the British Empire, they were technically protected under English common law as well as "laws of God and nature." But, Adams argues, without protection from common law, representation, and equal treatment, they must adhere to the ultimate claims of the "laws of God and nature."

Four years later Thomas Paine produced a pamphlet that in some ways echoed Adams yet had a wider and longer-lasting impact. *Common Sense* (January 9, 1776) was the most widely read pamphlet of the Revolution. In it Paine argues in favor of American independence from Great Britain and for the creation of a republican form of government over a hereditary monarchy. He calls for an end to reconciliation efforts and bases this assertion on the right of human beings to decide how they wish to be governed.

Paine implies that the controversies over taxes and other specific abuses are indicators of this greater issue. He paints with broad strokes: "Europe, and not England, is the parent country of America. This new world hath been the asylum for the persecuted lovers of civil and religious liberty from every part of Europe. Hither have they fled, not from the tender embraces of the mother, but from the cruelty of the monster; and it is so far true of England, that the same tyranny which drove the first emigrants from home, pursues their descendents still" (*Reader* 81–82). The colonies were the obvious, almost predestined, location for this experiment in human rights to occur. "The cause of America is in a great measure the cause of all mankind," and this should not be taken lightly (66). Paine writes that the colonists have a singular opportunity to create a government based on "common interest" as opposed to the tyranny of the few (67). Governments, including that of the English, are fundamentally flawed because they afford a place for a monarchy and aristocracy which limit the "common interest" and the possibility of democratic governance (69). Paine notes that those Englishmen who defend such a government must do so out of national pride and not out of rational arguments (71). American Loyalists might also fear the kind of revolutionary and democratic government Paine desires—one rooted in the "common" people. He calls for equal representation, a unicameral legislature, and protection of basic human rights including "freedom and property to all men, and above all things the free exercise of religion, according to the dictates of conscience" (91).

Throughout *Common Sense*, Paine employs sensationalist rhetoric to engage his audience, reminding them of the violent experiences of some colonists: "The blood of the slain, the weeping voice of nature cries, 'TIS TIME TO PART'"; the colonies must unite and move from "argument to arms" (83, 80). He reminds readers of the events of Boston and speaks to those who still seek reconciliation, "Hath your house been burnt? Hath your property been destroyed before your face? Are your wife and children destitute of a bed to lie on, or bread to live on?" (85). But these painful violations should not simply lead the colonists to seek retributive justice. Throughout *Common Sense*, Paine reminds readers of the opportunity they have to set a new example for the world by asserting their human rights: "'Tis not the affair of a city, a country, a province, or a kingdom, but of a continent—of at least one eighth part of the habitable globe. 'Tis not the concern of a day, a year, or an age; posterity . . . will be more or less affected, even to the end of time, by the proceedings now" (80). Paine recognizes that the colonists' actions could have universal implications and change the course of history. "O ye that love mankind! Ye that dare oppose, not only tyranny, but the tyrant, stand forth! Every spot of the old world is over-run with oppression" (93). There is no place for freedom anywhere on earth, he claims; the colonies must be "an asylum for mankind." In a later edition of *Common Sense* Paine invokes the story of Noah and writes: "We have it in our power to begin the world over again. . . . The birth-day of a new world is at hand" (109). Harvey J. Kaye writes that *Common Sense* united the colonists in such a way that they were no longer Britons, "but Americans, fighting not for British rights but for human rights. Thus, separation would not be a desperate, criminal, or treasonous act but an inspired, moral, and patriotic one" (43). The violence they would and did perpetuate would be just.

Because of its vast readership—over 150,000 copies were sold in a few months after the first printing—*Common Sense* exemplifies the important place literary communications had in fomenting the American Revolution.[2] The pamphlet was read aloud, shared, and distributed throughout the colonies. Many pamphlets were published during this period, but Paine's had a particularly significant influence because it relied on an argument based on, as he writes, "simple facts, plain arguments, and common sense" (79). Most importantly, "Paine end[ed] the impasse that loyal resistance impose[d] on colonial argumentation" (Ferguson 110). Paine not only asked the public to join together to create a government, he did so in a simple manner that spoke to them, using rhetorical tools they could connect with, in particular, the Bible. At the same time, Paine could be quite irreverent, as when he describes the far from noble English line of hereditary succession: "A French bastard landing with an armed banditti, and establishing himself king of England against the consent of the natives, is in plain terms a very paltry rascally original" (76).

Thomas Paine presented the cause of human rights in a way that spoke to and for a broader audience, causing the colonial public sphere to open, if only slightly. This was due, in part, to Paine's unimpressive, working-class background—he was an authentic revolutionary. Until he entered the fray, most pamphleteers were "lawyers, merchants, planters, and ministers" (Foner 85). Paine's humble origins and his keen eye for inequality intermingled in a simple but powerful rights argument that spoke to the colonial working classes—a group not often represented in European governments of the eighteenth century. In Philadelphia, Paine developed close ties to the artisan classes of the city. They were literate and politically engaged and in significant ways sparked the revolution.

On top of his working-class roots, Paine was well informed and attuned to the Zeitgeist, especially the ever-popular Locke-rooted rights discourse. But not all the political leaders of the Revolution found Paine's rhetoric appealing. John Adams believed his argument for republican government unoriginal—except for what he perceived as his working-class language, not that he saw that as a positive (Foner 82). His writings, the conservative Adams believed, were far too democratic in tone. Yet Paine made it clear to all of his readers that for the Revolution to occur, a broadly defined public must push it forward. He empowered his readership, saying that they were intelligent enough and had the "common sense" to do so.

Empowering the public to hold the British in low esteem is a theme of American Revolutionary literature because it both helped prepare the way for an eventual break with the British and prepared for the written declaration of that break. Thus, the colonial public was not offended by the bold claims of the Declaration of Independence. They were ready for them. When Thomas Jefferson penned the first draft, he employed Paine's democratic brand of rights discourse and carried it to a magnificent climax by giving the colonial public the opportunity "to assume among the powers of the earth, the separate and equal station to which the laws of nature and of nature's god entitle them." Human rights were central in Jefferson's text, particularly the right to be treated with dignity: "We hold these truths to be self-evident, that all men are created equal, that they are endowed by their creator with certain unalienable rights, that among these are life, liberty and the pursuit of happiness.—That to secure these rights, governments are instituted among men, deriving their just powers from the consent of the governed,—That whenever any form of government becomes destructive of these ends, it is the right of the people to alter or to abolish it, and to institute new government." When governments infringe upon the human rights of people, the people have the right to begin anew; as Locke notes in the *Second Treatise*, the people have "a right to resume their original liberty" (12.222). Thus, the Declaration of Independence acknowledges that natural rights violations are not "light and transient cause[s]"; such violations are reason enough for the colonists to separate from the English. The list of "abuses" that follows in the Declaration serves as evidence to a "candid world" that theirs is a just cause and not a move based on the whims of a few self-appointed spokespersons. The whole colony speaks as one for they have suffered the abuse of the British together and now wish to become a sovereign among sovereigns.

To become such, their argument had to be rooted in legitimate claims. Thus, Jefferson presents King George as one of the first great villains of American literature, accusing him of "repeated injuries"—port blockades, justice obstruction, dissolution of legitimate legislative bodies, the imposition of military order, and so on—that had limited colonists' freedom. They had "petitioned for redress," but to no avail. It was their human right, then, to leave the government of the British and begin anew. But the international community was not the only intended audience of this declaration. It was primarily meant to establish the consent of the colonists to this project. Rough estimates assume that in the American colonies one-third were loyalists, one-third were patriots, and one-third were indifferent. Therefore, commitment and consensus were literary imperatives, and Jefferson fostered a literary consensus by creatively molding his sources, the ideas of a number of European philosophers, into "something specifically American" (Ferguson 35).

When the Declaration of Independence was published, it had a very public introduction to the American people and was read aloud to large groups in towns throughout the united colonies, including New Brunswick, Philadelphia, and Halifax. When readers finished, attentive audiences cheered. The Declaration served as a signal of political and cultural independence for these cheering colonists; now this diverse assortment of human beings thrown together in the New World was exercising its right to speak freely and on its own behalf. Yet the Declaration of Independence was part of a larger literate phenomenon through which the public sphere widened in eighteenth-century America. Larzer Ziff notes that during the latter half of the century, print publications became more egalitarian in general. He offers the example of James Hector St. Jean de Crèvecoeur's *Letters from an American Farmer*. The narrator, Farmer James, is urged by his minister to write his "letters" just as he speaks and to describe that which he knows, that which is around him. It does not matter that the author is not much of a farmer; what matters is the appearance that someone as lowly as a farmer *could* write and publish. While groups like farmers and artisans who previously had little political voice were now participants in the American public sphere, significant populations were still excluded and their voices were edited out of the first public document of the United States. Jefferson's first draft of the Declaration was closely scrutinized by the Continental Congress; his denunciations of slavery were famously expunged in an effort to appease slave states like South Carolina that did not appreciate his musings on this topic. This draft accused King George of waging "cruel war against human nature itself, violating its most sacred rights of life and liberty in the persons of a distant people who never offended him, captivating and carrying them into slavery" (*Writings* 22). Of course, Jefferson's language was rather contradictory; slavery was the fault not only of the British but also of quite a few colonists.

In spite of, or because of, this reason, this language had to be removed from the final draft. Mentioning human rights and African slaves in the same sentence was beyond the limits of what Judith Butler calls "the domain of the speakable" (*Excitable Speech* 141). The exclusion of Jefferson's denunciations of slavery from the Declaration of Independence is a trademark of what Robert Ferguson calls the "consensual literature" of the Revolutionary period: public consensus was needed in order for the colonies to break away, to take such a great risk. And the consensus—or at least the dictates of a powerful few—was that slaves were not a part of that public. Thus, Jefferson, the new nation's great scribe, "learned that on the question of slavery one yielded to older and more cautious men, and especially to outspoken objections from any segment of the planter class" (D. Davis, *Problem of Revolution* 173). The remaining reference to slavery, which comes at the tail end of the list of abuses, is quite revealing. In the final version, "the rhetorical climax of the long train of alleged abuses was the accusations that George III had attempted to stir up 'domestic insurrections'—that is, slave rebellions like those the British governor Dunmore had encouraged by proclamation in Virginia in 1775 to undermine the colony's plantation economy" (Armitage 56). The movers and shakers of this period, the wealthy landowners, wished to make clear their desire to retain colonial order. Counter-narratives emanating from below, from "the domain of the unspeakable," would not be tolerated. One should not lose sight of the fact that this document, which so evidently sought to stifle legitimate human rights claims, would later be recast as a template for emancipation and human rights. Howard Zinn explains: "The point of noting those outside the arc of human rights in the Declaration is not . . . to lay impossible moral burdens on that time. It is to try to understand the way in which the Declaration functioned to mobilize certain groups of Americans, ignoring others. Surely, inspirational language to create a secure consensus is still used, in our time, to cover up serious conflicts of interest in that consensus, and to cover up, also, the omission of large parts of the human race" (73). In a sense, the debate concerning the relative importance of the Declaration is ongoing as those living in the United States of American continue to debate who gets to be human, who gets to have human rights. We have yet to reach consensus on such matters.

But consensual literary practices were absolutely necessary when, in the years following the Revolution, the leaders of the new nation turned "the people themselves into the authors of the Constitution" (Ferguson 131). Divisions had to be settled and political and cultural unity had to be established. James Madison, Edmund Randolph, James Wilson, and Gouverneur Morris wrote drafts of the Constitution, but the document's concision and its use of the first-person plural signified the people of the United States as its singular author. It begins, "We the People of the United States, in Order to form a more perfect Union, establish Justice, insure domestic Tranquility, provide for the common defense, promote the general Welfare, and secure the Blessings of Liberty to ourselves and our Posterity, do ordain and establish this Constitution for the United States of America." The text assumes the voice of the people and in so doing assumes the right to create their government. In turn, "by constituting the government, the people's text literally constitutes the people" (Warner, *Letters* 102). Yet, again, in the name of consensus, women, Native Americans, and slaves were not considered "people"; they were not allowed the security of "liberty" or, for that matter, "justice." The democratic potential of the new republic was momentarily laid to rest as private interests were met in the name of unity. Most noticeably, the Constitution met the peculiar needs of wealthy Southern planters in Articles 1 and 4 by offering a "shocking adaptation of the mathematical penchants of the Enlightenment" (Ferguson 150). Like the Declaration of Independence, the Constitution was supposed to represent the zenith of rights discourse during the Revolutionary period. This was a document that practiced power by establishing a discourse "situated at the level of 'it is said'" (Foucault, *Archaeology* 122). It was meant to embody ultimate meaning. And yet the Constitution serves as textual representation of a public rupture in human rights, a rupture that has always existed and has created permanent friction between the ideals of human rights and the awful realities of human behavior.

DISCOURSE OF DISSENT AND DISCONTENT

The debate among whites before and after these public documents were produced reveals widespread confusion and ambiguity regarding the human rights of enslaved or free blacks. The written record indicates persistent dissent as opposed to the apparent consent of the Declaration of Independence and the Constitution. Though the abolition movement—often considered the *first* international human rights movement—reached its peak in the nineteenth century, rights discourse appeared in concert with calls for an end to slavery throughout the eighteenth century. Throughout the American Revolution many writers were unafraid to highlight the hypocrisy of those who owned slaves while simultaneously advocating liberty from England. And there were many in England who seized upon this glaring contradiction. Horace Walpole exclaimed, "If all the black slaves were in rebellion I should have no doubt in choosing my side, but I scarce wish perfect freedom to merchants who are the bloodiest of all tyrants. I should think the souls of Africans would sit heavy on the swords of Americans" (qtd. in Gay 409). While fellow Brit Samuel Johnson wondered aloud, "How is it that we hear the loudest yelps for liberty among the drivers of negroes?" (454).

But such questions were also asked by writers in the colonies and in the early United States. American Hugh Henry Brackenridge expressed his disgust with the institution of slavery in an essay entitled "Thoughts on the Enfranchisement of the Negroes" in the December 1779 issue of *United States Magazine*. He writes, "It casts a shade upon the face of this country that some of those who cultivate her soil are slaves; slaves not to Britain, but to men who are themselves free" (104). Brackenridge reclaims the term "slaves," bandied about by many patriots, and reminds the reader of its actual meaning. He pleads that it is not the destiny of some to suffer on earth—the world can be otherwise. Others argue, he notes, that, materially, slaves are better off: "Yes, but they are in a worse situation as to liberty, which is (a phrase common in our ears every day) a most valuable blessing."[3] Brackenridge's was part of an ever-growing din of public condemnations of chattel slavery by writers arguing from many perspectives of slavery's immoral nature and clear erasure of human rights.

The narrative of rights discourse in early American literature covers broad territories and is richer than the often-edited arguments for independence from Britain. This other narrative analyzes restrictions to human freedom—and in this case "human" does not mean only white and male—employing a rights discourse with religious and secular Enlightenment roots. James Otis's 1764 "Rights of the British Colonies Asserted and Proved," for example, cites Locke's premise that "the natural liberty of man is to be free" as reason enough for abolishing slavery as well as for allowing the colonies to be independent. But Otis then acknowledges the great "giver" of this human liberty by writing that "this gift of God cannot be annihilated" (104). In an effort to explain this contradiction, anti-slavery advocates of the eighteenth century employed a variety of forms including essays and poems in a range of tones from moderate to sentimental to damning.

Perhaps more revolutionary than "Common Sense," Thomas Paine's 1775 essay "On African Slavery" marries religious and secular arguments to condemn slavery.[4] Paine understood well how to appeal to a wide audience, and in this particular essay religion is his bait. He chastises "Americans" directly, writing "that many civilized, nay, Christianized people should approve, and be concerned in the savage practice, is surprising ... though it has been so often proved contrary to the light of nature, to every principle of justice and humanity" (*Reader* 52). And "most shocking of all" are those pro-slavery advocates who use the Bible in order to support the practice (53). Few arguments have convinced such hypocrites that the practice is evil. Perhaps they would respond if they themselves were enslaved? Paine writes, if slaves "could carry off and enslave some thousands of us, would we think it just?" (54). He thus appeals to the interrelatedness of all people and the Golden Rule. Respecting this "law" is the only way to ensure that the dignity of all humans is respected.

But Paine knows he must offer more compelling arguments, other than the traditional Christian mantra for human dignity, in order to protect himself from hostile critics. Thus, Paine establishes that he is not alone in this analysis of slavery and cites John Locke, among others, in a "succession of eminent men" condemning the practice (52). Following Locke's cue, it seems, he argues that the slave trade opposes the laws of nature—that man is "an unnatural commodity." Slavery is a violation of the human right to freedom: "As these people are not convicted of forfeiting freedom, they have still a natural, perfect right to it; and the governments whenever they come should, in justice set them free, and punish those who hold them in slavery" (54). Paine again echoes Locke by noting that there is no way of knowing if slaves are prisoners of war. Therefore, "the slave, who is proper owner of his freedom, has a right to reclaim it." Paine writes that his purpose is not to simply argue against the practice—he wishes to ask Americans to consider the contradictions between this practice and the reality they wish to create. Sounding like Johnson, he notes, "With that consistency, or decency they complain so loudly of attempts to enslave them, while they hold so many hundred thousands in slavery; and annually enslave many thousands more, without any pretence of authority, or claim upon them?" (55). Amidst the rhetoric of revolution, Paine places this contradiction front and center—the colonists call for justice because of England's wrongs while perpetuating a gross injustice of their own.

Paine wonders if all those involved in the slave trade will suffer God's wrath. Remember, this essay's target audience is *all* Americans, thus everyone living in the colonies is indicted and will potentially suffer divine retribution. Paine writes, "How just, how suitable to our crime is the punishment with which providence threatens us?" (55). With retribution looming, he takes up the possibility of resolving this injustice and wonders aloud how slaves could possibly be freed—the ever-present "what next" question. Paine favors a process involving a Winstanley-esque system of land redistribution to the slaves so that, "all may have some property, and fruits of their labors at their own disposal" (55). Resolution will require further steps, including providing Africans and slaves with an education in Christianity. Like the first Christians, Americans should spread the gospel, though Paine seems to feel that this time it should be done as an act of repentance: "what singular obligations are we under to these injured people!" It is as though he advocates for a public relations campaign, a "truth commission" of sorts, as a first step for repairing the damage wrought by slavery.

Less well known today than Paine's essay is David Cooper's pamphlet *A Mite Cast into the Treasury: or, Observations on Slave-Keeping*, published in Philadelphia in 1772. Cooper was a Quaker abolitionist but was hesitant to attach his name to this document and so it was published anonymously.[5] In an introduction to the piece, Cooper reminds the reader that the human mind is capable of rationalizing anything it favors, that there is no "absurdit[y] too glaring for it to unite or reconcile" (38). Even children are capable of such rationalizations as they see, from an early age, how poorly white people treat black people and thus from the beginning assume those with black skin are not the same as themselves in the eyes of God. Cooper follows many of the same conventions of anti-slavery writing that Paine follows and calls upon Christians to adhere to Jesus's "golden rule" (40). Most important to Cooper's argument is his premise that one cannot justify slavery because slavery is a violation of natural law—in particular, as it has been defined by Locke. In this manner he calls attention to his own connection to the transatlantic trade in Enlightenment discourse. Cooper asserts the equality of human beings: "for every individual of the human species by the law of nature comes into the world equally entitled to freedom at a proper age" (42). Anyone denying an adult of their freedom "commits acts of violence against the strongest laws of nature,—robs that individual of his inherent property, his freedom, a right which was never given by the universal Father to any one creature over one another" (42). Here Cooper makes powerful connections between Locke's natural law and divine law.

Cooper concludes the pamphlet with a postscript that presents the sources for his concept of natural law. He writes, "Civilians define it thus—'The law of nature is that which God at man's creation infused into him, for his preservation and direction; is an eternal law and may not be changed; is the law of all places, persons and times without alteration, and has the same forces all the world over; its object is the good and happiness of mankind'" (48). With decidedly religious overtones Cooper defines natural law as universal and requiring that all humans be treated with dignity; this would preclude the enslavement of others. To buttress the layman's definition of natural law, he notes that Locke, "that celebrated master of reason, in his treatise on government, speaks much to the present purpose" (48). Cooper then cites a number of his favorite passages from Locke's *Second Treatise* and closes with Locke's thoughts concerning ultimate possession, allowing the philosopher to speak for himself: "Every man is born with a right of freedom to his person, which no other man has a power over; but the free disposal of it lies in himself" (49).

In another pamphlet published in 1783 Cooper follows a similar tack, noting that in Africa those now enslaved were free before being captured by "the more savage Christians" (*Serious Address* 64).[6] Because of this, slaves have the human right to their freedom: "With equal justice may negroes say, By the immutable laws of nature, we are equally entitled to life, liberty and property with our lordly masters, and have never ceded to any power whatever, a right to deprive us thereof" (64). This line of reasoning is based on Locke's premise that one can choose to give up these rights or not. Notably, this text appears in a column aligned side by side with the arguments white colonists are making concerning their treatment by the

British. Cooper makes a poignant and timely visual connection regarding the dissonance created by white colonists who argue for liberty when they, in fact, are depriving others of it. He notes that the language of the Declaration of Independence is "the language of the supreme council of America, in vindication of their rights as men, against imposition and unjust control" (69). But it is a flawed language; and Americans, those seeking to defend the "rights of humanity," must reconcile this issue.

More often than not, though, prominent political figures of the Revolutionary period and the early nation were ambiguous with regards to the peculiar institution. Patrick Henry, the man who shouted, "Give me liberty!" sums up this confusion best in a letter to Robert Pleasants dated January 18, 1773. Henry wrote this letter shortly after reading an anti-slavery tract composed by Quaker abolitionist Anthony Benezet. He wonders, "In a country, above all others, fond of liberty ... [w]ould anyone believe I am the owner of slaves of my own purchase! I am drawn along by the general inconvenience of living here without them. I will not, I cannot justify it.... I know not when to stop" (402). There were lines some Revolutionary leaders did not want to cross, indignities they did not wish to present to their constituents, steps they were unwilling to take. And, yet, beneath this pragmatic front was the recognition that they were advancing a terrible trade. The path for the new nation was uncertain because their political, social, and economic lives were tied up in this abhorrent trade in one way or another. Thus, many remained hopelessly discontent, vexed, and unsettled over the issue.

Thomas Jefferson is a prime example of public and private discontent over slavery, discontent that did not end when his commentaries on the subject were edited from the Declaration of Independence and would resurface in his *Notes on the State of Virginia* (1781). Here he presents a rational and proper discussion of his home state based on his own empirical observations—as any product of the Enlightenment would. One discovers Jefferson's interest in cataloging, his meticulousness, his penchant for exploration, and, ultimately, his almost obsessive commitment to enquiry. With exquisite precision Jefferson provides a detailed picture of the state of Virginia as he sees it as well as his own vision for the political future of that state and of the United States of America. Jefferson's vision does not include industrialized cities like those developing in Europe. His would be a nation of farmers because, he writes, "Those who labour in the earth are the chosen people of God" (170). For Jefferson, farms are a means to preserve what Leo Marx calls "rural virtue" and are not necessarily dynamic financial catalysts for the new nation (126). Rapid economic growth is less important for Jefferson than social and political stability. Yet, there is one significant problem with which the new nation will have to contend as it seeks social and political stability: slavery.

The new nation, and Jefferson himself, must confront the issue head-on—in particular, what to do with thousands of slaves who have endured years of servitude and indignation. In "Query 14: Laws," Jefferson calls for the resettlement of freed slaves because he believes it will be difficult for them to integrate with "society" for myriad reasons. He cites "deep rooted prejudices entertained by the whites; ten thousand recollections, by the blacks, of the injuries they have sustained; new provocations; the real distinctions which nature has made; and many other circumstances, will divide us into parties, and produce convulsions which will probably never end but in the extermination of the one or the other race" (*Notes on the State of Virginia* 145). In addition, he believes there are physical and moral differences between whites and blacks that will prevent true integration, a concern that reveals his racism and his ignorance of the living conditions of slaves. He writes that blacks smell worse compared to whites; require less sleep; are "at least as brave and more adventuresome. But this may perhaps proceed from a want of forethought" (146). Jefferson claims that blacks are incapable of deep consideration and emotion. They do not know how to truly love—theirs is "more an eager desire"—and "their griefs are transient." He concludes, "In general, their existence appears to participate more of sensation than reflection" (146). When the reader assumes that this racist litany could not get any worse, Jefferson notes that blacks are "in reason much inferior, as I think one could scarcely be found capable of tracing and comprehending the investigations of Euclid" (146).[7] He adds that even Native Americans are capable of producing rich stories and art, but that he has never heard such from blacks (147). He discounts the work of black writers Phillis Wheatley and Ignatius Sancho and adds that "Epictetus, Terence, and Phaedrus, were slaves. But they were of the race of whites. It is not their condition then, but nature, which has produced the distinction" (149). Jefferson concludes that blacks are incapable of cultural production, a significant assertion from the author of the Declaration of Independence.

Frank Shuffleton notes the fact that these claims are posited in "Query 14" amidst a discussion of legal codes: "In all European colonies the discourse of the law had focused specifically on black bodies and addressed the possibility of blacks as producers of culture only insofar as to prevent them from creating it" (xxvii). Blacks may not have been capable of producing what Jefferson would have considered "culture" because they were prevented from doing so; they were, more often than not, prevented from acquiring the literacy skills Jefferson would respect. Nor did they have the right to freely communicate with one another.

But something happens to Jefferson in "Query 18: Manners," and this man of reason becomes slightly unhinged. The task of the query is to describe "the particular customs and manners that may happen to be received" in his state. His response to this is illuminating. Jefferson writes that slavery has clearly had "an unhappy influence on the manners of our people" (168). The master-slave relationship is an ugly power play of "despotism" and "submissions." Jefferson is concerned by such relationships because children inevitably learn from their elders. The children of slave owners who are "nursed, educated, and daily exercised in tyranny, cannot but be stamped by its odious peculiarities." He wonders what effect this will have on the future of his state and on the new nation. One group is allowed willy-nilly to abuse the rights of another group, and this abused group becomes resentful. And the abusers believe they have a God-given right to treat their slaves as they wish. Jefferson's prose rushes to a difficult conclusion. He writes, "Indeed I tremble for my country when I reflect that God is just: that his justice cannot sleep for ever: that considering numbers, nature and natural means only, a revolution of the wheel of fortune, an exchange of situation, is among possible events: that it may become probable by supernatural interference! The Almighty has no attribute which can take side with us in such a contest.—But it is impossible to be temperate and to pursue this subject through the various consideration of policy, of morals, of history natural and civil" (169). A man who several chapters earlier presents his own rational analysis of the complete inferiority of blacks and the best solution for dealing with the "Negro problem," loses himself in a flurry of exclamation points and cries to heaven. For this champion of reason, "it is impossible to be temperate" and to clearly analyze the pertinent issues. Like Kurtz, he cries out in horror, recognizing that, in fact, the "Negro problem," the "Negro" hand, is everywhere. It is necessary to the production of his text and even—"I tremble for my country"—the developing nation. Given Jefferson's private affairs, he would recognize this awful fact.

What will become of this nation if God truly is just? Jefferson's exclamations reveal a keen awareness of possible resolutions, including full-scale insurrections, that could occur. Robert Ferguson reminds us, "Because the early Republic is still a Bible culture, God appears therein as the best available symbol of order and purpose against chaos and confusion" (78). And for Jefferson, who appears incapable of articulating his discontent, he sees no other recourse than to bring God into the equation. When faced with the limits of reason, his only outlet is the almighty. Jefferson concludes this brief chapter expressing his hope that a peaceful resolution will come soon, though he offers none. However, a limited resolution did occur when the U.S. Congress voted to end the importation of slaves. In an address to Congress on December 2, 1806, Jefferson offered praise for this first step to halt the importation of slaves: "those violations of human rights which have been so long continued on the unoffending inhabitants of Africa, and which morality, the reputation, and the best interests of our country, have long been eager to proscribe"(528).

The problem of slavery apparently "unhinged" quite a few writers at this time. Farmer-author J. Hector St. John de Crèvecoeur's *Letters from an American Farmer* (1782) describes the twin abuses of the slave trade—the excesses of its practitioners and the tortures inflicted on the slaves themselves—in what many view as the turning point in this book. Though not actually an epistolary novel, Crèvecoeur's letters are addressed to the American people even though at times he speaks harshly of some of them. In "Letter 9" the author depicts the lavish lifestyles of residents of Charles Town, South Carolina. The port city is "the center of our beau monde" and has a wealth that is surprising given the youth of the city (163–164). Yet despite all the "joy, festivity, and happiness in Charles Town, would you imagine that scenes of misery overspread in the country?" (165). The residents of Charles Town think little of the lives of slaves who live in a world completely controlled by their masters: "nothing but terrors and punishments are presented to them; death is denounced if they run away; horrid dilacerations if they speak with their native freedom; perpetually awed by the terrible cracks of whips, or by the fear of capital punishments" (170). Crèvecoeur, a sometime farmer, is appalled with the practice of slavery in the South, which he views as inhumane and unnatural. Slavery in the North is more humane and harmonious with the work of the farm. In South Carolina, "the owners of the soil have consigned to slaves the labor that would integrate them with their land" (Ziff 24). Such alienation from the soil leads to alienation from the natural order, from humanity, from proper care and treatment of others. Crèvecoeur condemns humanity for the practice of slavery and writes that the worldly pleasures that do exist are not enjoyed by the innocent: "Almost every where, liberty so natural to mankind is refused, or rather enjoyed but by their tyrants" (175). Joseph Brown Ladd, a sometime doctor and occasional poet from Charleston, would concur. In a letter from the last decade of the eighteenth century, he confides that Charlestonians are obsessed with "the pleasures of the table" (224). "Bacchus," he adds, "is a deity much respected in this country" (225).

Crèvecoeur delivers his most bitter denunciations of slavery in South Carolina when he describes a horrifying scene encountered one day when traveling to have dinner with a planter. Somewhere in the woods outside of Charles Town—he does not indicate the exact location—the author heard "a sound resembling a deep rough voice" and then noticed "something resembling a cage, suspended to the limbs of a tree; all the branches of which appeared covered with large birds of prey, fluttering all about, and anxiously endeavoring to perch on the cage" (176–177). He shot at the buzzards out of habit and quickly discovered "a negro, suspended in the cage, and left there to expire! I shudder when I recollect that the birds had already picked out his eyes, his cheek bones were bare; his arms had been attacked in several places, and his body seemed covered with a multitude of wounds. From the edges of the hollow sockets and from the lacerations with which he was disfigured, the blood slowly dropped, and tinged the ground beneath. No sooner were the birds flown, than swarms of insects covered the whole body of this unfortunate wretch, eager to feed on his mangled flesh and to drink his blood" (177). The author was shocked by this "living spectre" that asked him for water and wished he had a "ball" in his gun because if he did he would kill him. He gave him water and the slave thanked him and asked if he could put some poison in the water. Not sure how to respond, the author left the scene of the crime and continued his journey. When he arrived at his destination, he learned from his hosts that the slave in the cage had killed the plantation's overseer. They claimed that "self-preservation" requires such cruel punishments and defended "slavery with the arguments generally made use of to justify the practice; with the repetition of which I shall not trouble you at present" (178). Christopher Iannini believes this "rhetoric of 'self-preservation'" indicates that planters "viewed the slave's resistance, not as a random and isolated act, but as symptomatic of the genuine threat that revolt posed to the plantation order" (230). Despite his apparent disgust, Crèvecoeur broke bread with the planter, a man whose wealth was dependent on cruelty.

Earlier in the letter, this kernel of truth is not lost on the author as he makes astute connections among the various and persistent trading evils in the greater Atlantic world. In this way, his argument takes on universal dimensions and is more than an indictment of the South Carolina planting class. Like Voltaire's outspoken and mutilated "Negro," Crèvecoeur denounces an economy that uses "gold, dug from Peruvian mountains," to purchase slave ships and, ultimately, to disrupt families in "some harmless, peaceable African neighbourhood" (165–166). Both Voltaire and Crèvecoeur critique the inhumanity of the free market, the alienation of person from product, through the figure of the abused "Negro." And in both instances Europeans encounter slaves almost in total isolation—in transit and on the outskirts of a colonial city. Both Farmer James and Candide are faced with a troubling dilemma, what to do with or to this suffering human? In both instances the protagonists seem impotent when confronted with such obvious violations of human rights. "Good heavens!" cries Candide. "Oh, Nature, where art thou?" asks Farmer James (166). They are perplexed, unsure what to make of slavery in the age of enlightenment. How should it be addressed? All these white commentators do is cry to God and nature for mercy. They push on—ignoring the clear evidence of torture and abuse in front of them. On the contrary, the slave Crèvecoeur encounters is no passive observer. He, like the American colonists, is in a state of rebellion or, as Locke acknowledges, a constant "state of war" (*Second Treatise* 4.24). This slave was punished in the above manner because he killed his overseer, because he sought his freedom. Indeed, *he* was a true rebel—one who witnessed and experienced horror and sought to establish a counter-narrative in the public sphere.

PROUD CAROLINA AND THE BELLY OF HELL

During the eighteenth century, South Carolina emerged as a literary type—an over-indulgent, cruel, and tainted land, an extension of the West Indies. The colony and state's relationship with the slave trade drew scathing denunciations from those living in or visiting the state and experiencing chattel slavery directly, as one finds in Crèvecoeur, as well as from those who had never been to South Carolina. In letters, poems, and addresses, South Carolina, as spirit and as public, is excoriated directly. At times it is simply invoked so as to produce a nod of understanding from the reader. When Crèvecoeur describes his stay in South Carolina, he establishes his credentials as someone who truly knows slavery and the diseased landscape in which it thrives, the hot and humid summers, the torpid planters, and the anguished cries of tortured slaves—a deadly and sinful mixture, indeed. This is the picture, produced out of reality, that these writers wished to paint. Cruelty and opulence—tortured bodies versus pampered ones—were central themes for this peculiar genre of literature.

Not willing to risk publicly outing themselves, many Americans revealed their distaste of slavery in private letters, and an epistolary record of egregious human rights violations emerges throughout the eighteenth century. The letters of Francis Le Jau of the Society for Propagation of the Gospel in Foreign Parts (SPG) are particularly enlightening. Le Jau writes in the early days of the colony, when many of South Carolina's planters were recent émigrés of Barbados, a place known for enforcing a strict code on slaves—codes South Carolinians also found useful. In a letter dated February 20, 1712, Le Jau describes his dismay with a law establishing cruel and unusual punishments for runaway slaves—castration for men and cutting off the ears of women (108). In other instances, he explains, planters make use of apparently "medieval" torture apparatuses: "I must inform you of a most cruel contrivance. A man has invented to punish small faults in slaves. He puts them in a coffin where they are crushed almost to death, and he keeps them in that hellish machine for 24 hours." A year later Le Jau notes that such cruelties continue in the colony unabated. He knows he has been called to teach the gospel to slaves, but the planters in his flock are not interested in saving the souls of mere "Negroes." "They hamstring, maim, and unlimb those poor creatures for small faults"; and further, "I am at a loss when I see them in a praying posture knowing that at the same time they do not love their neighbour" (129–130).

Le Jau, like many in the Society for Propagation of the Gospel, is not openly opposed to slavery; he simply dislikes such punishments. However, his denunciations are extraordinary for someone behind enemy lines, so to speak. Le Jau's solution for resolving these abuses comes from Exodus 21, "which sets a slave at liberty if he should lose an eye or a tooth when he is corrected" (108). This passage from Exodus includes the famous pronouncement in the King James Version, "Eye for eye, tooth for tooth." In effect, he sets a precedent—the black body is worth less than the white body. If a slave loses an ear, the owner would lose his slave—not his own ear. But Le Jau ultimately concludes that not all slave owners are cruel, writing that "some good planters are of my opinion" concerning the horrors of slavery

(108). Like other SPG ministers, Le Jau worked for reform in an effort to win the trust of slaves so that he might convert them (D. Davis, *Western Culture* 218). The discipline he sought was spiritual rather than physical, and it was a discipline that many planters believed would work in their favor because, ultimately, the faith proselytized by Le Jau and company taught that a slave should respect the authority of his or her master—on earth and in heaven.

Some "good planters" were, in fact, of Le Jau's opinion. Later in this century of revolutions, one reads of the commencement of a few *quiet* revolutions with regards to slavery. In a letter dated August 14, 1776, Henry Laurens writes to his son John of his hatred for slavery—despite the fact that he owned many and had, for years, played a major role in their importation. He blames the British for establishing slavery in South Carolina and for exacerbating conditions by continuing to sell slaves to American planters. The elder Laurens exclaims, "You know, my dear son, I abhor slavery!" (405). He explains that he was born in a country where laws supported the slave trade—including the Fundamental Constitutions of Carolina. He hopes change is in the making "when, from principles of gratitude as well as justice, every man will strive to be foremost in showing his readiness to comply with the golden rule." Sounding much in the vein of his colleagues Henry and Jefferson, Laurens knows not where to turn as "Great powers" within the state oppose his unpopular opinions. David Brion Davis notes that, perhaps, British port blockades were the true cause of this change of heart (*Western Culture* 136). The progressive sentiments of his son John, though, are not as dubious. John served under Washington during the war and offered to organize a slave regiment with men culled from South Carolina plantations. These soldiers would, for the price of their service, gain their freedom at war's end. The plan was quickly put to rest by South Carolina legislators. When the younger Laurens was killed in battle late in the war, his ideals seem to have died with him—rare was the voice of dissent from within the Palmetto State in the late eighteenth century.

This was not so outside South Carolina. In Sarah Wentworth Apthorp Morton's unfinished poem "Beacon Hill: A Local Poem, Historic and Descriptive" (1797), the poet celebrates each state's participation in the Revolutionary War. When she addresses South Carolina, she exclaims:

> CHILD OF THE SUN, proud *Carolina* rise!
> And say what chief thy haughty hand supplies!

> Canst thou contend for freedom, while yon vale
> Pours its deep sorrows on the sultry gale!
> Thus rise with patriot heart supremely brave,
> Nor heed the scourge, that breaks thy shackled slave!—
> What boots the fleecy field, and ricey mead,
> If mid their bloom the culturing captive bleed!
> (*Beacon Hill* 194)

Morton exploits the contradictions. She praises South Carolinians for their struggle during the war, but chastises them for allowing slavery to continue. Like Crèvecoeur, she notes that South Carolinians treat their guests kindly and share in their abundance even though "the rich banquet, and the costly cheer, / Are fan'd by sighs, and moisten'd with a tear!" (195). She makes it clear that their wealth was built upon the suffering of others. In addition to the divisiveness of plantation slavery, she points out that there are also bitter class divides in the state. In a note to the reader at the bottom of the page, Morton reminds that "The original construction of Carolina was framed by the celebrated Mr. Locke, of an aristocratical form" (195). Even though the state apparently exudes more democratic principles, "there is no state in the union, in which the distinction of rank and situation is so tenaciously observed." This class divide and the figure of the hospitable Southerner will later become an integral part of plantation tradition literature and be described by writers like William Gilmore Simms and Thomas Nelson Page as a positive aspect of plantation society. Here it is a negative indicator of an opulent culture completely and utterly full of itself.

In many cases in eighteenth-century America, though, the loudest and most resounding cries for abolition came from the more radical wing of the Christian church.[8] In fact, Christian colonists began declaring their opposition to slavery publicly in the seventeenth century. In 1688 members of the Germantown Meeting signed a petition condemning the practice, and in 1693 Quaker George Keith denounced slavery and asserted that skin color does not preclude membership in the human family. These Christians recognized the practice of slavery as an affront to God's creation and, like Paine and Cooper, based their arguments on the Golden Rule: "Therefore all things whatsoever ye would that men should do to you, do you even so to them" (Matthew 7:12, King James). This "rule"—a statement about equality and human dignity—was one that rights advocates, both secular and religious, could claim. The Golden Rule was, in general, an important part of eighteenth-century rights discourse—though some took it more literally than others. These Christian writers, though, rarely displayed *Christian* forgiveness. They produced magnificent jeremiads that condemned the sinner and called forth God's wrath like the Old Testament prophets, predicting the possibilities of justice on earth or in death. From the more moderate, like Samuel Sewall and John Woolman, to the most radical, like Ralph Sandiford and Benjamin Lay, Christian writers valued human life and human rights and promoted immediate manumission. These were the renegades, the vanguard of human rights discourse in the eighteenth century.

Though perhaps the best known, John Woolman was not the only Quaker advocating for the abolition of slavery. Woolman's "testimony" was a part of a chorus of members of the Society of Friends demanding change in the practices of their fellow Quakers, Pennsylvania residents, and humankind. Two of the loudest voices in that chorus were those of Ralph Sandiford and Benjamin Lay. Repulsed by Quakers who owned slaves, both authors produced jeremiads denouncing slave owners in the Society of Friends. Perhaps, as Jean Soderlund writes, later advocates like Woolman were "gentler, and more persuasive leaders than Benjamin Lay and Ralph Sandiford," but Sandiford and Lay established a framework for advocates like Woolman or Anthony Benezet to seek change through more "official" channels (47). Because they demanded an end to a practice that supported the economic livelihoods of many, they were hardly appreciated in their day. These two fighting Quakers are particularly relevant to this conversation because both become anti-slavery zealots after experiencing slavery firsthand in South Carolina and in South Carolina's close cousin, Barbados. Their tenure in these locales where slavery sounded a similar tone pushed both men over the edge. Both Lay's and Sandiford's responses to the slave trade were published by that intrepid Pennsylvanian, Benjamin Franklin, and speak not only to the problem itself but to its possible resolution—radical or violent action.

In 1729, ten years before the Stono Rebellion, Ralph Sandiford published *A Brief Examination of the Practice of Our Times* without receiving permission from the Philadelphia Society of Friends. The book made its way to "the chief justice of the province, who threatened him with severe penalties, if he permitted it to be circulated" (Vaux 64). Sandiford ignored the orders and distributed his book widely. As advocate and author, Sandiford "shames and blames" through breathless, never-ending sentences that are reminiscent of English religious radicals Abiezer Coppe and Gerrard

Winstanley.⁹ This comparison is not a stretch; as a Quaker, Sandiford is literally a descendent of the English radical religious tradition. Through his writing he signals that he is no liberal nor is he an adherent of prayerful forgiveness like John Woolman.

Such views did not win allies within the Quaker leadership—many of whom were actively involved in slavery. Sandiford may have been correct, but he was not good for business. Sandiford's book opens with a dedication in which he establishes himself as an authority on slavery, having experienced the practice firsthand through his involvement in Atlantic commerce. He claims that he once spent some time in South Carolina after a series of disasters at sea, including a run-in with pirates and a leaking ship. Thus, upon arrival in South Carolina he was destitute and hoped to subsist on the kindness of strangers. He soon met a wealthy man who asked him to join him in a business venture, but when he discovered the source of the man's wealth, he lost interest in the partnership: "his riches being the product of Negro and Indian Slaves, which would have made me a debtor and an oppressor in the creation."¹⁰ Davis writes that after this discovery, Sandiford "tried to escape the taint of evil by refusing to share his employer's riches" (*Western Culture* 320). His experiences with slavery in South Carolina and throughout the Atlantic world must have made deep impressions, as *A Brief Examination* is simply one denunciation of slavery after another. He argues that it is incongruous for Quakers, a once oppressed group, to repay the God who has protected them by supporting the oppression of other humans (36). Quakers should be setting an example and furthering the rights of all people. Slavery, Sandiford argues, is a cruel theft of liberty, "And what greater unjustice can be acted, than to rob a man of his liberty, which is more valuable than life" (6). Humans have a right to liberty and have no right to sell others into bondage. There is no just reason for taking these people from their homes and making them slaves. Sandiford is clearly dipping into the well of secular human rights discourse, though his faith fuels his argument. He notes that by setting a poor example, Quakers have lost many possible Christian converts, adding that God does not care about the color of those brought into the fold (23–24). This is key, as Sandiford's understanding of rights is rooted in the belief that God loves and judges all humans equally; all can be saved by the "Prince of the Law of Liberty" (47).¹¹

But Sandiford is most interested in pointing out the consequences of supporting slavery and, thus, places himself within the prophetic tradition.¹² He notes that long ago when leaders veered from God's path, "the Lord often raised his prophets and ministers to testify against their practices" (56). Sandiford channels, so to speak, these Old Testament prophets who were "Sons of Thunder against all persecution and oppression, whether in liberty, or estate, or person, that all might enjoy freedom, both inwardly and outwardly" (59).[13] Bold testimony is necessary in order to scare people away from the practice, Sandiford notes, because slavery will produce horrible repercussions in life and death. God's justice is swift. Look at what happened, he says, to South Carolinians who enslaved Native Americans. He writes, "Every sin brings its own suffering; as we may observe by our neighbouring province of South Carolina, when the inhabitants in the commerce with Indians, would force their wives or captives from them, though for debt, for which they sold them for slaves; which when the Indians beheld, it soon raised the same property in them, to the loss of many lives, and the demolishing of the situations" (22–23). Violence begets violence and slavery begets slavery. Pennsylvania's Quakers are on thin ice as long as they participate in the trade. Exhausted from his diatribe, he exclaims, "Ah! my Friends! the consideration of these things had been sorrow of heart (beyond what may be mentioned) to those that have considered the worth of souls" (68).

Prophesying justice was no easy task, and Sandiford received little praise during his lifetime for this polemic and was reprimanded and ostracized by the Society of Friends for not receiving proper publication permissions. He was forced to retire to a farm outside of Philadelphia, where he died in 1733 at age forty. Benjamin Lay, Ralph Sandiford's confidant and co-conspirator, was convinced that Sandiford's early demise was the result of his banishment. As if fueled by his friend's mistreatment, Lay vaulted himself into the public sphere and earned a reputation among Pennsylvania Quakers as a radical in his own right. "If Ralph Sandiford lashed Quaker slaveowners with whips, Benjamin Lay chastised them with scorpions" (Drake 43). Davis describes his language as "violent," an apt description of his words as well as his public actions (*Western Culture* 292). Lay's general presence in the world must have also attracted attention. He stood no more than four feet seven inches tall, was hunchbacked, had a long beard, and wore clothing of his own making. In the latter part of his life, he lived in a cave outside of Philadelphia and would not eat meat or anything produced by slaves. Lay was famous for mid-meeting eruptions that led to frequent forceful removals from Friends meeting houses.[14] Thomas Drake cites minutes from one such meeting in which Lay is described as being a "disorderly person." Drake notes, "The word 'disorderly' here had a double meaning, the one in general usage, and the special Quaker meaning of being out of the good order of discipline in the Society of Friends" (45). Lay's disorder attracted attention, which was exactly what he hoped for. Because of his prophetic passion, Lay could not have viewed his actions as anything out of the ordinary—no more so than the act of purchasing a human being.

Lay's writing resembles his theatrics in its immediacy and urgency, unlike the more edited texts produced by other anti-slavery advocates. *All Slave-Keepers that Keep the Innocent in Bondage, Apostates* (1737) is an epic diatribe cobbled together from Lay's notes and journals.[15] The book is a somewhat formless denunciation of slavery and all those even loosely connected to it. Benjamin Rush comments, "This book contained many pious sentiments and strong expressions against negro-slavery; but even the address and skill of Dr. Franklin were not sufficient to connect its different parts together so as to render it an agreeable and useful work" (308). According to some accounts, Lay gave Franklin a disorganized (or disorderly) manuscript and told him to print it in whatever order he wished. The result is a rambling document with dated entries appearing in no particular order and for no particular reason—except to get his message out to the reading public. As a writer, Lay's concern is less with form than with content, yet the chaotic layout of this text may be the most proper form for a tempestuous account of Quaker complicity with slavery.

In most instances Lay begins his thoughts *in medias res*. Like a street preacher, his pace is quick, and line of reasoning "disorderly," with endless references to scripture and citations from the writings of John Milton, George Fox, William Penn, Samuel Sewall, and many others. Despite his impoverished upbringing and likely minimal education, Lay is adept at engaging with texts and using them to support rational arguments. But often he begins passages with phrases like "Something came into my mind this day," as if the spirit has moved him to write. God, he claims, is the source for his writing because, for Lay, truth cannot found in literature but "in him, not out of him, no, no, no, not a great way of, but in Christ" (253). He is decidedly uninterested in secular universalism. "Divine wisdom exceeds all literature and humane wisdom," he writes (191). Rational thinking has led some to believe slavery is not wrong. Lay claims it as his "duty to inform them what I can by word and writing, and then leave it to the Lord" (94). In other words, he can write of the truth, but until individuals discover it through some spiritual awakening, they will still be lost. And the truth, he writes, is that some Quakers are hypocrites. Friends, he notes, "pretend not to love fighting with carnal weapons, nor to carry swords by our sides, but carry a worse thing in the heart" (10).

Lay acknowledges his firsthand experience with slavery in Barbados as well as the "foul" stories he heard when employed as a sailor on the Atlantic (77). And in a moment of truth and reconciliation, he confesses his own sins and his complicity with the slave trade when he describes his stay in Barbados with his wife, Sarah. The couple was friendly to all the slaves on the island and provided what aid they could. But Lay describes a time when he caught one stealing from his store and beat him. He writes, "I have been sorry for it many times," and admits that the mistreatment of slaves by everyone around him may have led him to respond in such a manner (40). He adds that slavery breeds such cruelty as well as a general laziness. Slaves bring horses to the children of slave owners "for young madam and sir to ride on, impudently and proudly gossiping from house to house, stuffing their lazy ungodly bellies" (31). Lay is at no loss for words pointing out the wretchedness of a slave-based society: "Mamon, Mamon, Mamon, as though Satan ruled in them . . . riding, drinking and galloping about from house to house, smoking, snuffing, chewing tobacco" (197). Such opulent and carnal delights are, in Lay's mind, symptoms of a sick and unredeemable people. These slave keepers will be judged soon; "the Lord hasten the time, faith my soul" (53). He holds no hope for God's mercy if slavery does not end soon:

> And my dear, my very dear Friends, I must say, I must say, and it is experience and certain knowledge of my own soul, that except people will be willing to come to a separation, a separation, a separation
> from this thing,
> to wit, Negro practice
> they never can nor will see the evil of it, as it really is in itself. (32)

For Quakers, the dangers of not divorcing themselves from slavery are clear, and Lay sees grave trouble ahead. His prophecy relies heavily on the Book of Revelation, in particular, chapters 12 and 13, of which he offers his own thorough interpretations. Like the end of days described in Revelation, slavery could "bring sudden destruction upon us" (178). To bring his own argument to a "sudden" and resounding halt, Lay concludes with a reproduction of a passage from Milton's *Paradise Lost* (Book 12, lines 505–551): "Wolves shall succeed for teachers, grievous wolves," writes Milton, "Who all the sacred mysteries of Heav'n / To their own vile advantages shall turn" (Lay 402). Lay implies that the "wolves" have arrived in the guise of Quaker leaders who permit slavery.

Quite the social entrepreneur, Lay distributed his book widely, visited many community leaders, and shared his message in churches throughout the Philadelphia area and beyond. His loud accusations caught the attention of many and, in one instance described by Roberts Vaux, "curiosity, associated with respect for him, induced Governor Penn, Dr. Franklin, and some other gentlemen to make a visit to Lay" (32). He was, as noted above, friends with Sandiford and Franklin but also with Anthony Benezet, on whom he made a deep and lasting impression. And Lay references many well-known writers throughout his book in order that his argument not appear solitary; he wishes to be seen as part of a growing consensus, a developing discourse of human rights. As Foucault notes, "The frontiers of a book are never clear-cut.... [I]t is caught up in a system of references to other books, other texts, other sentences: it is a node within a network" (*Archaeology* 23). Benjamin Lay's public text is, indeed, a node within an ever-widening and ever-influential network. He is a boisterous pioneer laying the groundwork for a growing network of dissent. And for this network to develop Lay used whatever methods he could to get attention, "some of which were so extravagant as to induce the belief that his intellect was partially diseased" (Vaux 24). He was, in appearance, action, and ideology, an outsider. Thus, his life and the life of his colleague Sandiford serve as textbook examples of the regulatory powers of a discourse, literally and figuratively. The Society of Friends, like the architects of the new nation, could seek personal and religious liberty in North America while denying freedom to others whom they did not consider completely human. "Disorderly" figures who pressed this issue were unwelcome by the many slaveholders in South Carolina who feared the loss of power and privilege that would accompany a more thorough democracy.

Years later, in 1805, another Quaker, Ann Tuke Alexander, had these issues in mind when she penned "An Address to the Inhabitants of Charleston, South Carolina." This address, she claims, is motivated by "gospel love" (213). Yet this "gospel love" that has moved her to write after experiencing South Carolina's chattel slavery regime in person is an angry, tough love. She writes to South Carolinians of things "awfully important, as they regard your real interest, both in time and in eternity." Alexander is upset by the sight of her "fellow-creatures, of the African race, deprived of their natural liberty, and of almost every means of improvement of those faculties bestowed upon *them* as well as ourselves." Citing Paul's assertion in Acts that God made all humans "of one blood," she argues that slavery is "repugnant to every principle of humanity and justice." South Carolina faces the possibility of God's judgment "for the blood of thousands," for the sins of the state (214). There is still hope and they may avoid judgment, but this appears unlikely as God wishes to "undo the heavy burdens" and "let the oppressed go free." There is little evidence that South Carolinians read her letter.[16] Dissenting voices from outside South Carolina had little, if any, influence on the legal practices supporting chattel slavery within the state, and there were few voices within the confines of the state's public sphere willing to raise significant opposition. Of course, there were also few mechanisms for the slaves themselves to speak publicly—yet they did anyway. There was no column in Lewis Timothy's paper for them, but slaves asserted their rights and sought to undermine the plantation system throughout the eighteenth century.

We have examined eighteenth-century anti-slavery discourse fueled by arguments that range from sentimental to secular and from moderate Christian to radical Christian. However, another genre of argument existed—slave-originating public acts of violence. In some sense, these rebellious acts take on a literary nature because they function as texts or "public addresses" that seek to shape and transform the public sphere. These literary acts form new meanings, counter-narratives, rather than simply reverse the conversation. Those at the helm of the plantation system were well aware of the threat of such counter-narratives and of the constant possibility of rebellions. Benjamin Lay argues that the master class, through its own sins, will bring about their own destruction. He writes, "These rich grown, ever poor, over wealthy, ever needy, ever grasping, never satisfied, brim-full yet always empty, ever labouring, yet always idle, ever diligent, yet always negligent, ever waking, yet eternally asleep, ever living, panting and breathing after more, more, more, a little more, I say ever living yet eternally dead, and there let 'em lie and stink still, if they will not be awakened. But I had much rather they should" (229). Clearly, the declarations of independence made by slaves and radicals like Benjamin Lay were beyond the "the domain of the speakable," straying into this discomforting territory (Butler, *Excitable Speech* 139). But polite public presentation in action or in writing had no place in a world that permitted the horrors of slavery, and Lay's prophecy of divine retribution was not off the mark. One wonders, though, if perhaps it was not "supernatural interference," but the actions, the consistent "revolutions," of slaves themselves that led to the demise of chattel slavery.

These revolutions were not peripheral events but were central to the early American experience and to the development of human rights discourse. Only two years after Lay published his treatise, a group of slaves near the Stono River, South Carolina, would take up arms against their oppressors in the most violent insurrection in colonial North America, revealing the true nature of human rights discourse in early America, quite appropriately in John Locke's backyard. Months before this declaration of independence, in January of 1739, a group of Scots who had settled in Darien, Georgia, proclaimed slavery a practice contrary to human rights and a seedbed for future strife. They wrote, "How miserable would it be to us, and our wives and families, to have an enemy without, and more dangerous ones in our bosom!" ("Number IX" 427). Slavery, they asserted, is "shocking to human nature," and they wondered aloud if the introduction of slaves might lead to some eventual divine retribution. They would rather "some of our countrymen" be encouraged to come to the province—a labor plan they believed to be more sustainable. Apparently, their pleas, like so many in this century of revolutions, went unheard.

Chapter 3

★ ★ ★

CLAIMING RIGHTS
The Stono Rebels Strike for Liberty

> At this time there were above forty thousand negroes in the province, a fierce, hardy and strong race, whose constitutions were adapted to the strong climate, whose nerves were braced with constant labour, and who could scarcely be supposed to be contented with that oppressive yoke under which they groaned.
> —Alexander Hewatt, *An Historical Account of the Rise and Progress of the Colonies of South Carolina and Georgia* (1779)

ONE OF THE EARLIEST CONTACTS Europeans had with the land that some natives called *Chicora* was during a reconnaissance mission supported by a Spanish planter named Lucas Vásquez de Ayllón. These Spanish explorers invited a group of Native Americans onto their ships and then proceeded, without warning, to set sail for Hispaniola. In some ways this auspicious beginning would serve as the opening salvo in the continuous warfare of slavery that would eventually entrench itself in the sands of Carolina. From the moment a group of English investors gained control of the territory in 1663—a gift from King Charles II—slavery was essential to the economic viability and social underpinnings of the colony. The Fundamental Constitutions of Carolina, Locke and Shaftesbury's utopian road map, established a society comprised of enslaved human beings and pseudo-aristocratic overlords. In 1670, when Sir John Yeamans became South Carolina's first English slave importer, the colony was imbued with high hopes and visions of neo-feudal grandeur. But the late seventeenth century reality was that the colony, an outpost really, was struggling to survive. The primary occupants were former Barbadians who had been pushed out because of that small island's spatial limitations. But South Carolina was no ready-made Eden; like Barbados, it had its own set of obstacles. The brutal work of clearing land was often disrupted by outbreaks of disease (malaria, smallpox, yellow fever), and the unforgiving humidity of midsummer hampered the process further. The colonists struggled to find a cash crop, one that could help them replicate the success of West Indian plantations. They eventually took notice of a plant their African slaves were cultivating in their small gardens. This plant, rice or *oryza sativa*, was soon introduced on a much greater scale, and the labor and skills of African-born slaves became essential because these planters knew little of this crop. They needed individuals with knowledge of the arduous process of rice cultivation and would buy them if necessary (Wood 56).[1]

For these slaves brought to South Carolina, their experience must have been demoralizing from the moment they were captured. Rumors often circulated that they had been sold to cannibals who were going to eat them. Some, perhaps, believed this literally, but John K. Thornton notes that this was also a way of saying that they, the slaves, were "victims of a plot involving greedy and selfish people" (*Africa and Africans* 316). Traffickers of human beings were cannibalizing Africa, destroying families, and disrupting social networks. The trauma of surviving the machinations of such greed and selfishness must have tested the strongest wills and bodies. Slaves suffered without fresh air, water, and sufficient food for weeks. Sickness and death were commonplace. Chained bodies, both living and dead, rested in excrement with little light as ships with lovely names like *Bonetta, Dove, Morning Star*, and *Judith* lurched about on their journeys to the Americas. About one-sixth of African slaves died during this passage, their bodies dumped in the ocean along the way. Some corpses were not discovered until the ships had reached their destinations. This prompted a 1769 proclamation in Charles Town prohibiting slave ship captains from throwing bodies into the harbor because so many were washing ashore, creating an unbearable smell and health hazard.

Olaudah Equiano describes the conditions on slave ships in his narrative: "The shrieks of the women, and the groans of the dying, rendered it a scene of horror almost inconceivable" (35). The predicament of capture, the loss of control, the theft of humanity that was chattel slavery, led many to commit ultimate acts of free will, asserting their humanness through suicide. "One day," Equiano writes, "when we had a smooth sea and moderate wind, two of my wearied countrymen, who were chained together ... preferring death to such a life of misery, somehow made through the nettings and jumped into the sea" (36). Others would refuse to eat and were beaten harshly for such acts of protest (77). When Equiano's ship finally arrived in Barbados, he learned that the rumors that they were to be sold to cannibals were unfounded: "They told us we were not to be eaten, but to work" (37).

After a period of "seasoning" or quarantine on Sullivan's Islands, slaves were sold and transported to their new homes, where they immediately began working. In eighteenth-century South Carolina, this work was based on the "task system," which required slaves to complete a certain amount of labor before the end of each day. Some historians claim this management system provided slaves with a reasonable amount of leisure, but it did not necessarily make their lives carefree. Slaves were still required to finish their tasks—not a simple proposition. A former slave from the Upstate of South Carolina, Milton Marshall, remembers, "All of us had to go to work at daylight and work till dark. They whipped us a little and they was strict about some things" (Hurmence 43). Sam Polite, a former slave from St. Helena, provides specific details about the task system. He says, "When horn blow and morning star rise, slave have for get up and cook. When day clean, they gone to field.... Every slave have task to do, sometime one task, sometime two task, and sometime three. You have for work till task through. When cotton done make, you have other task. Have to cut cord of marsh grass maybe. Task of marsh been eight feet long and four feet high. Then, sometime you have to roll a cord of mud in cowpen" (Hurmence 77).[2] Even though these anecdotes of slave work experiences are from the nineteenth century, we can imagine similar situations in the eighteenth. Slaves worked—*constantly*. It was not until the Negro Act of 1740 that planters were required by law to let slaves rest on Sundays—but even that law was overlooked during harvesting times. Besides working in reptile-infested rice fields, slaves were responsible for the labor-intensive process of pounding the rice. A 1733 issue of the *South Carolina Gazette* contains a notice of a business partnership interested in constructing "an Engine or Machine to clean Rice." The author of this notice claims that the labor required to remove the husk from the rice grain has caused great financial hardships to many planters because the excessive work has killed "a large Number of Negroes."[3]

The first slaves in South Carolina spent most of their time clearing land and herding cattle on the frontier and, thus, led fairly autonomous existences. This changed as planters began to cultivate rice for export. With increased agricultural production came an increased desire to control the daily lives of slaves. Peter Wood notes that the "machinery for their containment multiplied: tickets were required, patrols were strengthened, punishments were enforced . . . rewards were offered to buy the loyalty of slaves" (268). This was especially apparent in the 1730s, as South Carolina saw a major influx of slaves imported by men like Joseph Wragg, Richard Hill, Benjamin Savage, John Guerard, Benjamin Godin, and others (Donnan 278–279). So many slaves were imported, in fact, that the colony earned a pretty penny on import duties. Charleston's St. Philip's church, a prominent tourist attraction today, was paid for, in part, by these duties as well as those on rum and brandy, which were also quite popular with South Carolinians (Rogers 56).

On September 29, 1729, the Lords Proprietors officially relinquished their control and South Carolina became a royal colony. As the colony developed from an outpost to a center of agriculture in the Atlantic world, disease, heat and humidity, and storms were common themes. The focus on rice production did not improve the colony's health as the actual process for cultivating rice, involving significant amounts of standing water, provides excellent breeding grounds for malaria. But for planters enjoying the boom of the 1730s, the financial benefits of Lowcountry farming outweighed these potential pitfalls. Besides, they spent much of the year in Charles Town while slaves worked their lands.[4] From roughly May to November, during the harshest months, slaves worked under the supervision of drivers.

By 1739 South Carolina's lieutenant governor, William Bull, had a difficult situation on his hands.[5] Sickness had become a way of life in the preceding years. On September 26, 1739, Robert Pringle writes, "We have been afflicted in this town for these two months past with a great sickness & mortality by a malignant fever, which has carried off a great many people" (135). A letter from the colony in the *Boston Weekly News-Letter* from late September 1739 explains: "A terrible sickness has raged here, which the doctors call a yellow bilious fever, of which we bury 8 or 10 in a day; the like never known among us" ("A Letter" 2). In addition, relations between Spain and Britain were dissolving rapidly, especially since Spain had published a royal edict in 1738 promising freedom to any slave who could escape to Florida. Rumors abounded that Spanish priests were coming on shore to spread word of this edict in hopes of fostering escapes or, worse, outright insurrection. This was a quite problem for the white population of South Carolina as African slaves outnumbered whites almost two to one.[6]

THE STONO REBELS STRIKE FOR LIBERTY

NEGROES RISING IN CAROLINA

South Carolina was a disaster waiting to happen—but which "disaster" would happen first? An astute observer from the nearby colony of Georgia named William Stephens writes of his neighbors, noting that "in the midst of these hostilities from abroad, it was now their great unhappiness to have a more dangerous enemy in the heart of their country to deal with" (412). This "more dangerous enemy," about twenty Kongolese slaves led by a man named Jemmy or Cato,[7] gathered before dawn on Sunday, September 9, 1739, and made their way to Stono Bridge.[8] Their destination was Hutchenson's storehouse, about fifteen miles outside of Charles Town next to a road that followed the coastline southward.[9] The men were likely former members of a public road construction crew that, apparently, had had sufficient autonomy while working and used that space to plan a rebellion.[10] They broke into the storehouse, a breach that pushed these former slaves into new territories of freedom. Now rebels, they attacked and killed the two storekeepers, Mr. Gibbs and Robert Bathurst. As a sign of their intentions, they cut off the storekeepers' heads and placed them on pikes, following the precedent set by white colonists who, with increased frequency in the 1730s, placed the heads of unruly slaves on public display—a cultural carry-over from Europe.[11]

Now armed with guns and powder taken from the storehouse, they broke into the home of Mr. Godfrey, whom they killed along with his son and daughter ("Account" 234). As they left Godfrey's house, they set it on fire—again signaling their open rebellion to all those who could see. Next the rebels "passed Mr. Wallace's Tavern about daybreak, and said they would not hurt him for he was a good man and kind to his slaves." They then plundered the house of Mr. Lemy and killed all those within. The rebels continued to move southward along the Pons Pons Road. At this point, either together or in smaller splinter groups, the rebels simultaneously attacked plantations later called Laurel Hill and Morris's Nook, belonging to Thomas Elliott and Thomas Rose, respectively.[12] These incursions, which would have required the rebels to go far off the main road they had been on, did not go exactly as planned. Some slaves on these plantations either protected the whites or encouraged the rebels to keep moving. But the biggest hitch in their plans was yet to come. Before noon, by mere coincidence, they encountered South Carolina's lieutenant governor, William Bull, who was traveling through St. Paul's Parish on his way back from a trip to Granville

County. Bull hastened away to inform the local militia. Eighteenth-century historian Alexander Hewatt claims that, it being Sunday, Bull stopped at the Presbyterian Church at Wiltown, where Archibald Stobo held forth (73).[13] According to Hewatt, the men left the women behind in the church, "trembling with fear," as they rushed to engage the rebels. They were led by a militia leader named Captain Bee.

The rebels kept on marching, apparently heading toward Spanish Florida, where they expected to find freedom. After running into Bull, they traveled about ten miles before attacking other plantations. Perhaps they were recruiting others to join them in their freedom struggle during this period. Or maybe they were just playing it safe. Nevertheless, the record claims that "several Negroes joined them, they calling out liberty, marched on with colours displayed, and two drums beating, pursuing all the white people they met with" ("Account" 234). The rebellion was growing. There were between sixty and one hundred rebels on the move, and one can imagine they were excited by their bold display. After this brief break in action, the rebels attacked plantations belonging to Colonel Hugh Hext, Royal Sprye, Thomas Sacheverell, Mr. Nash, and James Bullock (Halifax).[14] At the time, these plantations were on tracts of several hundred acres; they would eventually grow in size through marriage and death. On this day, however, the relative closeness of the plantations allowed the rebels to make multiple attacks in succession. They moved quickly, pillaging and burning every house and killing all slave owners and their families—twenty or more in total. An account in the *Boston Weekly News-Letter* claims the rebels "sacrificed every thing in their way" ("A Letter"). The rebellion was bloody, and the actions of the slaves were total. According to a Ranger serving under Oglethorpe, they "went on killing what men, women, and children they met, burning of houses and committing other outrages" ("A Ranger's Report" 222–223).

Shortly after taking these last plantations, the rebels assembled in an open field near the Edisto River, now known as Battlefield Plantation, and began dancing and playing drums—continuing the call for others to join them.[15] But the colonial militia caught up with them, and an intense battle ensued during which eyewitnesses claim the rebels fought like well-trained soldiers, using flags and fighting in military formation. "They behaved boldly" but were outnumbered and the rebellion was vigorously put down ("Account" 235). According to one version of the Stono narrative, this boldness was often quite dramatic. In one incident a rebel "came up to his master. His master asked if he wanted to kill him. The Negro answered he did at the same time snapping a pistol at him, but it misfired and his master shot him through the head" ("A Ranger's Report" 223). Who was this man? Could it have been Jemmy or Cato? Some of the rebels were more pragmatic than bold, and rather than confront their masters and face certain execution, they fled the scene—one was not captured for several years.

In the wake of the rebellion, Captain Charles Fanshawe of the H.M.S. *Phoenix* offered his assistance to the militia, but it was apparently not required; the white militia, most likely better armed, had put an end to the rebellion (Duncan 786). Historian George Howe claims that if not for the Presbyterians at "Wiltown, matters would have been much worse" for white colonists (228). In truth, the rebellion upset the colonial order and the alarm bells were sounded. A messenger from South Carolina reached Stephens in Georgia and explained that "the country thereabout was full of flames: our letters also informed us, that they were fearful lest it prove general" (Stephens 412). These letters note that South Carolina was offering rewards for slaves, dead or alive. A letter from Minister Andrew Leslie to the Society for the Propagation of the Gospel in Foreign Parts (SPG) reveals the general uncertainties and anxieties many felt after the rebels had killed members of his parish "in a most barbarous manner" (Leslie). He continues, "Several of my principal parishioners, being apprehensive of danger from the rebels still outstanding carried their families to town for safety, & if the humour of moving continues a little longer, I shall have but a small congregation at church" (Leslie). Leslie's letter was read during a London meeting of the SPG on April 18, 1740. According to a report of this meeting, there was a "second engagement on the Saturday following," involving groups of rebels still roaming the countryside (*American Papers*).

Those rebels that did not escape were rounded up and immediately executed. The white colonists killed over forty people that day, placing their cut-off heads on "every milepost they came to" ("A Ranger's Account" 223). Or, as Robert Pringle writes, "most of the gang are already taken or cut to pieces" (135). A notice in the *Pennsylvania Gazette* acknowledges that this public display served as "terror to the rest" of the slaves. Some rebels were simply hanged. The author of "An Account of the Negroe Insurrection in South Carolina" applauds the "honour of the Carolina planters, that notwithstanding the provocation they had received from so many murders, they did not torture one Negro, but only put them to an easy death" (235). Given white planters and their overseers' predilection for torture, this is, indeed, surprising.[16] South Carolina colonists were fond of meting out horrific punishments; many were from the West Indies and believed that harsh reprisals were the only mechanisms for maintaining order. But perhaps they were tired of all they had seen on that day and wished to expedite the process. Notes from another meeting of the SPG, this one on July 18, 1740, indicate that Andrew Leslie was definitely tired of all *he* had seen (*American Papers*). He resigned his post in the Stono area, "his health not permitting him [to] live in Carolina."

REBELLIOUS COMMUNICATIONS

When describing the ways in which slaves in South Carolina communicated with one another, Walter Edgar writes, "The African American grapevine in South Carolina was quite effective. It is possible that because blacks were able to communicate with one another so quickly, they were able to launch the Stono Rebellion to coincide with whites' apprehension about the war with Spain" (166). Edgar is correct in describing the rapidity of communications among slaves and their possible comprehension of political events. A close reading of this brief rebellion reveals that the rebels demonstrated a propensity for multiple layers of communication and organization that must have frightened whites. These African slaves used "uncanny networks" of communication to foment the most successful rebellion in the colonial South.[17] In this sense, an uncanny network refers to multi-layered communications techniques used over a variety of physical and social geographies in ways unimagined by the dominant political power. The Stono rebels used such networks not only to organize their own escape, but to launch a wider insurrection—despite being embedded within a nervous and vigilant community. Their rebellion, then, can be viewed as a chain of sophisticated communicative acts.

The events of the Stono Rebellion itself have been pieced together by many historians, most using Peter Wood's interpretation in *Black Majority* (1974) as a jumping-off point. These analyses explore the various actions of the rebels and describe the meanings of these acts, though often in isolation from one another. Taken as a whole, though, these communication acts reveal a shocking complexity. An uncanny network also functions as a *social network*, what Mario Diani calls "a network of meanings," and relies on a shared discourse and fosters interdependence (5).[18] Diani writes that simple exposure to certain media can foster a communication network (8). Natalie Zemon Davis echoes this sentiment when she writes that print functions as a "carrier of relationships" (66). The media used by the Stono rebels included drums, flags, weapons, military formations, shouts, and, perhaps, print—and each of these media communicated not only relationships, but a message. Building on the rich historical interpretations of Stono, I believe that the totality of these acts demonstrates a specific desire on the part of the rebels and reveals larger connections to the continuous acts of rebellion among slaves and other subaltern peoples in the Americas in the eighteenth century. In this sense, we may view Stono within a larger early American, Atlantic, or global cultural context. As Herbert Aptheker and others have explained, slaves in the Atlantic world were not docile, taking slavery as their burden in this temporal world. In the 1730s there were insurrection conspiracies in the Bahamas (1734) and Antigua (1735), a war was fought between colonists and maroons in Jamaica (1730), and rebellions took place in St. John (1733) and Guadeloupe (1737).[19] There were rumors, conspiracies, or actual occurrences of slave rebellion in South Carolina in 1720, 1730, 1732, 1733, 1734, 1737, 1738, 1739, and 1740.[20]

To begin to understand the circumstances and meaning behind one of these rebellions, that of 1739, we must first ask, Where did these bold rebels come from? What were their origins, culturally and historically? Understanding their roots will allow us to imagine how this rebellious moment was organized and communicated among Lowcountry slaves. Such questions inevitably lead one to the debate over the depth of African cultural carryovers among African Americans.[21] Philip D. Morgan argues that "slaves did not arrive in the New World as communities of people; they had to *create* communities" (442). This seems to echo Sterling Stuckey's assertions about the development of a Black Nationalist culture among African Americans through shared traditions such as the ring-shout. There is also the idea—represented by Melville J. Herskovits and others—that slaves transmitted their particular African cultures wholesale, despite the agonies of the Middle Passage. But perhaps culture is more fluid than either of these two camps allow. Humans exist in the borderlands, in liminal spaces where culture survives and transforms. And if one argues that African slaves transmitted their uniquely African cultures intact to the Americas or that they created a completely new culture, one denies the realities of the historical record. Nowhere is this more evident than in the observations Mark M. Smith and John K. Thornton have made in relation to the Stono

Rebellion.[22] Their work acknowledges that the particular cultures of the Stono rebels had been in flux for some time prior to their arrival in South Carolina. Much of west-central Africa had undergone dramatic cultural changes beginning with the advent of the Portuguese slave trade. The stress of this trade significantly transformed the social dynamics of the Atlantic half of the continent and increased opportunities for sharing cultural practices among unlikely peoples.

An examination of the Stono Rebellion reveals a variety of cultural influences on the rebels. The author of "An Account of the Negroe Insurrection in South Carolina" recorded these influences for posterity: "Amongst the Negro slaves are a people from the Kingdom of Angola in Africa, many of these speak Portuguese [which language is as near Spanish as Scotch is to English] by reason that the Portuguese have considerable settlement, and the Jesuits have a mission and school in that kingdom and many thousands of Negroes there profess the Roman Catholic religion" (233). Any notion of a "pure" Kongolese culture persisting on either side of the Atlantic at this moment is, perhaps, false. This account reveals that the Stono rebels had been participating in a dynamic cultural climate, precipitated by Atlantic capitalism, both in west-central Africa and in South Carolina. Thornton reminds us that the Middle Passage did not erase this cultural heritage—especially in eighteenth-century South Carolina, when large-scale plantations were emerging. He notes that "in the eighteenth century African culture was not surviving: It was arriving. Whatever the brutalities of the Middle Passage or slave life, it was not going to cause the African-born to forget their mother language or change their ideas about beauty in design or music; nor would it cause them to abandon the ideological underpinnings of religion or ethics—not on arrival to America, not ever in their lives" (*Africa and Africans* 320). The plantation system prompted the arrival of thousands of new slaves in the decade prior to the Stono Rebellion. This is important for two reasons. First of all, there is evidence demonstrating that African-born, or "outlandish," slaves were more likely to escape in groups and were also more likely to escape shortly after their arrival (G. Mullin 34). More important than the fact that South Carolina had a significant influx of new slaves in the 1730s is the specific origin of those slaves. The records from ships in Charles Town during that period reveal that the majority of imported slaves were from the Kingdom of Kongo or, as this area along the west-central African coast was often called at the time, Angola. Today this would include parts of Gabon, Congo, Cabinda, the Democratic Republic

THE STONO REBELS STRIKE FOR LIBERTY

of Congo, and Angola.[23] Ships docking in Charles Town harbor were making many trips to this part of the world.

Reports of the rebellion indicate that South Carolinians were aware of the origins of the rebels. One writer blames the insurrection on "Some Angola Negroes" ("Account" 233). Thornton clarifies the origin of the Stono rebels, writing that they were likely "from the Kingdom of Kongo," or what is now Angola ("African Dimensions" 1103). The Royal African Company's trade there focused on "the town of Kabinda, just north of the Zaire River," the center of a popular trading network that extended across the continent (1104). Thus, we cannot rule out the possibility that slaves arrived in this port from places far beyond the boundaries of the Kingdom of Kongo. The popular belief, though, was that the Stono rebels were from Angola or Kongo. A report in the *Boston Gazette* claims South Carolina residents thought the rebellion was indicative of "a general Plot thro' the whole Province, but it does not yet appear that it was ever laid deeper than for the nation of Angolas" ("Letters"). One can only imagine why the rebellion led to a strong aversion to the importation of Angolan or Kongolese slaves that lasted well into the 1790s.

Knowledge of the specific origins of many of the rebels should be central to any understanding of how the Stono Rebellion was executed. Thornton provides ample evidence to support this claim, noting that accounts of the events demonstrate that the Kongolese "background of the slaves contributed to the nature of the revolt" ("African Dimensions" 1103). The first action of the rebels—breaking into a storehouse in order to arm themselves—gives one a clue as to their backgrounds. Clearly, they had experience with weapons and knew what to do with them once they obtained them. There was frequent fighting in the Kongo during the first half of the eighteenth century, and these wars often "resulted in the capture and sale of many people, no small number of whom would have been soldiers with the military" (1103). Thus, former soldiers may have instigated the rebellion. Reports of the rebellion add to this hypothesis as they indicate that the rebels acted like well-trained soldiers. And like a military regiment they chose a leader: "One who was called Jemmy was their Captain" ("Account" 233). Hewatt notes the militaristic qualities of the rebels: "they elected one of their number captain, and agreed to follow him, marching towards the south-west with colours flying and drums beating, like a disciplined company" (72). But this military experience could not have been gained in the colony because by this time there were "restrictions against slaves possessing firearms, and slaves no longer served in the militia" (Thornton, "African Dimensions" 1108). Thornton notes that "some, perhaps most, had probably served in the wars in Mbamba five years earlier and knew well how to use such weapons" (*Kongolese* 212). Thus, there is a greater likelihood that the rebellion instigators had gained their military experience in Africa.

But several accounts claim that the rebels, unlike a "disciplined company," seemed to scatter when the real fighting with the militia began in an open field by the Edisto River. On the contrary, Thornton argues that the slaves were likely scattering in order to better position themselves for battle in keeping with skirmish warfare tactics ("African Dimensions" 1113). Another tactic that contemporary writers apparently misunderstood was the rebels' use of hand-to-hand combat, a style of fighting akin to dancing. This may explain why they appeared to have "set to dancing" ("Account" 234). According to another account, the planters "found them in an open Field where they were Dancing being most of them drunk with the Liquors found in the Stores" ("Ranger's" 223). Historians of the eighteenth and twentieth centuries have echoed these festive interpretations; the rebels were merely celebrating prematurely.[24] Rather than celebrating, it is possible that the rebels were dancing a "war dance" or *sangemento* (Thornton, "African Dimensions" 1112). Such dances were an important part of military training and war preparations. Richard Cullen Rath notes the importance of hand-to-hand combat in Angolan and Kongolese cultures, a dance-like practice from which Brazilian *capoiera* gets its roots (87). Rath wonders if this "dance" helped the rebels overcome the two men at the storehouse to get their guns and ammunition (88) Perhaps they used the hand-to-hand combat skills that they learned while soldiers in Africa.

Flags and drums were also part and parcel of warfare in the Kongo. These communication technologies added sights and sounds to the rebellion and helped organize and signal the troops, so to speak. A flag hoisted in the air while a large group of rebelling slaves marched across their masters' lands, in the direction of freedom, would have served as a visual aid for witnesses throughout the countryside—a message of the rebels' intentions and their desire to be noticed. Thornton contends that these "colours displayed" may have had some connection to military unit flags ("African Dimensions" 1111). Drums, perhaps more than one, sounded these intentions to those not in the rebels' sightlines. For slaves, the message delivered by the rebel drums that Sunday morning would have been quite clear. Rath notes that slaves often used "instrumental soundways . . . to craft autonomous agendas in colonial America" (77). The rebels' agenda was rebellion. For whites within hearing, the sound of the drums must have been disconcerting. Drums had been a source of unease among Europeans, who, from their earliest contact with Africa, feared the use of drums (79). In the minds of most Europeans, drums were linked with rebellion or warfare, and because of these violent associations their use was subject to regulation. Laws banning the use of drums by slaves were established in 1688 and again in 1717 in Jamaica, in 1699 in Barbados, and in 1711 and again in 1722 in St. Kitts. A similar law would go into effect in South Carolina in the aftermath of the Stono Rebellion.

Perhaps their military training, beyond teaching tactics and weapon use, helped some of the rebels to stay focused even in moments of high intensity. Peter Charles Hoffer notes the importance of the dramatic incident cited above from "A Ranger's Report," when a rebel was asked by his former master if he wanted to kill him, and the rebel replied in the affirmative (154). The rebel's gun misfired and his former master shot him dead. Hoffer believes something revolutionary is revealed in this slave's actions because "before he cocked and aimed the pistol—he looked straight at his master. Eye-to-eye contact of this sort was relatively rare; ordinarily the slave did not look directly at the master, but down to the side" (155). The author of "An Account of the Negroe Insurrection in South Carolina" writes that the slaves "behaved boldly" (235). But one wonders what connotation "boldly" holds in the mind of this author. On one hand, it could signal a breach of one's social standing, a presumption. On the other, it could also signal courage, stout-heartedness in the face of danger.

Such courage was, perhaps, supported by the knowledge that in nearby Florida lived political and religious allies. The problem of slaves escaping to Florida had infuriated South Carolina's planters for some time. This exodus began when the Spanish promised freedom to any slave who escaped to their colony. The Spanish hoped to lure slaves to St. Augustine to annoy the English, to get more soldiers, and to populate a buffer town established for escaped slaves called Gracia Real de Santa de Mose.[25] Fort Mose, as it is sometimes called, was the destination of choice for South Carolina's slaves. On November 21, 1738, twenty-three slaves fled to the town from Port Royal. Many slaves must have gained knowledge of Florida and the Spanish offer of freedom through word of mouth. But where did this message originate? William Stephens's journal offers one clue as he describes the capture of a Spaniard in July 1739. This man, it was believed, "had been employed a pretty while, in corrupting the Negroes of Carolina; and was certainly with Don Pedro at Charles-Town, at the time when he lately came thither in his Launch" (413). The Spanish were apparently sending spies, some who may have been priests, into the English colonies to spread the good news.[26]

The slaves who encountered and who could communicate with Spanish priests or spies were likely those from the Kingdom of Kongo, with Roman Catholic roots and a working knowledge of the Portuguese language. Language apprehension and religious conversion went hand in hand in the Kingdom of Kongo (Thornton, "African Dimensions" 1107). Literacy, in this sense, was mostly the realm of the upper classes, though in the eighteenth century Portuguese was an important state and trade language. Therefore, it would have been possible for a person in the lower class of this society to have some general understanding of or exposure to the language. Facility with Portuguese would have allowed South Carolina's Kongolese-born slaves to communicate with priests fluent in a similar Romance language. Such a scenario is not far-fetched. Francis Le Jau of the SPG writes in letters from 1710 and 1711 of slaves who had been baptized by Catholic priests in Africa, indicating that such slaves had been thriving in South Carolina for some time before the rebellion (69, 102). This eager minister claims that two such slaves in his parish "are very desirous to Abjure the popish heresy's" (102). But converting these Catholics may have been easier said than done as the faith had played a central role in Kongolese culture since King Nzinga Nkuwu was baptized as João I in 1491 (Thornton, "African Dimensions" 1106). The rebels' connections to Catholicism, then, may have played a significant role in their nascent culture as well as in their organizing efforts. Mark Smith asserts that the slaves rebelled "when they did because of their specific veneration of the Virgin Mary" and their understanding of the church calendar ("Remembering Mary" 518). They believed the date on which they rebelled to be a holiday in honor of the birth of Mary. And Smith lends further evidence to his assertion, arguing that the flags the rebels waved, if white, may have been "associated closely with Mary in Kongolese iconography" and thus served as a source of unity and strength for the rebels (530).

It is important to note, however, that Kongolese Catholics held beliefs rooted in the Kongo, not Rome. Most experts claim that "the Kongolese simply added Christian labels to their indigenous beliefs" (Thornton, "African Dimensions" 1106). One notorious example of this uniquely Kongolese theology is the Antonian movement of Dona Beatriz Kimpa Vita at the beginning of the eighteenth century. Dona Beatriz claimed to receive prophetic visions from St. Anthony of Padua, who had taken over her body while she was struggling with an illness. She believed that she was given a direct connection to God, who ordered her to develop a Kongolese-based Catholicism. Dona Beatriz opposed European missionaries and proclaimed that Jesus, Mary, and Saint Francis had been born in Kongo. She was eventually burned by loyalists of King Pedro IV in 1706, though her followers continued to spread her ideas throughout the first decades of the eighteenth century—ideas that may have reached the ears of some of the Stono rebels. If these Kongolese rebels did, in fact, adhere to such a quasi-Catholic belief system, their approach to death and dying—their belief in an afterlife—may have strengthened their will to rebel. Margaret Creel, in her examination of religious ritual among Lowcountry Gullah communities, acknowledges that "belief that one's spirit consciously existed after death was also common" among numerous African cultures (53). The Gola people, she writes, believed that "death destroyed the body but did not affect the soul, or 'heart.' The dead would awake, arise, and join their departed relations and friends" (Creel 53). To such believers, death by gun, rope, or fire would not have been frightening.

While there is much evidence pointing to the Kongolese origins of the Stono rebels, there is also the possibility that the rebellion was a collaboration between acculturated, South Carolina–born, and outlandish slaves, if only to a small extent. Peter Wood writes that "in the first half of the eighteenth century Negroes in South Carolina were more unified by the common ground of Old World ancestry and recent migration than they were set apart by contrasting routines" or belief systems (104). This unity could have sparked a collective effort to foment insurrection and would have encouraged slaves to share useful information with one another. As I noted in chapter 2, Wood suggests that "calculations might also have been influenced by the newspaper publication, in mid-August, of the Security Act which required all white men to carry firearms to church on Sunday or submit to a stiff fine, beginning on September 29" (313).[27] This act was published on the front page of the August 11–18 edition of the *South Carolina Gazette*:

> *After the twenty ninth day of September, which will be in the year of our Lord, one thousand, seven hundred and thirty-nine, every white male inhabitant of this province . . . who by the laws of this province, are or*

shall be liable to bear arms in the militia of this province, either in times of alarms or at common musters, who is possessed of ten slaves in this province, and who shall on any Sunday or Christmas day in the year, go and resort to any church, or an other public place of divine worship within this province, and shall not carry with him a gun or a pain of pistols in good order and fit for service, with at least six charges of gun powder and ball, and shall not carry the same into the pew or other seat where such person shall sit, remain or be in such church or other place of worship as aforesaid, every such person shall forfeit and pay the sum of twenty shillings current money for every neglect of the same.

The law was unequivocal. It was established to protect the colony from slave rebellions. Through this order, the newspaper continued, "the Inhabitants of this Province may be better secured and provided against the Insurrections or other wicked Attempts of Negroes and other Slaves." Did some slaves overhear discussion of the new law or, perhaps, come across a copy of the newspaper? If this was the case, it would imply at least some communication between acculturated and outlandish slaves and some level of literacy in the English language.

In the earliest days of the colony, many slaves were introduced to European forms of literacy when they had the initials of the Royal African Company branded on their bodies. These letters signified ownership, property, and force. In the twenty-first century "to brand" carries the innocuous connotation of naming or claiming a company or product. Its roots, though, are in livestock and human bondage. In medieval and early modern Europe, criminals were branded for committing a variety of acts. Later, slave trading companies and slave owners would brand newly acquired human property so as not to confuse their "property" with that of another. The use of language, in this sense, was a mark of total power. But there is evidence that slaves were able to gain literacy in unique ways and use that knowledge to undermine slavery. Earlier I discussed the relationship of Catholicism to the possibility that some Kongolese slaves were able to understand, read, or speak Portuguese and, in turn, comprehend Spanish. But what of the English language? Could some slaves have understood English enough to read the proclamation in the *South Carolina Gazette*?

At the beginning of the eighteenth century, Le Jau indicates that there were some slaves who knew the English language quite well. Le Jau's February 1, 1710, letter describes an encounter with several slaves who "speak very good English" (69). Their dexterity with languages may have been cultivated, in part, by pastors like Le Jau, who were interested in teaching slaves English to facilitate religious conversion. Or, perhaps, they learned English from schoolteachers. One such teacher arrived in Le Jau's Goose Creek community and was encouraged by the minister to teach black children as well as white children (95). But non-religious education efforts were few and far between. Protestant missionaries were, in fact, the most vociferous supporters of slave literacy.[28] Michael Mullin writes that in the eighteenth century, "Christianization everywhere shared one basic feature: the promise—and increasingly for many the actuality—of literacy, of learning to read the Bible, which evangelicals insisted was the word of God and the vehicle for conversion and salvation" (211). Le Jau was not the last of the SPG to support educating slaves. In 1742, South Carolina minister Alexander Garden asked the SPG to help him buy two slaves who could be taught to read and write. These slaves would then teach other slaves, and, in this manner, Garden hoped more slaves would learn to read the Bible. He established a school in Charles Town with two African American teachers named Harry and Andrew. By 1750, Andrew was deemed unfit for the project and sold with "the proceeds applied to the purchase of books" (Olwell 121). By 1768 Harry also fell by the wayside and was sent to an asylum. Robert Olwell wonders if the effects of Harry's double-consciousness, straddling the liminal regions of literate and oral cultures, pushed him to insanity or to unpredictable behavior that at the time would have been perceived as such (130). Forced to choose between the English-based Christian culture they were supposed to be teaching and that of their families, these two slaves appear to have unraveled. They may have felt disconnected from their communities, communities that in the South Carolina Lowcountry were in the process of developing their own customs and languages. In fact, pidgins that used a substantial amount of English were in development prior to the Stono Rebellion. Wood explains that because there was such a high concentration of African Americans in the Lowcountry, many were able to retain their African languages, or parts of them, while acquiring English. Within this context a unique dialect, today called Gullah, developed.

Besides these few instances, it is difficult to measure the extent of English-language literacy among slaves. Janet Cornelius's research of Federal Writers Project slave narratives reveals the various difficulties of measuring slave literacy in the *nineteenth* century. Those who taught slaves to read and write could not do so openly; "Patrols, mobs, and social ostracism faced owners who taught their slaves" (Cornelius 173). Similar mechanisms of social control were in place in the eighteenth century, much to the chagrin of the SPG.[29] There were exceptions. In letters from 1741 and 1742, Eliza Lucas Pinckney reveals that when not researching the best ways to cultivate indigo, she was teaching some slaves how to read and write and wanted to train her most successful students to be schoolteachers (12, 34). But most planters believed that if slaves could read and write in English, they would try to use that skill to their own advantage—an obvious fear that manipulated language could foster "autonomous agendas" in the same ways that drums could. SPG meeting minutes from April 15, 1737, include a report on a letter from Rev. Mr. William Johnson of Barbados describing his trouble with "the instruction of Negroes" (*American Papers*).[30] The minutes note Johnson's claim that planters believed that teaching slaves to read and write "enables them to carry on plots against their common safety" and references a recent "diabolical design" in Antigua organized by literate slaves. Johnson added that in Barbados those slaves that can read and write often use their skills to forge passes, aid runaways, and steal. Gerald Mullin cites a runaway slave advertisement placed by William Macon Jr. in the *Virginia Gazette*, February 9, 1769: "[Peter] by some means has learned to write a little, and has frequently wrote passes for himself and other Negroes to go a little distance, and I am apprehensive he has done the like again" (93). Cornelius acknowledges the ultimate effects of slaves learning to read for religious purposes: "Reading the Bible for oneself enabled a slave to undercut a master's attempts to restrict Christian teaching to carefully selected Biblical passages" (171–172). These "selected" passages underscored subservience and respect for one's master rather than salvation.

The appropriation of the English language in order to plan and execute the Stono Rebellion is one more example of the unique ways slaves manipulated new and old communication technologies in order to assert their own agenda. In this embryonic moment of the modern world, African American slaves—both acculturated and outlandish—took advantage of all available tools in an effort to circumvent the boundaries of their defined lives. In his analysis of antebellum slavery from 1830 to 1860, Cal M. Logue calls such communication "creative resistance," noting that "even when one person is enslaved by another, she or he is able to find feasible and effective strategies of rhetorical retaliation" (32). Amidst the stress and struggle of plantation slavery, slaves learned how to use language and a variety of cultural literacies to resist. Logue observes that "blacks learned to remain in a state of rhetorical readiness, constantly alert for signs of harm and opportunities to be pursued" (37). They learned to perceive changes in the social climate of whites so that they might act to gain some advantage over their own lives or simply to avoid punishment or harm. At a moment of extreme social anxiety the Stono rebels created uncanny networks that fostered a counter-narrative to that of those in power in South Carolina. In this narrative, slaves were intelligent human beings claiming their natural or human rights despite an oppressive environment. This rebellion exemplifies the social possibilities embedded within moments of cultural and technological transformation—in this case the transformations brought on by a growing Atlantic capitalist economy and its development of international communications networks. At Stono, a counterpublic emerged promoting a revolutionary alternative to the offered discourses of the South Carolina white colonial public. And this counterpublic effectively piggybacked, although unwillingly, on the infrastructures of capitalism—most notably the slave ship. The Stono rebels, then, rose up on September 9 and delivered their rebellious communication to the people of St. Paul's Parish, South Carolina, and to the world.

THE MESSAGE OF THE MEDIA

Judith Butler writes, "The claim of human rights is articulated in a speech situation in which someone can speak in a language that is not only understood but also engaged, received, and responded to" (1659). Despite themselves, the colonial government understood the message of the Stono rebels. An official account of the rebellion can be found in the record of the South Carolina Commons House of Assembly. This account, dated July 1, 1741, describes the methods the rebels used to kill whites as "the most cruel and barbarous manner to be conceived" ("Report" 83). It paints the rebels as foolhardy and marching "so slow, in full confidence of their own strength," that the militia had time to track them down, not imagining that their plan could have been deliberate, that they were moving slowly in order to recruit others to join them. When the militia finally met the rebels in battle, "the number was in a manner equal on both sides and an engagement ensued as may be supposed in such a case wherein one fought for liberty and life, the other for their country and every thing that was dear to them" (83). The words slip so easily from the author of this passage—a moment of rupture that is, perhaps, unintentional. Nevertheless, one could interpret the passage to read thus: the rebels sought the romantic goal of human liberty whereas the whites sought to maintain their way of life, a system of forced enslavement, monoculture, and dislocation from which they were benefiting handsomely.

But this passage from the Commons House record includes other equally pertinent revelations of the mental state of whites in South Carolina—after the rebellion, they were scared. Slave rebellion or retribution was a constant danger. Indeed, "on this occasion every breast was filled with concern. Evil brought home to us within our very doors awakened the attention of the most unthinking. Every one that had any relation, any tie of nature; every one that had a Life to lose were in the most sensible manner shocked at such danger daily hanging over their heads. With regret we bewailed our peculiar case, that we could not enjoy the benefits of peace like the rest of mankind and that our own industry should be the means of taking from us all the sweets of life and of rendering us liable to the loss of our lives and fortunes" ("Report" 84). It is worth quoting this passage in full. Each sentence uncovers the planters' deepest fears. "Evil is brought home" to South Carolina, comes to reside in a place that, until this bold manifestation, was simply a business venture. But now they are shocked that "nature" could be so cruel, so turned upside down, that their "own industry" could cause their downfall. Their public "shock" is quite shocking, given the plethora of rebellions prior to Stono. Of the Haitian revolutionaries C.L.R. James writes, "The slaves had revolted because they wanted to be free. But no ruling class ever admits such things" (95). The ruling class in South Carolina was not about to admit that fact. The emphasis was eventually placed on the role of the Spanish as the primary instigators of the chaos caused by the Stono Rebellion, thus negating the true subjects of this narrative—the slaves themselves.

In 1779 Alexander Hewatt observed that the greatest concern of most whites after the Stono Rebellion was that if the rebellion had spread, "the whole colony must have fallen a sacrifice to their great power and indiscriminate fury" (74). But amidst his discussion of South Carolina's status post-Stono, Hewatt offers a hint of a solution to the colony's woes that was unusual at the time: "Slavery, in general, like several other enormities, ought to be ascribed to the corruption and avarice of men, rather than to any principle of nature and humanity, which evidently testify against it" (92). Slavery, he suggested, is an unnatural state of oppression—a sign of human depravity. Forty years after Stono, during the heady moments of the American Revolution, Hewatt seems to suggest a different kind of response to slave insurrection. But no white person made this kind of suggestion in the immediate wake of Stono even though South Carolina's black population was clearly pointing out the need for radical change.

The actions of the Stono rebels during the insurrection give rise to speculations about their ambitions and ideals. Eugene Sirmans downgrades the events' importance, saying that "it was less an insurrection than an attempt by the slaves to fight their way to St. Augustine" (*Colonial* 208). Escapes to Florida were common at this time—over 253 from 1732 to 1739 (Pearson 36). If so many slaves were escaping, though, why did the Stono rebels not seize the opportunity to simply flee? Why did they attack the colony's infrastructure so violently? Robert Olwell asserts that, viewed as a whole, "their actions . . . suggest that striking a blow against slave society rather than seeking refuge with the Spanish was their primary objective" (22). The written evidence indicates that these rebels had ambitions other than organizing a large-scale jailbreak. First of all, they stopped at each house they passed, killing the inhabitants, destroying property, and setting the houses on fire. Some whites who had been kind to slaves were spared. This process consumed time and raised alarm—deliberate destruction is not conducive to a quick and clandestine escape. Secondly, the rebels gathered in a field in plain view, beating drums and dancing—drawing evermore attention to themselves. These Kongolese rebels may have performed, as Thornton notes, a *sangemento*, a dance that is also considered a declaration of war ("African Dimensions" 1112). One does not declare war if one seeks a quick escape. Finally, this was not a small insurrection, nor did the rebels try to limit its size in order to escape detection; they wanted others to join their struggle. Gerald Mullin acknowledges that it was more likely that in most situations less acculturated slaves, the apparent instigators of this rebellion, viewed "slavery as a collective problem" (36). Such slaves were also more likely to run away or rebel in groups. This is important. The Stono rebels were clearly calling others to join them as they marched and gathered because they saw their struggle as one shared equally by all slaves.

There is further evidence that these rebels asserted their intentions and their rights in a rather unique way. An account of the rebellion attributed to General James Oglethorpe places the rebels firmly within the developing rights discourse of the eighteenth century. As the rebels marched, "several Negroes joined them, they calling out liberty, marched on with colours displayed, and two drums beating, pursuing all white people they met with" ("Account"). This account was published in March 1740 issues of the *Gentleman's Magazine* and *London Magazine*, popular London-based miscellanies, as well is in the *Scots Magazine*, based in Edinburgh. Oglethorpe's words were read widely, with the calls of the Stono rebels resonating throughout the English-speaking world. These publications, especially *Gentleman's Magazine*, were not marginal. Jürgen Habermas notes the direct contribution it made to the development of the bourgeois public sphere. He writes that with the introduction of journals like *Gentleman's Magazine*, "the press was for the first time established as a genuinely critical organ of a public engaged in critical debate" (60).

As I noted in chapter 1, their shouts of "liberty" may be a creative rendering of the events by this account's author. On the other hand, is it possible that these former slaves were aware of what they were shouting? Is it possible they chose this word because of its connection to their intrinsic belief in human freedom, to a belief in natural or human rights? Later that century a former slave named Toussaint L'Overture would write, "Do they think that men who have been able to enjoy the blessing of liberty will calmly see it snatched away?" (qtd. in James 196). Amidst those tumultuous years in Haiti, the priest Boukman gave a prayer before the beginning of the rebellion in which he asked the Haitian rebels to, in an English translation, "listen to the voice of liberty, which speaks in the hearts of us all" (James 87).

The exact words the Stono rebels chanted or what white South Carolinians believed they heard will forever remain a mystery. But we can speculate and, by doing so, re-imagine what motivated the rebels to act; we can re-imagine how their shouts resonate in the present. In English the word "liberty" would have signaled a desire for a condition of freedom or release from bondage. Or it could have been used in a Lockean sense, for example, when Locke writes that when a government acts in a manner that does not support the public good, the people have "a right to resume their original liberty" (*Second Treatise* 12.222). Here "liberty" signifies a will to start anew, to begin again as a free human being. Thornton wonders if the word held a particular religious connotation to the Stono rebels. If they were still thinking in Kikongo, the word would have been "*lukangu*, whose root, *kanga*, also meant 'salvation' to a Christian" (*Kongolese* 13). He points out that the word was used in prayers central to Dona Beatriz's Antonian movement. If any of the rebels took part in that movement, they may have remembered Beatriz's zealous efforts to restore the kingdom to its past greatness—and the social conditions out of which those efforts grew. While not attacking the slave trade directly, Dona Beatriz "blamed the elite of the country for its problems, which she ascribed to their greed and desire to rule" (Thornton, *Africa and Africans* 316). In a country such as the Kingdom of Kongo, fraught with political struggle, the development of a ground-up religious movement that veered away from the doctrines of the elite is not surprising.

The use of religious faith as a catalyst for a freedom struggle launched by slaves was also a possibility in colonial America. During the centuries of American slavery, slave owners feared, with good reason, that slaves would use religion to support their freedom struggle. There was also the possibility that whites would read their Bibles closely and, in so doing, espouse their own radical theologies that might undermine the status quo. In 1741 an apparently unstable white preacher named Hugh Bryan emerged in the backwoods of South Carolina in the wake of George Whitefield's evangelizing tour through the colony.[31] Bryan is said to have preached prophetic sermons to large groups of slaves using Exodus—a narrative of a struggle for freedom from bondage—as his principle text. Bryan claimed that the recent spike in disasters in the Charles Town region was an indication of God's displeasure with the colony's economic practices. Due to the large numbers of slaves hearing this particularly damning message, rumors spread that he was organizing slaves, for what purpose white colonists were unsure. When Bryan's evangelizing caught the attention of colonial officials, he was forced to recant all he had preached.

Francis Le Jau speaks of an incident involving the advent of a similar apocalyptic vision for South Carolina, though this time it came from the mind of a slave. The slave, whom Le Jau describes as "the best Scholar of all the Negroes in my Parish," was apparently literate enough to read on his own (70). Upon reading in a book "some descriptions of the several judgmts. that Chastise Men because of their Sins in these latter days, that description made an Impression upon his Spirit, and he told his Master abruptly there wou'd be a dismal time and the Moon be turned into Blood." One wonders if he had somehow come across an anti-slavery tract—Samuel Sewall's famous work had been produced ten years earlier—though this is speculative. It would seem more likely that this slave had discovered a passage in the New Testament like Acts 2:19–21: "And I will shew wonders in heaven above, and signs in the earth beneath; blood, and fire, and vapour of smoke; The sun shall be turned into darkness, and the moon into blood, before that great and notable day of the Lord come: And it shall come to pass, that whosoever shall call on the name of the Lord shall be saved." Le Jau continues that several other slaves heard of this man's vision and rumors spread that he had been given said book by an angel. The reverend quickly dispelled these rumors among the slaves. Le Jau writes that African slaves "have not judgment enough to make good use of their learning." After a scare that put the colony and his job at risk, Le Jau offers that he would prefer that "those that run in the search after curious matter had never seen a book."

But "curious matter" was circulating among the South Carolina public in the decade prior to the Stono Rebellion. Great Awakening revivalists were distributing literature throughout the colonies prior to George Whitefield's arrival. Frank Lambert writes that Whitefield "circulated about a hundred publications in the Atlantic world, including the American colonies" (13). Both the published tracts and sermons of the revivalists frightened more than one South Carolinian because of their possible impact on slaves. In the April 10–17, 1742, issue of the *South Carolina Gazette* an anonymous writer claims that rather than teaching slaves a passive form of Christianity, revivalists are "filling their heads with a parcel of cant-phrases, trances, visions, and revolutions, and something still worse, and which Prudence forbids to name" (qtd. in Lambert 15–16). Was the idea of rebellion that "something still worse"? Religion played a significant role in many slave rebellions, including those of Haiti and Nat Turner as well as in Denmark Vesey's plot. In these revolts connections were made between faith and practice, between understanding religious doctrines and transforming one's lived experience—a sort of liberation theology.[32]

But religious faith was not necessary for slaves to assert and display their human desire for freedom. This desire was played out again and again in the many rebellions that took place in South Carolina from the very beginnings of Atlantic slavery until the end of the Civil War. One of the first slave rebellions on American soil took place in 1526 when Africans brought by Spanish pioneers to South Carolina rebelled and, perhaps, went to live in nearby Native American villages. The Spanish, led by Lucas Vásquez de Ayllón, had established a colony called San Miguel de Guadalupe, which was populated by five hundred Spaniards and one hundred African slaves and was located somewhere near the Pee Dee River. Aptheker writes that months after settlement there was a small slave rebellion and the colony spun out of control. At this point, a number of Africans apparently went to live with the Native Americans (163). The remaining colonists soon left, leaving the former slaves behind.

Colonization and other commercial developments in the Atlantic world were the apparent cause of many such rebellions as lower-class workers suffered tremendous exploitation by the developing economy. Peter Linebaugh and Marcus Rediker employ the term "the many-headed hydra" to describe this developing network of cooperative protest. They write that "the heads, though originally brought into productive combination by their Herculean rulers, soon developed among themselves new forms of cooperation against those rulers, from mutinies and strikes to riots and insurrections and revolution. Like the commodities they produced, their experience circulated with the planetary currents around the Atlantic, often eastward, from American plantations, Irish commons, and deep-sea vessels back from the metropoles of Europe" (4). Rebellions, it seems, were par for the course in eighteenth-century European colonies. In the 1730s and 1740s there were rebellions in British, French, Spanish, Dutch, and Danish colonies (191). During this span of twenty years, "the magnitude of the upheaval was, in comparative terms, extraordinary, encompassing more than eighty separate cases of conspiracy, revolt, mutiny, and arson" (192). Most involved enslaved Africans, but some—like the Irish-led Red String Conspiracy of Savannah in March 1736—involved other subaltern groups. There is reason to believe that slaves from different parts of the Atlantic world were communicating and learning about these disturbances from one another. For example, Le Jau writes that in 1713, slaves in South Carolina plotted an insurrection similar to one that took place in New York in 1712 (136–137). In 1793, there were reports that slaves in South Carolina became unruly after learning of the events in Haiti (Aptheker 96).

There is some evidence that the Stono Rebellion, like that of Haiti, made waves throughout the British colonies on the Atlantic Seaboard. Reports of the incident were published in Boston newspapers, and Jill Lepore claims that New Yorkers "knew about the Stono Rebellion in South Carolina in 1739" (53). A reference is made to Stono in a proclamation signed by James Oglethorpe and published in the *New-York Weekly Journal* on April 28, 1740. Oglethorpe explains his rationale for preparing to attack the Spanish at St. Augustine, who "do continue to foment and countenance the slaves in rebellion, burning of houses, murders, and other cruelties, of the success of whole proclamations, the late massacre in this province has been too sad a proof" (Oglethorpe). Perhaps the knowledge of what happened in

South Carolina helped cultivate the famous multiracial conspiracy that was uncovered in New York in 1741. This incident was, coincidentally, preceded by arsons in New Jersey and followed by an attempted arson in Charles Town.[33] Apparently, the Stono Rebellion fostered resistance within South Carolina. In June of 1740 over 150 slaves rebelled near Ashley River. In June eight years later a plot was uncovered among slaves living on plantations along the Cooper River. Edward Ball notes that this plot was organized by a slave named Agrippa owned by James Akin (148). Ball asserts that "everyone recalled the Stono events eight years before; then the black rebels had been slaughtered, but what was to prevent the revolt from succeeding this time?" (149). After interrogating the slaves involved, blame was pinned on the gossip of four women who were "sold and deported" (152). Was this a case of hysteria, or did the whites remember the Stono rebels, as Ball claims, and not want to take any chances? And did the *slaves* remember them as well?

Nonetheless, South Carolina was never immune to such movements from below. Vincent Harding writes, "In South Carolina there was never a time when organized attempts at black uprisings did not seem a part of the landscape" (*There Is a River* 33). The slave rebellion, in this sense, becomes a form of natural justice or pathetic fallacy as the natural world of South Carolina responds violently to the practice. Or perhaps, as one Salzberger emigrant in Georgia offers, rebellions were retribution from God. In an account of the incident from September 28, 1739, Johann Martin Boltzius writes that James Oglethorpe had told them that "the Negro rebellion had begun on the day of the Lord, which these slaves must desecrate with work and in other ways at the desire, command, and compulsion of their masters and that we could recognize a *jus talionis* in it" ("Diary" 226). The members of this Lutheran community were staunch opponents of slavery and must have been receptive to the idea that white slave owners had been subject to a God-ordained *jus talionis* or "right to retaliation" for overworking their slaves.

But theories of divine retribution imply an outside force at play. The rebels, in this case, are not the subjects of their own destiny. Perhaps, then, we could imagine the actions of the rebels as *jus bellum* or "just war." One could argue via Locke that the slaves, because they were not legitimate prisoners of war and because they lacked rights within the context of the social contract—from which they were excluded—would have every right to rebel against those who "governed" them and to wage a just war. Can we justify the Stono rebels' declaration of war, then, as a truly legitimate, rational, and appropriate response to the Middle Passage, enslavement, and gross violations of human rights? For some whites, at the time, the rationale behind the slaves' rebellion was obvious. In a letter to the British Admiralty office dated October 4, 1739, Captain Charles Fanshawe claims that the Stono Rebellion was "revenge for particular severity's they conceived they had received from their masters and overseers" (qtd. in Duncan 778). But was it more than just a moment of revenge?

Harding refers to Stono and all other American slave rebellions as being part of "the Other American Revolution." He believes, "Every serious challenge to the system of white domination and exploitation, each act of resistance and rebellion, each attempt to fashion an independent black vision of new humans and a new society has been an element of the continuing revolutionary tradition" (*Other American* xv). The vision of this other American revolution is rooted in what is, in the bourgeois capitalist tradition, a radical notion of human dignity and equality—a notion that was furthered by the constant attempts by African American slaves to overturn the violent status quo of human bondage. We may never know precisely what these rebels understood of natural or human rights philosophy, the human right to freedom and liberty, but can imagine that—after the putrid smells of the Middle Passage, the hunger, the sickness, the disease, after the weeks of seasoning on Sullivan's Island, after the back-breaking work of rice cultivation—they were formulating their own ideas, their own human rights discourse. Sterling Stuckey believes this discourse is rooted in an African nationalism that was born on slave ships, "the first real incubators of slave unity across cultural lines ... fostering resistance thousands of miles before the shores of the land appeared on the horizon—before there was mention of natural rights in North America" (3).

Stuckey is right to acknowledge the African roots of American human rights discourse. Large-scale disruptions of the developing plantation system often began in Africa. An incident in 1729 involving the slave ship *Clare* comes to mind. At this juncture in history, Africans must have been keenly aware of the purpose of the large ships steered by white men that were constantly roaming their shores. The *Clare* "having completed her number of Negroes had taken her departure from the coast of Guinea for South Carolina; but was not 10 leagues on her way, before the Negroes rose and making themselves masters of the gunpowder and fire arms, the captain and ships crew took to their long boat, and got shore near Cape Coast

Castle. The Negroes run the ship on shore within a few leagues of the said castle, and made their escape" (Donnan 274).[34] But many ships did make their way across the Atlantic, depositing their human cargo in places like Charles Town. In South Carolina and throughout the American colonies, the universal, human belief in the pursuit of freedom did not die, but, in fact, developed and transformed. Rebellions were truly human reactions to capture and enslavement, but such actions take on added significance in America because they were the first steps in the development of the abolition movement—the first international human rights campaign.[35] In this sense, ships served as incubators for new visions of reality and were essentially bridges to modernity (Gilroy 17). But this modern vision of "liberty" was one wholly different than that of Europeans. Kenneth Stampp makes a similar theoretical leap when analyzing the oral histories of former slaves, writing that "untutored slaves seldom speculated about freedom as an abstraction. . . . An ex-slave explained simply what freedom meant to her: 'I am now my own mistress, and need not work when I am sick. I can do my own thinkings, without having any to think for me,—to tell me when to come, what to do, and to sell me when they get ready.' Though she may never have heard of the doctrine of natural rights, her concept of freedom surely embraced more than its incidental aspects" (88–89).[36]

There are, however, more appropriate narratives—at least for this particular study—detailing the history of slave resistance and the quest for human rights. The best evidence, perhaps, is the oral narrative of George Cato, who claimed to be the great-great grandson of Cato, the rebellion leader. This account, "The Stono Insurrection Described by a Descendant of the Leader," was recorded and transcribed in dialect by Stiles M. Scruggs as part of the Federal Writers' Project in 1937. Cato's account demonstrates that the Stono narrative had such force and power that it persisted over time, passed on by several generations of African Americans. It is notably similar to white-produced written accounts of the rebellion. The details are familiar: about one hundred slaves rebelling on September 9, 1739; the initial slaying of two men in a storehouse by the Stono River; the arson and killings; the run-in with Bull; and the final showdown in the field.

Cato places much emphasis on the heroism and selflessness of his ancestor, who "was plum willin' to lay down his life for de right"; what he did was not "for his own benefit as it was to help others" (Cato 98). The rebellion leader was willing to put his life and freedom at risk in the service of his community. He was bold and stood firm when the white militia arrived.

He struggled to maintain order among the rebels, despite the fact that they were outnumbered and that, according to the speaker, they were busy dancing and drinking.[37] George Cato claims, "Commander Cato speak for de crowd. He say: 'We don't lak slavery. . . . [W]e not whipped yet and we is not converted' . . . He die but he die doin' de right, as he see it" (100). He died "doin' de right," fighting for what he intrinsically believed to be correct. Cato also notes that "long befo' dis uprisin', de Cato slave wrote passes for slaves and do all he can to send them to freedom," highlighting the importance of having a literate rebellion organizer—a key factor in the Prosser and Vesey conspiracies and in Nat Turner's rebellion in the nineteenth century (100). But it was an oral culture that allowed the Stono narrative to survive, stored, as it was, in the Cato family's intellectual and bodily archive and protected for over 198 years (98). One imagines the narrative instilled in family members a sense of pride in their past—direct lineage to a powerful leader with the necessary skills to take such a bold step. Pearson points out that, besides Cato/Jemmy, no other rebels are identified in direct accounts of the rebellion—a sign, perhaps, that he held a position of prominence on a plantation or among local slaves (37). The Stono leader possessed the same qualities that David Robertson ascribes to Denmark Vesey: organizational and ideological leadership, both necessary for rebellion in a slave society (20). Robertson calls Vesey "a prophet of the Enlightenment of the eighteenth century, during which he gained his physical majority and his literacy" (135). One could say the same of Jemmy.

Stono decidedly follows Aptheker's "conclusion that discontent and rebelliousness were not only exceedingly common, but, indeed characteristic of American Negro slaves" (374). But Stono shares the philosophical basis of myriad other subaltern rebellions—the intrinsic belief in the dignity of the human being. The rebels' declaration of "liberty" and George Cato's narrative can be read as principal literary acts that participate and shape this discourse of human rights. Indeed, Stono provides unique insights into the United States' ambiguous relationship with human rights and struggles to achieve them. At once Stono is an act of violent rebellion and an act of political and historical significance, a narrative of one group's attempt to assert its freedom, its dignity, and, I believe, its right to communicate that message. When the rebels shout "liberty," they are not murderers but are freedom fighters.[38] They are participants in the Atlantic world, in projects of modernity, and in the development of human rights discourse.

In his work exploring the roots of African American fiction, Jon-Christian Suggs claims that "the law's ability to shape—its historical force as the sole yet ever elusive determinant of African American social identity—presets the narrative base for all African American fiction" (9). One might also read George Cato's narrative—the narrative of the African American as an actor within the Stono Rebellion—as a response to legal status and part of the development of African American literature. The lives of the Stono rebels had been circumvented by laws which deemed them less than human. The rebels were confronting this legal status head-on, manifesting their full humanity through the unique cultural practices that one discovers in the written record.[39] The rebels asserted their right to communicate, their right to be human, in a variety of ways—through their own cultural practices (flag, religion, language) and by subverting the communication technologies of whites (reading the laws, cutting off heads, and destroying homes and property). These actions provide a counter-narrative to the laws governing African Americans in South Carolina.

The Stono Rebellion and the many other American slave rebellions (recorded and not) were important contributions to the struggle for international human rights in the eighteenth century. It has been well documented that slaves rebelled in less spectacular ways—poisonings, work slow-downs, tool-breaking, petty larceny—but the public nature of bold acts of violent resistance like Stono helped shape a discourse of rights championed by black and white abolitionists. Slave rebellions like Stono are equally as important to an understanding of contemporary human rights discourse as the events of the American and French revolutions, though they are too often excluded due to a common perception that they lack texts that can transmit their essential narratives. But African American slaves left a variety of cultural impressions—texts, if you will— that demonstrate a sophisticated understanding of their predicament and an innate desire to transform it. In addition to this record that has been lifted from beneath the words of white writers is the transmission of a discourse of human rights into early African American literature.

Chapter 4

★   ★   ★   ★

NEGRO ACTS
*Communication and African American
Declarations of Independence*

> But above all, are there no dangers attending this mode of treatment?
> Are you not hourly in dread of an insurrection?
> —Olaudah Equiano, *The Interesting Life of Olaudah Equiano*

FOR A COLONY TRYING TO ESTABLISH its presence among the growing community of British colonies on the east coast of North America, a violent slave rebellion would be horrible press, to say the least. American colonists were generally aware that slave rebellions were common in the West Indies but wished to ignore the potential and actual rebellions in their own backyard. After Stono, the *South Carolina Gazette* exerted a media blackout, but word of the event leaked nonetheless, and letters and reports written by white South Carolinians depicted heightened anxieties and desires for swift retribution.[1] Stories of the rebellion appeared in Benjamin Franklin's *Pennsylvania Gazette*, several Boston newspapers, and in at least seven British periodicals.[2] Possible references to the rebellion appeared in the *New-York Weekly Journal* and, perhaps, George Whitefield's diary.[3]

These stories and letters reveal the usual post-disaster finger pointing, with most fingers pointing directly at the Spanish in Florida. In a letter to John Richards of London, Robert Pringle writes, "I hope our government will order effectual methods for the taking of St. Augustine from the Spaniards which is now a great detriment to this province by the encouragement & protection given by them to our Negroes that run away there" (135). The rebellion, he claims, was provoked by the Spanish and had nothing to do with the social order of the colony. The decidedly dramatic official report of the event, published by the South Carolina Commons House of Assembly in 1741, exhibits a general fear of a disrupted society and an intense hatred of the Spanish: "On this occasion every breast was filled with concern.... With regret we bewailed our peculiar case, that we could not enjoy the benefits of peace like the rest of mankind and that our own industry should be the means of taking from us all the sweets of life and of rendering us liable to the loss of our lives and fortune" ("Report of the Committee" 84). The "peculiar case" the report refers to is the existence of slave rebels in their midst and the hostile Spanish in nearby Florida. The Commons House report concluded that the Spanish were the greater evil: "With indignation we looked at St. Augustine (like another Sallee) that den of thieves and ruffians! Receptacle of debtors, servants, and slaves! Bane of industry and society!" (84). The Spanish were hangers-on, Catholics, and, worst of all, disrupters of Atlantic capitalism who had the audacity to offer freedom to escaped slaves.

At the time, rumors were rampant that Spanish priests had come on shore and told slaves this good news. In his journal, William Stephens of Georgia describes an encounter with a suspicious character captured in Savannah and believed to be a Spanish spy (378–379). Knowledge that the Kongolese slaves involved in the Stono Rebellion may have had some exposure to the Portuguese language and to the Catholic faith in Africa made these speculations more promising. Another Georgian, Benjamin Martyn, also suspected that the Spanish were involved in the rebellion, but he seems to think their reasons for resistance were more basic (84). And if slaves received such offers of freedom again, he writes, they would once again try to escape "certain slavery to liberty and better treatment." The fact of the rebellion, then, heightened the colonists' sense of urgency and emboldened them to join forces with Oglethorpe of Georgia to attack Spanish Florida. The campaign, which lasted from the following May to July, was a fiasco. Despite the failure of the Georgia-Carolina expedition, the Stono Rebellion did provide South Carolina with extra support from Great Britain in their efforts to disrupt the Spanish colony. It focused British attention on the problem of having colonial territories within close range of their enemy. But this episode represents more than scapegoating on the part of South Carolina's leading citizens; it marks, in some ways, the culmination of a series of choices regarding human rights made by white colonists that would have disastrous effects on the lives of countless human beings for generations to follow.

In his analysis of the diaries of several perpetrators of the late-nineteenth and early-twentieth-century atrocities in the Belgian Congo, Adam Hochschild notes that "we can sometimes catch the act of forgetting at the very moment it happens. It is not a moment of erasure, but of turning things upside down, the strange reversal of the victimizer mentally converting himself to victim" (*King* 295). A similar moment occurs after the Stono Rebellion. Recall the words of the official report cited above: "On this occasion every breast was filled with concern.... With regret we bewailed our peculiar case, that we could not enjoy the benefits of peace like the rest of mankind." A "peculiar" narrative turn occurs. South Carolina has been victimized by the slaves, by the Spanish, but not by the actions of slave traders, slave owners, or the colonial government that permitted the practice. In the Commons House Journal from November 8, 1739, William Bull blames the Spanish in St. Augustine, writing, "As the protection our deserted slaves have met with at that castle has doubtless encouraged others to make the like attempts and even rise in rebellion, so the demolition of that place, would free us from the like danger for the future" (Easterby 2:16). Bull claims that the real problem is Spain, a problem that can be remedied. But more was going on here than sour relations with Spain, and the colonists knew it; choices had to be made about the human slaves in their midst. They had to decide whether to entrench their blossoming society within the context of slavery—or not.

The response was to entrench. The colonial government's first move was to strengthen the Patrol Act of 1737, and then it began a process of consolidating all slave-related regulations. Robert Olwell notes that "South Carolina's legislators deliberated carefully about the place of slavery in their society and their society's place within the Anglo-American world" (65). These careful deliberations led to "An Act for the Better Ordering and Governing of Negroes and Other Slaves in this Province," or more commonly referred to as the "Negro Act," which was signed into law on May 10, 1740. The Negro Act "looked toward a fundamental alteration in the character of Carolina society, with a less open and compromising slave system" (Wax 138). South Carolina's Negro Act was modeled, in part, on the thorough slave codes of Barbados and was later mimicked in Georgia and the Gulf states (Stampp 206). It remained largely in effect until the Civil War and included a few provisions meant to better the lives of slaves—preventing certain cruel punishments and limiting workdays—but, ultimately, it served to legally separate black people from white people as much as possible. This was a concrete step in the direction of creating a solid, legal foundation for a slave society. Eugene Sirmans notes, "The assembly had not changed the colony's basic slave laws since 1696, although it had re-enacted the slave code of 1696 three times and amended it twice. The old law was becoming obsolete and needed drastic revision" (*Colonial* 207). The revisions were, indeed, drastic.

The South Carolina government sought ways to stem the tide of the growing black population and imposed a temporary ban on slave importation from 1741 to 1743 and established stiff duties for when the ban was eventually lifted. In addition to limiting the number of black people entering the colony, it was thought prudent to increase the number of whites—or at least people who shared, or could be made to share, common cause with the white leadership's agenda. There had been various attempts to support the immigration of more Europeans into the colony, but these attempts were largely unsuccessful. The South Carolina government, therefore, decided to work with what was at hand. Rewards were established for slaves who informed on other slaves. Those slaves that helped their masters escape from the Stono rebels were publicly acknowledged in Charles Town so as to provide potential collaborators with positive role models; for white South Carolinians, this system of public reward functioned as a significant communication event.

The South Carolina Commons Journal records reveal that on November 29, 1739, over thirty slaves were rewarded for protecting their white masters during the rebellion and for assisting in the apprehension of rebels in the aftermath. According to the Journal, July, owned by Thomas Elliott, "had at several times bravely fought against the rebels, and killed one of them" (Easterby 2:64). He was awarded his freedom, some clothing, and a pair of shoes. Slaves named Ralph, Prince, Joe, Larush, Pompey, Mingo, Doctor, Cub, and Toby and eight unidentified men and one woman were given clothes and cash for opposing the rebels; many of them assisted in protecting Thomas Elliott. One wonders why these slaves did not join the rebellion. Perhaps the exigencies of slavery or the uncertainties of joining the freedom struggle led them to protect their lives or the lives of family members. It is also unclear to what extent slaves assisted whites and to what extent coercion was involved. The government's hope was that rewards such as these would disrupt unity among slaves and prevent further insurrection.

Equally as important, the government wished to collaborate with Native Americans. And so, the Negro Act offered rewards to Native Americans who captured runaways. As long as the Cherokee remained on the borders of the colony, slave owners sought to exploit native tracking skills in their efforts to capture runaways. This helped prevent escapes as well as the development of colonies of maroons like those that existed in Jamaica. More importantly, it fostered animosity between blacks and Native Americans. Gary Nash writes, "Indian uprisings that punctuated the colonial period and a succession of slave uprisings and insurrectionary plots that were nipped in the bud kept South Carolinians sickeningly aware that only through the greatest vigilance and through policies designed to keep their enemies divided could they hope to remain in control of the situation" (292). A unified force of excluded groups was a real possibility in colonial South Carolina. Though complicated by the dynamics of power and culture, there was some contact between Native Americans and African slaves, including instances of escaped slaves living among the Tuscarora, Yemassee, and Cherokee. But there were few major acts of public resistance involving Native Americans and African slaves working in concert. Nonetheless, in 1740, South Carolina officials wished to prevent these two potentially volatile groups from joining forces. They knew it was a possibility; they had heard stories of a black–Native American alliance in New York City in 1712 and did not wish to take chances.

But the colonial government believed the best way to stabilize the dynamics of the colony was to enhance the social position of poor whites; thus racism became a "realistic device for control" (Zinn 56). To that end, the Negro Act transformed the legal status of South Carolina's slaves from freehold property to chattel: "absolute slaves, and the subjects of property in the hands of particular persons" ("An Act for the Better Ordering" 397). Sirmans notes that after 1740 "slavery no longer rested upon custom" but in the *corpus jurus* (*Colonial* 209). The first slave act that went into effect in South Carolina was drawn up in 1696, but its definition of the legal status of African slaves was vague (Sirmans, "Legal" 466). This changed when the Negro Act was written: any black person within the colony would be assumed a slave unless they could prove otherwise. Any white person, planter or pauper, could stop any black person and demand proof of their status. This pass system codified difference, circumscribing lives, movements, and freedoms.

The relationship of slaves to property changed in other ways as well. The neuroses of the authors of these laws are revealed in crimes meted out to those who destroy property. For example, a slave who destroyed white property—a barn, a farm tool, a bag of rice—would be put to death. But a white person who destroyed a slave (also white property) would be fined. Essentially, black human beings, slave or free, were now singled out by law from other kinds of human beings. Colonial leaders believed their safety depended on making others, like poor whites and even Native Americans, feel socially significant in comparison to African slaves. This *was* the age of enlightened cataloging.

And so, the Negro Act enhanced the legal position of poor whites. That whites were empowered by this legal structure is revealed in reports of violent searches of slave quarters, which Robert M. Weir notes "was a recognized form of amusement for young men" (195). Weir continues, "Perhaps here—in the perversion or the laws making every white man a guardian of law and order—lay one of the tangled roots of vigilantism and nineteenth century lynching." A system rooted in terror was created. Colonists "terrified at what the large number of slaves might be able to do, attempted to terrorize the slaves into not doing it" (196). In his *Discourse on Colonialism* Aimé Césaire speaks of the dehumanizing effects of such structures of terror. He notes that "colonization works to *decivilize* the colonizer, to *brutalize* him in the true sense of the word, to degrade him, to awaken him to buried instincts, to covetousness, violence, race hatred, and moral relativism" (35). South Carolina's slave system and the structures that disciplined its practice worked in a similar fashion. The Negro Act established parameters that denied the humanness of black people and, one could argue, called into question that of whites.

But legal status is certainly not the only measure of human dignity—and the authors of the Negro Act were aware of this important fact. Human dignity also manifests in one's capability to communicate one's concerns and ideals. Therefore, the ultimate goal of the Negro Act was to prohibit any narrative emanating from the African American community that posited alternatives to the slave regime, to racism, to violations of human rights. Besides the pass system, strict regulations were placed on slaves' ability to communicate with one another: literacy and drums were outlawed and blacks could no longer congregate publicly. South Carolina was one of the first colonies to target communication technologies in its efforts to reduce human beings to chattel. Article 36 "restrain[ed] the wanderings and meetings of negroes and other slaves, at all times"[4] and prohibited the use of "drums, horns, or other loud instruments, which may call together or give sign or notice to one another of [the] wicked designs and purposes ... of strange negroes" ("An Act for the Better Ordering" 410). Article 45 claimed that "the having of slaves taught to write, or suffering them to be employed in writing, may be attended with great inconveniences" (413). Until Stono, access to these technologies by slaves was not deemed a serious enough threat to order to warrant legal prohibitions. Some South Carolinians, perhaps, believed that the rebels may have read the notice in the *South Carolina Gazette* on August 18, 1739, about the new law requiring all white men to carry their arms to church on Sundays. The rebellion broke out on a Sunday, weeks before this law went into effect. Others thought that the rebels motivated themselves and communicated their intentions by playing drums and having raucous gatherings. In an essay that was later reprinted as the introduction to the *Norton Anthology of African American Literature*, Henry Louis Gates Jr. and Nellie McKay acknowledge the importance of communications to the Stono Rebellion and the prohibitions set forth by the Negro Act, "a draconian body of public laws, making two forms of literacy punishable by law: the mastery of letters, and the mastery of the drum. . . . In the Stono Rebellion, both forms of literacy—of English letters and of the black vernacular—had been pivotal to the slave's capacity to rebel" (96).[5] If these modes of communication were used to launch the most successful slave rebellion in the colonial South, they would have to be controlled. In the process, these controls denied African Americans access to certain mechanisms for expressing their humanity in the public sphere.

These legal restrictions are not surprising given the growth of print and other communication technologies in the Western world at this time. During the eighteenth century, many Europeans and many American colonists began to recognize the importance of communication rights to their own political and/or revolutionary efforts, citing free speech, press, and assembly as necessary for bourgeois democracy. The first clear articulation of the human right to communicate freely in a broad sense came fifty years after the Stono Rebellion in Article 11 of the French Declaration of the Rights of Man and of the Citizen: "Free communication of ideas and opinions is one of the most precious of the rights of man. Consequently, every citizen may speak, write, and print freely."[6] Contemporary discussions of communication rights begin with Article 19 of the Universal Declaration of Human Rights, which asserts, "Everyone has the right to freedom of opinion and expression; this right includes freedom to hold opinions without interference and to seek, receive and impart information and ideas through any media and regardless of frontiers." Article 19 declares that human beings must be allowed the positive right to communicate freely with one another, to create their own narratives, to speak in first-person. Humans have the right to share "information and ideas" by using all kinds of media, across all boundaries, both geographic and national. Article 19, enhanced in part by the United Nations International Covenant on Civil and Political Rights (1964) and, perhaps, the Covenant on Economic, Social, and Cultural Rights (1966), has driven a larger discussion regarding a potential human right to communicate.[7] My understanding of this right is based on the comprehensive approach of Jean d'Arcy. From a comprehensive standpoint the right to communicate could encapsulate many human rights, including the right to assembly, to movement, to send and receive information, to associate, to express, to practice cultures, and to receive an education.[8] Speaking of the right to communicate as a comprehensive right highlights the significance of communication technologies in a networked and globalized society—like the eighteenth-century Atlantic—as well as the interdependence of many of these human rights.

D'Arcy claims that "those in power . . . have always known that he who effectively controls communications controls society" (15). The creation of the Negro Act after the Stono Rebellion was an attempt to "effectively" control society by controlling communications. South Carolina's leaders knew they had a significant problem on their hands—human beings, the source of their income, asserting their humanity. There is, as demonstrated in chapter 3, significant evidence that the Stono rebels took issue with their situations and were seeking to destroy what they knew of South Carolina plantation society. In this light, the immediate and total legal response of the South Carolina government to their insurrection becomes clear. One of the final provisions of the Negro Act, Article 56, absolves whites of any wrongdoing on that day and in the wake of the rebellion:

> *As the exigence and danger the inhabitants at that time were in and exposed to, would not admit of the formality of a legal trial of such rebellious negroes, but for their own security, the said inhabitants were obliged to put such negroes to immediate death; to prevent, therefore, any person or persons being questioned for any matter or thing done in the suppression or execution of the said rebellious negroes, as also any litigious suit, action or prosecution that may be brought, sued or prosecuted or commenced against such person or persons for or concerning the same . . . all and every act, matter and thing, had, done, committed and executed, in and about suppressing*

and putting all and every said negro and negroes to death is and are hereby declared lawful, to all intents and purposes whatsoever, as fully and amply as if such rebellious negroes had undergone a formal trial. ("An Act for the Better Ordering" 416)

This article permits a legal rupture in South Carolina, encoded in government policy and revealed in cultural practice. This rupture did not happen overnight—it was deliberate and calculated.

Some historians have argued that the Negro Act's influence was temporary. Donald Wax believes these laws did not lead to "long-lasting or permanent change.... Once the immediate danger had passed and memories were blunted, masters and slaves returned to their former ways" (143). And there is evidence that some slaves did flaunt their ability to communicate with other slaves. There were reports of slave gatherings and of slaves trading goods in the Charles Town market in 1742. With such evidence, Wax notes that in some ways, "slaves became a class of law-breakers.... Whites were forced by their bondsmen into fashioning their own compromises with the system. Private interests, often economic in nature, took precedence over the demands of the law" (145). In other words, there was a degree of compromise and fluidity between blacks and whites. And yet, despite such assertions, the Negro Act existed and was present in ways that not all could see. It was never completely forgotten. Shortly after uncovering Denmark Vesey's plot in 1820, officials in Charleston reminded city residents (white and black) of the Negro Act's existence. Appended to a pamphlet published in 1822 entitled *An Account of the Late Intended Insurrection among a Portion of the Blacks of This City* is Article 17 from the Negro Act, acknowledging that the punishment for those instigating an insurrection is death (31).

There are, of course, many instances of slave rebellions and of blatant disregard for the Negro Act throughout colonial and antebellum South Carolina history. This does not, however, change the fact that in the letter of the law blacks were always subject to the force and power of whites. A black person was automatically suspect, and social and political order rested on the presence of this ethos of divide and conquer—one that lingers with us in the present. Indeed, the effects of this legal order are telling. As noted above, the Negro Act included a few provisions to limit the cruelty of slave owners. But Alexander Hewatt writes in 1779 that the rights of slaves "as human creatures are entirely disregarded, and punishments are commonly inflicted according to the will of their master, however cruel and barbarous his disposition may be" (94). He says that they are punished "for the most trifling offences, and sometimes, O horrid! when entirely innocent" (96). Like Crèvecoeur he is reduced to the poetics of the exclamation mark in order to convey his repulsion.

Law was one mechanism for entrenching difference, for creating separate spheres rather than addressing the source of the problem. In the short run it created unity for some, but in the long run it helped breed resentment and enabled trauma to endure by setting patterns of social and cultural segregation that in some ways remain.[9] There is some evidence that slaves in South Carolina had a difficult time gaining access to reading and writing—the most privileged tools of communication in the American public sphere. Oral histories of former South Carolina slaves, most transcribed in dialect form in the 1930s, reveal this problem.[10] One former slave, Nellie Boyd, claims, "De slaves never learned to read and write" (qtd. in Rawick 64). Fairy Elkins points out one obvious reason for this: "We didn't have time to learn to read and write" (115). One interviewer asks Charlie Grant, "Did you all have books?" Grant replies, "No. Ketch Nigger wid book it wuz, 'What dat you got dere? Bring it here. Where did you git it frum?' Carry you to whipping post" (170). Nevertheless, some slaves, like the Stono rebels, figured out how to infiltrate white communication networks and used this knowledge to their advantage. Former slave George Fleming claims, "Twan't no seats in school fer de slaves, though. Some of de slick ones slipped around and lairn't de letters" (135). Hector Godbold adds to this, claiming that most slaves "ne'er know nuthin tall 'bout gwinne to school. . . . Jes pick up wha' l'arnin' we ge' heah, dere en eve'ywhey" (145).[11]

Richard Cullen Rath notes that the Negro Act's prohibition of drums was "analogous to taking pens, paper, and books from the literate. Such an action could have definite effects, but it would not render the literate population illiterate" (89). Despite their best efforts, white South Carolinians continued to have trouble with slaves who "slipped around." Even though African Americans lacked legal human rights, they kept their hopes of achieving those rights alive. The Negro Act limited access to the public sphere and to certain mechanisms of communication for blacks, but it could not prevent communication entirely. This is most dramatically revealed in the slave plots and rebellions that punctuate the history of American slavery. The Denmark Vesey plot of 1820 was the most public plot or act of slave rebellion in South Carolina post-Stono and involved both free blacks as well as slaves. Coincidently, this conspiracy was linked to literacy. After the plot was uncovered, Thomas Pinckney, writing under the pseudonym "Achates," acknowledges the danger of having blacks learn to read and write. The leading cause for the conspiracy, he believes, was the "improper indulgencies permitted among all classes of the negroes in Charleston, and particularly among the domestics: and, as the most dangerous of those indulgencies, their being taught to read and write: the first bringing the powerful operation of the press to act on their uninformed and easily deluded minds; and the latter furnishing them with an instrument to carry into execution the mischievous suggestions of the former" (Pinckney 7). In Pinckney's mind, literacy or access to such privileged communications must have come only through the aid of whites. He cannot imagine that blacks had their own communication networks or their own definition of human rights. As one co-conspirator during the "trials" attempting to uncover the Vesey plot notes, "Vesey said, we were deprived of our rights and privileges by the white people ... and that it was high time for us to seek our rights, and that we were fully able to conquer the whites, if we were only unanimous and courageous, as the St. Domingo people were" (*Account 1822* 39). Rolla Bennett's testimony, quite remarkable on its own accord, elucidates the conspirators' relationship to rights discourse. She claims, "I know Denmark Vesey, on one occasion he asked me, what news? I told him, none. He replied, we are free, but the white people here won't let us be so; and the only way is, to raise up and fight the whites" (34). At one meeting, Bennett explains, "Vesey said, we were ... to get arms; that we ought to rise up against the whites to get our liberties. He was the first to rise up and speak, and he read to us from the Bible, how the *children of Israel were delivered out of Egypt from bondage*" (34). Again, Vesey couches his plan within a familiar rights discourse. Like the Stono rebels, these black South Carolinians are signifying, speaking back to the rights discourse of the Christian church, of Locke, of the "founding fathers," with their own shouts of liberty. The white regime had intended to quiet black South Carolinians for good. Clearly, they failed.[12]

THE PERSISTENCE OF AN AFRICAN AMERICAN HUMAN RIGHTS DISCOURSE

The Stono Rebellion was one of many freedom struggles organized and executed by slaves in the Americas. It is, though, unique because of the presence of the word "liberty" in the historical record and the relationship of that word to the rebels' actions. If we are uncertain what they meant when they shouted, "Liberty!" we may find some answers in early African American literature. In this literature we see a discourse of human rights, of individuals asserting their right to freedom and their right to communicate that message. From the first moments that African Americans put pen to paper, there were echoes of the Stono rebels' cry. This constant working out of rights discourse—of rewriting and signifying—demonstrates and participates in a significant intertextuality among various African American literary texts.[13] African American writers from the twentieth century speak back to those of the eighteenth and nineteenth century and on back to enslaved blacks themselves. William Paulson calls such specific intertextuality a "network of discourse" and writes, "The making, reception, and recycling of works ... is a complex, indirect, and often subtle way of sending feedback signals within the ongoing life processes in which history is made. It is also a form of participation in networks of human communication and transmission that mobilize the past and the present, the dead and the living, the far and the familiar" (21). Networks of discourse can present, represent, and rehearse a conceptual conversation across borders and through time (123). Most importantly, such a network is "a hybrid space, subject and object, social and technical" (125). I place great emphasis on this notion of a network of discourse as "hybrid space"; such a network does not privilege any form of communication but instead elicits input from all corners. The discourse merges, blends, combines, connects, revolves, and evolves as it shapes a meaning unique unto itself. This concept inevitably asks us to extend our notion of texts, though I intend to demonstrate how this works through an examination of African American literary creations. I hope to show how African American literature contends with both oral and written communication networks as it seeks to respond to white concepts of human rights with its own. This literary record of rights discourse exposes the fact that African Americans were not completely shackled by the various legal regimes meant to suppress their freedoms and that a rich culture and a counterpublic persisted.

When W. E. B. Du Bois writes that "there are to-day no truer exponents of the pure human spirit of the Declaration of Independence than the American Negroes," he is speaking of the ways in which African Americans past and present seek to achieve the rights set forth in that declaration (16). From the first moments of slavery, African Americans embodied broken promises, and yet "few men ever worshipped Freedom with half such unquestioning faith as did the American Negro for two centuries" (12). Du Bois believed that this longing for freedom is expressed in the folk tradition, specifically, African American folk songs, calling these songs "the sole American music" and "the most beautiful expression of human experience born this side of the seas" (155). It is the singular American music because it is the only American music that clearly expresses the hope represented by the Declaration of Independence—these songs are the sole musical manifestations of humanity, of human rights. All else, he avers, is dross.

Coincidentally, Du Bois acknowledges that during the Civil War Northerners first encountered slave songs while stationed in South Carolina and were moved by what they heard: "The Sea Islands of the Carolinas ... were filled with a black folk of primitive type, touched and moulded less by the world about them than any others outside the Black Belt. Their appearance was uncouth, their language funny, but their hearts were human and their singing stirred men with a mighty power" (155). Listeners were stirred by such songs as "I Know Moon-Rise" or "Lay Dis Body Down":

> I know moon-rise, I know star-rise
> Lay dis body down.
> I walk in de moonlight, I walk in de starlight,
> To lay dis body down.
> I'll walk in de graveyard, I'll walk through de graveyard,
> To lay dis body down.
> I'll lie in de grave an' stretch out my arms;
> Lay dis body down.
> I go to de judgment in de evenin' of de day
> When I lay dis body down;
> And my soul and your soul will meet in de day
> When I lay dis body down. (Higginson 209)

Du Bois writes, "I know little of music and can say nothing in technical phrase, but I know something of men, and knowing them, I know that these songs are the articulate message of the slave to the world" (156). In such songs, such "Sorrow Songs," exists an acute understanding of "the ultimate justice of things" (162). In "Lay Dis Body Down," the speaker claims she will have redemption in death—that she will "lay down" at a time of her choosing. This has more to do with life choices than with word choices. Other slave songs are less ambiguous in their approach. Sam Polite recalls one song sung behind the backs of masters:

> Go way, Old Man
> Go way, Old Man:
> Where you been all day?
> If you treat me good,
> I'll stay till Judgment Day.
> But if you treat me bad,
> I'll sure to run away. (qtd. in Hurmence 80–81)

In such songs, slaves make commitments to freedom in this life or in the next. "Would America have been America without her Negro people?" Du Bois asks (163). And would our contemporary understanding of human rights be the same without the many examples of "declarations of independence"—in both thought and deed—in early African American letters?

Shortly after Thomas Jefferson's Declaration of Independence was published, another declaration of independence emerged, this one signed by a number of African Americans in Boston,[14] including a man named Prince Hall, an important community organizer among free blacks of that city.[15] With Jefferson's text fresh on people's minds, these African Americans claim that like whites, "they have in common with all other Men, a natural & unalienable right to that freedom, which the great Parent of the Universe hath bestowed equally on all Mankind" (Hall, "To the Honorable Council" 1061). The writers make the obvious correlation "that every principle from which America has acted in the course of her unhappy difficulties with Great Britain, pleads stronger than a thousand arguments in favor of your Petitioners" (1062). In the midst of the revolutionary moment, they are calling on the white revolutionary leaders to recognize their particular Americanness. Twenty years later, Prince Hall would make similar assertions in his "A Charge Delivered to the African Lodge, June 24, 1797, at Menotomy," in which he asks all listeners to promote "a fellow feeling for our distres'd brethren of the human race, in their troubles, both spiritual and temporal" (76). Hall prescribes patience, for now, "for were we not possess'd of a great measure of it you could not bear up under the daily insults you meet with in the streets of Boston. . . . [H]ow are you shamefully abus'd" (73). Yet patience, like prayer, will take one only so far, and he offers the example of Haiti, where only years before slaves suffered horribly; "but blessed be God, the scene is changed.... Thus doth Ethiopia begin to stretch forth her hand, from a sink of slavery to freedom and equality" (74). Hall leans in a radical direction while seeking solidarity and reforms. His efforts for social justice were not limited to orations. He spent most of his life organizing the black community, creating mechanisms for socializing and sharing resources since the white community offered little meaningful assistance or entrée into their social circles or support networks.

African American preacher Lemuel Haynes shared Prince Hall's quest for a realization of the Declaration of Independence's promises in his "Liberty Further Extended: Or Free Thoughts on the Illegality of Slave-Keeping," written around the time of the Declaration. Haynes turns the screws on white Americans who ignore the contradiction of shouting for liberty while maintaining plantation slavery. Thus, he chooses the following line from the Declaration of Independence as his epigraph: "all men are created equal, that they are endowed by their creator with certain unalienable rights." Like Hall's African American community in Boston, Haynes speaks directly to Jefferson's text. Yes, he says, "Liberty, & freedom, is an innate principle.... Liberty is a jewel which was handed down to man from the cabinet of heaven, and is coaeval with his existence" (18). It would follow, then, that because liberty is natural and God-given, any human, including "a negro may justly challenge, and has an undeniable right to his ... liberty: consequently, the practices of slave-keeping, which so abounds in this land is illicit" (19). Color or nation should not be determining factors for one's freedom; human rights are "aspiring principles placed in all nations."

Haynes's numerous biblical citations—the obvious Calvinist thread throughout—are reminiscent of Olaudah Equiano's narrative, also from this period. Equiano notes that slavery increases the depravity of human beings: "it is the fatality of this mistaken avarice, that it corrupts the milk of human kindness and turns it into gall" (80). Slavery "violates that first natural right of mankind, equality, and independency; and gives one man a dominion over his fellows which God could never intend!" Despite his own ambiguous relationship to the practice, Equiano believes slave traders are "invaders of human rights" (89). Haynes makes similar arguments as he addresses slave traders directly at the conclusion of his essay. He castigates them and blames them for the potential failure of the revolutionary project: "If you have any love to yourselves, or any love to this land, if you have any love to your fellow-men, break these intolerable yokes... for god will not hold you guiltless" (29–30). He asks, essentially, who the real, authentic man is.

Another engagement with patriotism appears in the well-known works of Phillis Wheatley, who famously touted her patriotism and faith in an effort to seek justice for African Americans. Kidnapped as a child, most likely from the Senegal-Gambia region of West Africa, she was brought to Boston as a slave in 1761. Her masters recognized her brilliance at a young age, and, unlike many slaves, she was taught to read and write. She became the pride of the Wheatley family—a curio, a sideshow act for guests. In 1773 she published a volume, entitled *Poems on Various Subjects, Religious and Moral*, in London. Her poems were well-known throughout the colonies. Julian D. Mason Jr. claims that "Wheatley's poems were indeed known among the prominent families of Charleston during and after the Revolution" (9). Mason notes that her book may have crossed paths with Declaration of Independence signer Edward Rutledge and Constitution signer Charles Cotesworth Pinckney. This curious connection is all the more curious because both men had close ties to slave trade, and Wheatley's poems reveal a discomforting recognition of the glaring contradiction of her status within the Revolutionary milieu. The poems also reveal a "double-consciousness," the result of living as a black woman among privileged whites.

Wheatley's poem "On Being Brought from Africa to America" demonstrates her complicated existence. On the one hand, the poem imitates a European and neoclassical form, perhaps borrowed from one of her favorite poets, Alexander Pope. On the other, however, the poem speaks to the poet's condition as slave and black woman. This tension invites multiple readings of this, one of Wheatley's earliest poems:

> 'Twas mercy brought me from my *Pagan* land,
> Taught my benighted soul to understand
> That there's a God, that there's a *Savior* too:
> Once I redemption neither sought nor knew.
> Some view our sable race with scornful eye,
> "Their color is a diabolic die."
> Remember, *Christians*, *Negros*, black as *Cain*,
> May be refin'd, and join th' angelic train. (53)

On the surface the poem proclaims the poet's thankfulness for being brought to America, where she was redeemed by the Christian faith. Her "benighted" or dark soul discovered the Christian God and Jesus. To the reader and those who would "view our sable race with scornful eye," those who believe "Negros" are stained with the mark of Cain, she reminds that they, too, can be saved. But is it really that simple? A closer reading of this poem—the kind that Rutledge and Pinckney did not do—reveals an indictment of racism and slavery as well as Wheatley's acute awareness of her identity as an African American. She focuses on race—"benighted," "sable," "diabolic die," and "black." And her race is bound to chattel slavery in the Americas and to the racism that assumes "Negros" are only capable of cultivating sugar cane and indigo, if we read "Cain" and "die" as puns. No, slaves are humans and deserve to be treated with dignity. Whites must recognize that they are capable of becoming practicing Christians.

Whites must also understand that slaves desire to be free, too. Wheatley's poem "To the Right Honourable William, Earl of Dartmouth,"[16] ostensibly a paean to Dartmouth, the king's secretary of state, includes a stanza that steps beyond her attempts to win Dartmouth's understanding for the colonists' revolutionary cause. She tells him that her "love of *Freedom*" is rooted in her own lived experiences (83). As a child she was "snatch'd from *Afric's* fancy'd happy seat," leaving her mourning family behind; those who did this were heartless "and by no misery mov'd." Wheatley implies that it was not the logic of Locke or the pamphlets of Paine that taught her to desire freedom and human rights, but her own life. And her authority as rights advocate comes not from her ability to craft verse but from her position in a racist society. She concludes this stanza by expressing her wish that "others may never feel tyrannic sway" as she has. This is an unusual moment amidst her imitative neo-classical verse of heroic couplets and over-wrought lines. The verse comes alive as Wheatley quite literally speaks truth to power. She would soon taste freedom as she was manumitted in October of 1773, shortly after her book was published. But this did little to increase her fortunes; life as a free black woman in Boston was harsh. In 1784, Wheatley passed away in poverty and was buried with her last surviving child, who died shortly after she did.

Clearly, Christianity exerted a significant influence on human rights discourse in early African American literature and on the ever-developing abolition movement. Yet there were other religious influences. Omar ibn Said's short narrative, originally written in Arabic in 1831, describes the author's life experiences and trials as a slave in South Carolina and his escape to North Carolina; it is one of the earliest extant texts written by a Muslim

American.¹⁷ In the interstices of this relatively straightforward account are veiled messages, what James C. Scott calls "hidden transcripts."¹⁸ Said describes his journey to the United States after his capture. He writes, "we sailed upon the great sea a month and a half, when we came to a place called Charleston in the Christian language. There they sold me to a small, weak, and wicked man called Johnson, a complete infidel, who had no fear of God at all. Now I am a small man, and unable to do hard work so I fled from the hand of Johnson and after a month came to a place called Fayd-il" (793). "Fayd-il" is Fayetteville, North Carolina, where Said was discovered praying alone in a church. After being imprisoned while the authorities tried to figure out what to do with this strange man who used coal to write in Arabic on the walls of his cell, someone tried to buy him and send him back to Charleston. He shouted, "*No, no, no, no, no, no, no,* I not willing to go to Charleston." Said was apparently content with life in North Carolina, perhaps out of fear of the alternative. He claims, "I reside in this our country by reason of great necessity. Wicked men took me by violence and sold me to Christians. We sailed a month and a half on the great sea to the place called Charleston in the Christian land. I fell into the hands of a small, weak and wicked man, who feared not God at all nor did he read (the gospel) at all nor pray. I was afraid to remain with a man so depraved and who committed so many crimes and I ran away. After a month our Lord God brought me forward to the hand of a good man, who fears God, and loves to do good, and whose name is Jim Owen" (794–795).

In its original form, Said's narrative begins with a series of passages from the Qur'an. He recalls from memory, "Do you not know from the creation that God is full of skill? That He has made for the way of error, and you have walked therein?" (791–792). He also remembers, "Say, 'Have you not seen that your water has become impure? Who will bring you fresh water from the fountain?'" (792). Said is essentially transcribing a section from the Qur'an, Surah 67: Al-Mulk. In English "Al-Mulk" translates to "sovereignty" or "dominion." This passage depicts the omniscience and omnipotence of Allah: "It is He who has made the earth subservient to you. Walk about his regions and eat of His provisions. To Him all shall return at the Resurrection" (400). It also includes this passage, "Say: 'He is the Lord of Mercy: in Him we believe, and in Him we put our trust. You shall soon know who is in evident error'" (401). Why did he transcribe this particular passage before his autobiography? Was this a critique of his enslavement among Christians? Sylviane Diouf points out that Said was still a slave when he wrote this text; "he still had to be very much on guard" (143). Much of the autobiography expresses how happy he is to be the slave of the Owen family, and yet a few lines, safely written in Arabic, got away.

Said apparently converted to Christianity at some point, though he continued to use religious faith as a mechanism for critiquing his social status. In an article from *North Carolina University Magazine* dated September 1854, the writer recalls hearing Said read and translate Psalm 23, which begins, "The Lord is my shepherd; I shall not want." This Psalm underlines God's protection, "goodness and mercy." Yet in an article published in the *Wilmington Chronicle* in January 1847, the author writes of an Arabic translation that Said did of Psalm 22, a Psalm that carries a rather different tone from Psalm 23: "My God, my God, why hast thou forsaken me? Why art thou so far from helping me, and from the words of my roaring? O my God, I cry in the daytime, but thou hearest not; and in the night season, and am not silent." The psalmist calls on God to protect him for "trouble *is* near." The speaker of this Psalm is abused, laughed at, and scorned, yet he still calls on God, finding strength in the thought of his redemption. He knows the world belongs to God, who is "the governor among the nations." In the end, "the meek shall eat and be satisfied"; they will be redeemed. Which Psalm did Said feel the greater connection to—the one that depicts the peace of God's presence or the one that depicts God's almighty power and justice? Was this small, admittedly meek man speaking to slaveholders, to the people of North Carolina and the United States of America? As Muslim and Christian, as African and American, perhaps Said is demonstrating, through the veil of these texts, a universal human desire to live freely with dignity despite the shackles of "Negro Acts."

In significant ways, early African American writers addressed an audience ill-prepared for rebellious narratives; and, thus, much of early African American literature signifies on the religious and political rhetoric floating around in the colonial public sphere. Hall, Haynes, Wheatley, and Said must use the tools at hand, like the Stono rebels. The most obvious and ready-made language available was the revolutionary discourse of human rights. There is evidence that some freed blacks in South Carolina saw something hopeful in the rhetoric of 1776. Three days before July 4, 1791, a group of free blacks petitioned the South Carolina senate. The document titled "To the Honorable David Ramsay Esquire President and to the rest of the Honorable New Members of the Senate of the State of South Carolina" was written by a bricklayer named Thomas Cole and two butchers named Peter Bassnett Mathews and Mathew Webb, "on behalf of themselves & others free-men of Colour" ("To the Honorable" 98). Like Prince Hall, they declared their relationship to the liberty project and claimed that like the "founding fathers," they, too, have human rights. They noted that the 1740 Negro Act limited their ability to provide testimony and that because of this many criminals "have escaped the punishment due to their atrocious crimes." They pointed out that they had been loyal to the United States and had paid taxes (99). Because they were free, they hoped to be treated as such: "they are ready and willing to take and subscribe to such oath of allegiance to the states as shall be prescribed by this honorable house, and are also willing to take upon them any duty for the preservation of the peace in the city" (99). The authors of this petition were well aware that they could only hope for limited changes in their social position. They wrote, "Your memorialists do not presume to hope that they shall be put on an equal footing with the free white citizens of the state" (99). Their bold request to be treated with dignity was ultimately rejected.

Chapter 5

★ ★ ★ ★ ★

THE HEIRS OF JEMMY
Slave Rebels in Nineteenth-Century African American Fiction

> The English language befriends the grand American expression....
> It is the powerful language of resistance.
> —Walt Whitman, Preface to *Leaves of Grass* (1855)

BENEDICT ANDERSON ASSERTS that a nation is "an imagined political community" (6). Such a nation "is always conceived as a deep, horizontal comradeship. Ultimately it is this alliance that makes it possible, over the past two centuries for so many millions of people, not so much to kill, as willingly to die for such limited imaginings" (7). Nations promote "fellow-feeling"; they create bonds of identity. As I note in chapter 1, Anderson also acknowledges that in early America "print-capitalism ... made it possible for rapidly growing numbers of people to think about themselves, and to relate themselves to others, in profoundly new ways" (36). He posits that these national identities are produced when people participate in the shared practice of reading—most notably, when they read newspapers. Newspapers foster a particular community identity because they are locally produced for daily consumption; thus, reading a newspaper can become a ritualized and unifying cultural activity (34–35).

Elizabeth McHenry writes that in the nineteenth century some African Americans also traveled this printed path to racial/ethnic or national identity—to the formation of an "imagined community." She examines the efforts of free blacks in the North to gain access to the press and printed texts and to establish networks of print distribution and communication. The goal of these free blacks was to counter the popular argument that they were ignorant and incapable of useful literacy and to create black literary communities. The press was "a strategy that leaders in the black community believed would open the doors of American society to black people"

(McHenry 86). African Americans used the press on behalf of the black middle and working classes to help establish an identity and presence in the United States. Certainly, the press was an important mechanism for *whites* to share information, trade, and take part in the ongoing narrative of nationhood, but the developing black press also served these purposes, allowing some freedmen to participate in that narrative or, perhaps, to create their own.

Samuel Cornish and John Russworm's *Freedom's Journal* (1827), the short-lived first African American newspaper, was one such attempt to establish a literary culture within the African American community and, in so doing, establish that community's legitimacy and its claims for equal treatment. The editors intentionally wrote copy that focused less on slavery, the most obvious and pressing concern in the African American community, and more on establishing readers. They believed that freedmen would be treated better if their day-to-day behavior changed—if they could participate in the "literary community," broadly defined. *Freedom's Journal* published a significant amount of "fluff" and was inexpensive, thus giving blacks ready material for reading and conversation. McHenry writes that Cornish and Russworm's goal was for African Americans "to understand the public uses to which literature could be put" (102). African Americans, they concluded, should be able to participate effectively in the larger public sphere—this would give them the clout to press other claims, perhaps their rights as human beings.

And yet, African Americans understood that being accepted by whites was not the only method for obtaining human rights. Human rights discourse manifests in much of nineteenth-century African American prose written by David Walker, Frederick Douglass, Harriet Jacobs, T. Thomas Fortune, and countless others. For such writers, African American identity rests on this discourse because only through the bold assertion of one's human rights could one hope to be treated as a human and, ultimately, as an American citizen. These writers pushed the ideals of the Declaration of Independence into the public sphere in hopes that America would truly become America, as Langston Hughes would write in the twentieth century. This human rights discourse, as it transformed and asserted itself, was not rooted in print culture alone; the claims expressed by the Stono rebels and other slave insurrectionists were also central to its development.

Writing about victims of the South African apartheid regime, Pumla Gobodo-Madikizela notes that "the mistake is to see the political as separate from the personal—to see discontinuities between them. In dealing with the past, the narratives that people construct about what happened to them, the stories of their suffering, reflect the continuities between their personal and their political lives" (102). In other words, the ways that individuals construct identities in the wake of gross human rights violations is not disconnected from the ways they imagine their political futures. In the United States of the early nineteenth century, African Americans, free or otherwise, suffered countless indignities. It is not surprising, then, that when African Americans began to write their stories, the constructed and represented human subjects that manifested in those stories were often assertive, educated, and willing to use violence as a method for gaining their human rights. These writers had many models from which to choose since the first part of the nineteenth century was an age of well-known rebellions and conspiracies: Gabriel Prosser (1800), the Louisiana rebellion (1811), Denmark Vesey (1822), and Nat Turner (1831).

Nat's Rebellion was particularly bloody, resulting in the deaths of some fifty-five whites and fifty-five suspected rebels who were executed by the state. Even more shocking is the fact that perhaps as many as two hundred African Americans were killed by angry mobs seeking revenge. Slave states were put on high alert, with organized and disorganized militias roaming the countryside, searching the quarters of both slaves and free blacks. Harriet Jacobs famously comments on the tension in the wake of Nat's Rebellion and in a fit of sarcasm writes, "Strange that they should be so alarmed, when their slaves were so 'contented and happy'! But so it was." (63). But black writers were not surprised by these violent slave rebellions and some even championed such actions themselves, marking a sharp divide from the conciliatory tone set by many African American writers in the late nineteenth century. In creating and rehearsing and retelling narratives of liberation, African Americans were preparing themselves for liberation. These heirs of Jemmy are not long-suffering Uncle Toms; they are actively engaged in striking for liberty. Like the rebels of Stono, they foster rebellion through literacy or education and violence, using communication technologies to promote resistance.

Bostonian David Walker's *Appeal . . . to the Colored Citizens of the World* is one important marker of this break. On September 28, 1829, this used clothing dealer published the first edition of his *Appeal* and set off alarms throughout the South when copies of it began to appear in port cities, including Charleston, South Carolina. Walker believed that the power of his text rested in its mere existence and that it would send a signal to slaveholders (and, perhaps, a chill down their spines). Living in Boston gave Walker access to sailors and longshoremen who could distribute his text up and down the eastern coast of the United States and beyond. When Charleston officials discovered the text in the possession of a white sailor named Edward Smith, he was fined one thousand dollars and given a one-year sentence. The concept of a black man writing must have troubled Charlestonians, but the contents and implications of the *Appeal* must have troubled them all the more. Walker writes that God is just and, in an apparent reference to Thomas Jefferson, that justice is nigh (8). His self-assuredness regarding this future justice captivates: "Whether I write with a bad or a good spirit, I say if these things do not occur in their proper time, it is because the world in which we live does not exist, and we are deceived with regard to its existence" (22). This biting prose does not tiptoe around the subject of a violent end to slavery.

And this is what makes his text so important. The rights of African Americans have been trampled upon and it is up to them to reclaim them. Walker asserts, "Yea, would I meet death with avidity far! far!! in preference to such *servile submission* to the murderous hands of tyrants" (16). His exclamations hark back to the "Spirit of '76," yet his claims have little to do with taxation or representation; he denounces the enslavement of humans and reminds whites that the United States belongs to the slaves who helped build it (67). Slaves, he writes, must not submit. They must "prove to the Americans and the world, that we are MEN, and not *brutes*, as we have been represented, and by millions treated" (32). Walker acknowledges the importance of literacy, of being able to declare one's humanity, but he also promotes violence as a necessary evil: "Remember Americans, that we must and shall be free and enlightened as you are, will you wait until we shall under God, obtain our liberty by the crushing arm of power?" (72). Walker taunts white Americans, writing that they have a choice as to how the liberty of slaves will be achieved—through violence or education.

Frederick Douglass's quintessential slave narrative depicts a struggle for literacy and freedom that also marks the territories slaves must cross in order to liberate themselves and their nation. Ultimately, freedom for Douglass is achieved via a kind of violence, wrestling with the brutal slave breaker Covey and wresting away his freedom by running away. This is his rebellion against the plantation system. Douglass describes his struggle to gain literacy—from lessons given by his master's wife to tricking young boys on the street to teach him—as a method of liberation. But his momentous encounter with Covey is his most important communicative act. This fight, he notes, "rekindled the few expiring embers of freedom, and revived within me a sense of my own manhood" (*Narrative* 50). Much has been made of the trope of masculinity dripping from this scene, indeed, from this narrative, but one could also read it as a success story, a narrative of achieving human dignity. Because he crosses the boundaries set for him by the plantation system, because he fights back, he recognizes his humanity again. Douglass writes, "You have seen how a man was made a slave; you shall see how a slave was made a man" (47). We know of the brutality of slavery and of its victims, he seems to say; now let us have narratives of victors. Narratives like Douglass's establish cultural heroes and human rights warriors.

One finds evidence of this vision of the human rights hero in the folk culture of the handful of African Americans in South Carolina (how many we may never know) who shared the narrative of the leader of the Stono Rebellion. George Cato's account, passed on through the eighteenth, nineteenth, and into the twentieth century, is an indication of the power and strength of human rights discourse within African American communities. The obstructive laws that limited communications among black South Carolinians were apparently surmountable. Such stories of slave rebellion became fodder for the first efforts of African Americans to create fictions of their American experiences and, thus, help them establish an identity rooted in revolution. In Cato's oral history, his ancestor takes a Mosaic stand against his oppressors and assumes a central role in the cultural tradition of some Lowcountry African Americans. He is a hero, a legendary warrior, a protagonist in a counter-narrative.

Heroic slave rebels cut in Jemmy's mold are key figures in two significant early African American works of fiction—Frederick Douglass's 1853 novella *The Heroic Slave* and Martin R. Delany's *Blake; or, The Huts of America*, written and published serially between 1859 and 1862. These first fruits of African American fiction are inextricably linked to slave narratives, folk stories, and other communication technologies of slave culture that doggedly promote "shouts of liberty" and human dignity; and open slave revolts are central to both of them. At the same time, though, they assert an intertextual relationship with eighteenth-century human rights theorists as well as nineteenth-century white abolitionists like Harriet Beecher Stowe. (Her *Uncle Tom's Cabin* promotes a kind of acquiescence that seems foreign to the protagonists of these two tales, however.) Through fiction Delany and

Douglass seek to "manipulate sentiments" and transform human rights discourse in ways that they were perhaps incapable of doing in prose.[1] In the process, they hope to create new histories for newly imagined communities to share.

"LIBERTY, THE INALIENABLE BIRTH-RIGHT"

In his 1852 address, "What to the Slave is the Fourth of July?" Frederick Douglass notes, "We have to do with the past only as we can make it useful to the present and to the future" (123). He recognizes the possibilities that past ideals—the ideals of the American Revolution—offer the present-day listener. His search for a usable past does not end with this July 4 oration; Douglass was quite serious about finding a form that would help his quest for re-imagining national identity. A year later he published *The Heroic Slave*, his only work of fiction and in some sense a response to the quiet martyrdom of Stowe's Uncle Tom. Douglass's work describes the events surrounding a slave rebellion and the repercussions of the rebellion itself—in particular the influence of the hero's leadership and spirit on white observers. A conscious storyteller, Douglass is creating a narrative of human rights meant to be told and passed on.

His story is based on the slave mutiny on board the *Creole* in November 1841. The ship left Hampton, Virginia, with 134 slaves meant for sale in New Orleans when one of these slaves, a man appropriately named Madison Washington, led an insurrection and directed the ship to Nassau, where all of the slaves were freed. Despite its heroic implications, this was a tricky narrative to reproduce. Maggie Montesinos Sale notes that "at the historical moment at which Douglass's novella was written, published, and received, slave rebellion was virtually unrepresentable in national forums, and further, the righteousness of such an act was unimaginable for most U.S. Americans" (175). But accounts from the period claim that Washington was a strong leader, organized, intelligent, and capable of maintaining order throughout the mutiny, even sparing the captain's life. Such a story would prove an excellent source for Douglass's fiction—here was a group of slaves who rebelled with limited violence unlike, for example, Nat or the Stono rebels. Washington was an insurrectionist any abolitionist could love.

Douglass's version of the story begins with Madison Washington speaking to himself in a Virginia pine forest in the spring of 1835. A "Northern traveler," Mr. Listwell, bears witness to this young slave's "soliloquy," this "sable preacher" in his "solitary temple" (*Heroic Slave* 29). Washington describes the trials of his life as a slave and his desire to run away with recognizable eloquence: "If I get clear, (as something tells me I shall,) liberty, the inalienable birth-right of every man, precious and priceless, will be mine" (28). The narrator places the struggle for human rights front and center and links Washington to the American Revolution and its Virginian leaders: "Let those account for it who can, but there stands the fact, that a man who loved liberty as well as did Patrick Henry,—who deserved it as much as Thomas Jefferson... lives now only in the chattel records of his native State" (25). Krista Walter notes that rather than complicate the narrative, Douglass does not question the motives of these "founding fathers" (3). She writes, "For Douglass the philosophical basis for the republic was unquestionably sound; its ideals simply had to be fully realized." Thus, as we witness Madison Washington's dramatic soliloquy, Douglass wants the reader to believe that he or she is witness to the private deliberations of an important man, a forgotten revolutionary cut from the same cloth as Henry, Jefferson, or the hero's namesakes. The only difference is that Washington is a strong, handsome black man who, as Douglass writes, "had the head to conceive, and the hand to execute" (28). By the end of part 1 of the novella both Washington and Listwell are determined to make changes—Washington will run away and Listwell will become an abolitionist. Both make "declarations" of their independence in Virginia, and in so doing Douglass claims that slaves have shared ideals and a virtual equality with the American patriots.

In part 2, Mr. and Mrs. Listwell are at home in Ohio five years later when Madison Washington shows up at their house as he flees to freedom. Listwell transports Washington to a ship that will carry him on to Canada. In so doing, this resolute Northerner risks his own freedom, a sign that his transformation is complete, that he has become an abolitionist. Before he concludes his journey to Canada, Washington describes the long process of his escape from slavery. He tells Listwell, "The fact is, sir, during my flight, I felt myself robbed by society of all my just rights; that I was in an enemy's land, who sought both my life and liberty" (39). Washington is not alone in his sentiments as he describes a scene in which he bears witness to the tormented musings of an old slave, alone in a forest, like Listwell so many years before. Washington hears this old man pray, "O deliver me! O deliver me! In mercy, O God, deliver me from the chains and manifold hardships of slavery!" (41).

The system that oppresses all slaves is on scandalous view in part 3 when Listwell, back in Virginia on business, arrives at a broken-down tavern on the outskirts of Richmond. The tavern has been taken over by ill-mannered men, the dregs of society, and, coincidentally, a bevy of slave-traders on their way to an auction in Richmond. The narrator explains that the tavern was once a grand establishment. Today, it is a lair of licentiousness full of gamblers, drunks, and slave-traders. The doubleness of Virginia—birthplace of revolutionaries and home to slavery—is made concrete through the description of this ramshackle locale (Stepto 111). What was once moral is now despicable. This becomes most apparent when Listwell learns about the impending slave auction and is later awoken from his sleep by the sounds of an arriving slave gang. Among this horrid lot is none other than Madison Washington. Listwell learns from his friend that he could not live in Canada without his wife and that he subsequently returned to Virginia for her. In the process she was killed and he was recaptured. The resolutions Washington and Listwell made in the first part—to be free and to help free others—are here re-affirmed. Listwell follows Washington's crew into Richmond in hopes of helping him escape again. Eventually, he slips some files into Washington's pocket and, thus, paves his path to mutiny. Through Listwell's actions, Douglass demonstrates the extent to which whites, in the era of the Fugitive Slave Law, can help slaves gain access to freedom. However, bringing a runaway to the border is one thing, but being an accessory to an insurrection is another. Listwell has come a long way intellectually since initially witnessing Washington's pastoral monologue.

In the novella's concluding section, the reader is introduced to another character who has been transformed by the words and actions of Madison Washington. The setting is a sailor's coffeehouse in Richmond. Washington and Listwell are present only in spirit as a conversation ensues among a group of sailors. One sailor named Jack Williams claims that he is ashamed by the recent slave mutiny on the *Creole*: "For my own part, I would not honor a dozen niggers by pointing a gun at one of'em,—a good stout whip, or a stiff rope's end is better than all the guns at Old Point to quell a *nigger* insurrection" (61). Tom Grant, first mate on the *Creole*, responds, "It is one thing to manage a company of slaves on a Virginia plantation, and quite another thing to quell an insurrection on the lonely billows of the Atlantic, where every breeze speaks of courage and liberty" (62). Coming from the pen of Frederick Douglass, this image of the sea as communication network, carrying a discourse of freedom, is appropriate given the author's own "naval" escape to freedom. At the story's conclusion, this idea of the sea as path to freedom is re-emphasized. Madison Washington speaks to Grant, saying, "Mr. Mate, you cannot write the bloody laws of slavery on those restless billows. The ocean, if not the land, is free" (68). Grant admits to his fellow sailors that he will never work on a slaver again—never participate in a trade that destroys the liberty of another human being (63). His declaration mimics Listwell's more radical assertion in the first part of the novella. Grant transforms, perhaps, because for the first time he has encountered a slave whom he believes to be, at the very least, a cultural equal. He was impressed with Madison Washington, especially his skill with language: "His words were well chosen, and his pronunciation equal to that of any schoolmaster. It was a mystery to us *where* he got his knowledge of language; but as little was said to him, none of us knew the extent of his intelligence and ability till it was too late" (65). "Too late" was when the slaves attacked amidst a raging storm at sea. Grant describes Washington as a merciful leader. At one point Grant tries to overpower Washington but is warned that Washington could have killed him before had that been his intention.

Washington's goals are clear: to take the boat to a place where he and the other slaves can be free and to rehearse and re-claim the "founding fathers'" discourse of human rights. He says, "God is my witness that LIBERTY, not *malice*, is the motive for this night's work. I have done no more to those dead men yonder, than they would have to me in like circumstances. We have struck for our freedom, and if a true man's heart be in you, you will honor us for the deed. We have done that which you applaud your fathers for doing, and if we are murderers, *so were they*" (66). Again, Washington could have easily killed Grant but chooses not to. He acts on behalf of human rights: "Acknowledging the natural rights of his male opponents, regardless of their race, tempers his bravery, physical prowess, and ability to fight for his freedom" (Sale 194). In the eyes of his oppressors, Washington, a black slave, becomes a moral human being. Grant tells his fellow sailors that he began to overlook Washington's "blackness" and contemplate the claims he was making (66). "It seemed," he says, "as if the souls of both the great dead (whose names he bore) had entered him." But Washington's claims, though acknowledging their theoretical roots in the American Revolution, are of a different nature; those men were not interested in promoting the rights of all humans, only those who were white and male. Grant—prophetically bearing the surname of a certain Union army general—admits he is in the process of transforming his understanding of slavery. He will not claim to be an abolitionist, but he has much to consider after witnessing the successful usage of "the principles of 1776" (68).

Madison, the hero, is a vehicle for Douglass's ideals, and the novella serves to "symbolically liberate rebel slaves whose story would otherwise remain trapped in the chattel records" (Walter 4). In so doing, he re-imagines the patriotic narrative of American history, though, significantly, concluding with the slaves' liberation in British territory as if to show readers how far off its original course the United States is. And yet this idealization of "Eurocentric historical and cultural perspectives, the belief in America's glorious origins, the projection of a kind of manifest destiny based on origins, and the necessary adherence to patriarchal values," is problematic (4). Douglass's focus on re-claiming this patriarchal identity clouds the production of any identity rooted in slave or African culture. Douglass makes it clear that his hero is black, but he also makes it clear that his ideals and his eloquent speech are befitting the founding fathers. This prevents Douglass from developing a human rights discourse unique to African Americans in *The Heroic Slave*, something which is central to Martin Delany's only—and unfinished—novel, *Blake; Or, The Huts of America*.[2]

SOULS "PANTING FOR LIBERTY"

Blake describes Henry Blake's escape from a Mississippi plantation and subsequent organizing efforts among slaves in the United States and Cuba. The novel is explicitly concerned with human rights, coming as it does in the wake of the 1857 Dred Scott decision, which stipulated that African Americans were not "citizens" and that they had no civil rights that should be recognized by the United States government. The only recourse for African Americans was to assert their rights as human beings, but such assertions were without a legal framework at the time, and there were few international organizations that could speak, let alone act, on their behalf. Thus, Delany emphasizes the need for solidarity among all people of African descent despite their geographic location and promotes a kind of Pan-African blackness. Delany's novel navigates the nations involved in and benefiting from the slave trade and the slave economy: the novel begins with a conversation among capitalists in Baltimore and concludes with one among black revolutionaries seeking to overthrow the plantation-friendly regime in Cuba.

The leader of this human rights struggle is Henry Blake, a heroic figure much like Madison Washington. Blake, we are told, is "black—a pure Negro—handsome, manly and intelligent, in size comparing with his master, but neither so fleshy or heavy built in person. A man of good literary attainments ... having been educated in the West Indies" (17). Blake was born free, but was kidnapped when young and sold into slavery in Mississippi. When his master, Colonel Stephen Franks, sells his wife, Maggie, Blake strikes for freedom and begins plotting a general insurrection, an effort which takes up most of the novel. Delany never clarifies Blake's actual plan, but he provides a few clues. Blake's "scheme, a matured plan for general insurrection of the slaves in every state," will require the development of a network of like-minded slaves (39). The reader follows the hero as he seeks out "true and trustworthy" slaves on plantations and shares his plan with them (41). In the process, the reader travels throughout the American plantation slave systems with Blake as witness providing a running commentary on the plight of African Americans in Alabama, Arkansas, Louisiana, Texas, Washington, D.C., Canada, and Cuba, among other places.

In "haughty South Carolina" he discovers that "the most relentless hatred appears to exist against the Negro, who seems to be regarded but as an animated thing of convenience or a domesticated animal, reared for the service of his master. . . . . To impress the Negro with a sense of his own inferiority is a leading precept of their social system; to be white is the only evidence necessary to establish a claim to superiority" (109). Delany notes that South Carolina's ruling class ethos of divide and conquer is exhibited in the "Brown Society," a prominent social club in Charleston used by whites to play mulattoes and blacks against each other. Remnants of post-Stono legislation abound and Negro codes are especially strict; Blake must be cautious while in the state (110). But memories of resistance persist in South Carolina, and we are reminded of this when Blake meets with a man who is "one of the remaining confidentials and adherents of the memorable South Carolina insurrection" (112). He tells Blake, "I been prayin' dat de Laud sen' a nudder Denmark 'mong us! De Laud now anseh my prar in dis young man!" (112).

Shortly thereafter, Blake makes his way north to the Dismal Swamp, where a conjurer named Gamby Gholar greets him, saying, "I been lookin' fay yeh dis many years" (112). Gholar lives with a group of "some of Virginia and North Carolina's boldest black rebels" who revere the names of Gabriel Prosser, Denmark Vesey, and Nat Turner; Gabriel's name, according to the narrator, functions as a "talisman" within this clandestine culture (113). Some of these slave rebels, they claim, were also soldiers in the American Revolution, Gabriel, in particular. The historical narrative crafted by these Dismal Swamp conjurers links famous slave rebels to the ideals of that first revolution—a revolution they continued through their separate insurrections and plots. But Blake is not ready to become another Denmark Vesey just yet. He has much work and traveling to do. Part of this work is a re-education, a course in the horrors of slavery. And Blake is witness and proxy-witness to numerous atrocities. In Cuba he encounters Lotty, a tired and apparently abused slave who turns out to be his wife. Lotty says her mistress "beats [her] like a dog," an action which has a tremendous influence on the behavior of her mistress's child, who has taken to beating his young servant, Pomp (167). As Jefferson acknowledges in *Notes on the State of Virginia*, Delany identifies the pedagogical nature of slavery, which creates brutal children who learn from brutal adults to treat black humans differently than white humans.

Despite bearing witness to numerous atrocities, the reader is repeatedly reminded of the persistence of human dignity among slaves. In fact, in the most painful, the most brutal, moments of the narrative, oppressed human beings assert their humanity, their tremendous "soul-beauty" (Du Bois 12). In chapter 16 several Southern gentlemen make a show of beating a young slave for a Northern visitor. The slave has been trained to make a variety of noises or songs with each slash of the whip: "the whole person being prepared for the purpose, the boy commenced to whistle almost like a thrush; another cut changed it to a song, another to a hymn, then a pitiful prayer," and so on (Delany 67). The Southerners watch with stoic amusement while their Northern guest shudders. Yet, in the midst of this horrific scene, Robert Reid-Pharr claims that something unusual occurs. Despite the whip's lash, "the boy's humanity is never absolutely squelched. Indeed, the crime for which he is punished is the fact of the indestructibility of some core self" (82). Reid-Pharr writes that the whipping itself "reveal[s] the boy's essential humanity, his genius." Through his wide-ranging performance in the midst of this whipping, the boy "creates an index of black humanity that finds its efficacy precisely in the fact that it refuses rationalist modes of thought and expression" (83). This child "hits upon a counter-discourse, aesthetic and mystical, that propels him into new ranges of meaning against which the protestations of his tormentors become altogether meaningless" (84). This counter-discourse exists beyond the range of the oppressors, beyond their understanding.

Delany shares a similar moment with the reader, though less dramatic, when Blake is in New Orleans. The songs of slave boatmen, he writes, are ever-present in that city. These boatmen are truly "men of sorrow" for they are able to witness so much freedom as they travel up and down the Mississippi but experience so little freedom themselves (100). The narrator tells us they are "fastened by the unyielding links of the iron cable of despotism. . . . [T]hey are seemingly contented by soothing their sorrows with songs and sentiments of apparently cheerful but in reality wailing lamentations." And yet they sing "as if in unison with the restless current of the great river," synchronized with the natural world which is forever exhibiting its own freedom. No greater communion exists, perhaps, than these slaves and this quintessential American river. The river floods the Delta, and these slave songs flood the air of New Orleans. They are an ever-present exclamation of and for humanity. While these songs are imbued with bitter sorrow, they are also representative of the boatmen's creativity—like the spirituals, they depict a tension between mourning and celebration. Blake, too, carries a somewhat ambiguous message: he seeks violent upheaval, "to scatter red ruin throughout the region of the South," in order to establish a society rooted in human rights (128). Despite the potential for brutality, the plan and the goal itself are intrinsic, in agreement with nature.

Throughout the novel, images of the natural world correspond to Blake's plan and to the goal of human liberty. Blake says that his plan is so natural: "So simple is it that the trees of the forest or an orchard illustrate it; flocks of birds or domestic cattle, fields of corn, hemp, or sugar cane; tobacco, rice, or cotton, the whistling of the wind, rustling of the leaves, flashing of lightning, roaring of thunder, and running of streams all keep it constantly before their eyes and in their memory, so they can't forget it if they would" (39). Blake reminds the reader later, "Equality of rights in Nature's plan, / To follow nature is the march of man" (293). Human rights are, as Gofer Gondolier thinks to himself, "heaven bequeathed, and endowed by God, our common father, as essential to our being, which alone distinguish us from the brute. The authority of the slaveholder ceases the moment that the impulse of the slave demands his freedom" (273). Yet, this is a challenge for a people "sorely oppressed, mocked and ridiculed, refused and denied a common humanity"

(284). When Maggie is eventually freed, Blake exclaims, "As God lives, I will avenge your wrongs"; as long as he is alive, it will be natural for him to seek freedom for all slaves (192). He continues, "Whatever liberty is worth to the whites, it is worth to the blacks; therefore, whatever it cost the whites to obtain it, the blacks would be willing and ready to pay, if they desire it." Delany links this struggle to white political revolutions. As he alludes to Gabriel's participation in the American Revolution, he seems to say that it is natural for black people to take part in revolutions. So innate is this struggle, then, that as people begin to recognize their common cause, their goal of equality and human rights spreads naturally. On one occasion we learn that Blake leaves a plantation "after sowing seeds from which in due season, he anticipated an abundant harvest" (73).

Communications between Blake and other slaves, and among the slaves themselves, are dazzling, seamless, discrete, and organic. Like the Stono rebels, they communicate in ways that whites cannot imagine. Slaves signify, in a sense, on more privileged communication technologies. Blake and his comrades use a variety of technologies—songs, ships, and vernacular culture—to foment solidarity in anticipation of the coming revolt. And they are ever attentive to the demeanor of whites in their communities. The narrator notes the hypersensitivity that slaves have to plantation events, to information and lack thereof: "The slaves, from their condition, are suspicious; any evasion or seeming design at suppressing the information sought by them frequently arouses their greatest apprehension. Not unfrequently the mere countenance, a look, a word, or laugh of the master, is an unerring foreboding of misfortune to the slave. Ever on the watch for these things, they learn to read them with astonishing precision" (11). Information also travels quickly from one plantation to another. In Arkansas, a slave woman knows Blake is coming before he gets there and Blake is surprised (89). The woman says she received the message from slaves who had seen him on another plantation at his last "seclusion." She adds, "Da all'as gwine back and for'ard and da lahn heap from dem up dah; an' da make 'ase an' tell us" (89). Delighted by this, Blake notes that the slaves in Arkansas must have "a good general secret understanding" among themselves. The woman replies, "Ah, chile! dat da is." In Cuba, "so completely were they organized, and systematic their plans, that whatever might be going on among them in Matanzas those in Havana were conversant with it," and so on across the island (282). Blake himself relies on his knowledge of the rivers and of steamboat routes to move about freely. His familiarity with horse racing provides him with another cover (a kind of cultural literacy) as he travels about the countryside. When he encounters others, he claims he is tracking down his master's runaway racehorse. On other occasions, Blake relies on cash and claims, "Money alone will carry you through the White mountains or across the White river to liberty" (84). When he tries taking a group of runaways on a ferry and is asked to show his "free papers," Blake replies, "Here are our free papers," and hands a wad of cash to the ferryman (140).

The ability of these slaves to move within a vast communications network reveals greater linkages among a disparate people. Blake is planning an insurrection that will go from the Rappahannock in the United States to the Cuato in Cuba, relying on "rhizomorphic, routed, diaspora cultures," cultures that somehow "speak" to one another (Gilroy 28). This insurrection cannot happen without the assistance of black people throughout North America and in the Caribbean—African American slaves, Afro-Cuban slaves, freed men and women, and middle-class mulattoes. They all face the difficulty of living within the omnipresent legal confines of white power and racism. When Blake leads the fugitives to Canada, the narrator makes it clear that despite their having reached a place of ostensible freedom, they will still face the injustice of racism and be "excluded from the enjoyment and practical exercise of every right" (153). The only resolution is to pursue *black* unity everywhere. Paul Gilroy recognizes that "the version of black solidarity *Blake* advances is explicitly anti-ethnic and opposes narrow African-American exceptionalism in the name of a truly pan-African, diaspora sensibility" (27). This proposed unity is based less on a common past and more on a common fight to end slavery, situating "the black Atlantic world in a webbed network . . . [that] challenges the coherence of all narrow nationalist perspectives" (28–29). This black nationalism anticipates Pan-Africanism and, later, global justice movements and human rights campaigns. In fact, the novel illustrates the globalization of human rights discourse.

The weight of the world, then, rests upon the protagonist's shoulders: "A mighty undertaking, such as had never before been ventured upon, and the duty devolving upon him, was too much for a slave with no other aid that the aspirations of his soul panting for liberty. . . . [C]ontemplating his mission, a feeling of humbleness and a sensibility of unworthiness impressed him, and that religious sentiment which once gave comfort to his soul now inspiring anew his breast" (Delany 69). Blake's contact with diverse cultures is a learning experience that leads him to a personal transformation—especially in regards to his own relationship with organized religion. As part of the establishment of a unified front against slavery, Blake transforms religion for his purposes and denies white faith practices. When he learns that Maggie has been sold, he denies his faith completely and replies to Daddy Joe's protestations: "Tell me nothing about religion when the very man who hands you the bread at communion has sold your daughter away from you!" (20). He seeks salvation on Earth. In New Orleans a man at a gathering asks Blake to lead the group in prayer, and he claims, "I am not fit, brother, for a spiritual leader; my warfare is not Heavenly, but earthly; I have not to do with angels, but with men; not with righteousness, but wickedness" (103). But there is evidence that Blake has begun a transformation early in the novel when he claims, "We must now begin to understand the Bible so as to make it of interest to us" (41). His faith is one of personal connection to God, yet rooted in the promotion of a communal response to oppression. As he travels alone on a riverboat through hostile territory, he seeks solace in faith and "[throws] himself in tribulation upon the humble pallet assigned to him, there to pour out his spirit in communion with the Comforter of souls on high" (124). Henry Blake is determined to find a new form for religious expression.

He eventually recognizes that the fact that the Dismal Swamp conjurers believe that he is one of their own is important for his organizing efforts. The use of conjure "makes more ignorant slaves have greater confidence in, and more respect for, their headmen and leaders" (126). His interest in folk religion, then, appears as only a desire to bring more people into his plan. It is not until he is in Cuba, though, that he sees the full potential faith can offer his movement, though not the kind of faith embodied in traditional white churches. To Placido he says, "Let us at once drop the religion of our oppressors, and take the Scriptures for our guide and Christ as our example" (197). By submitting to the master's religion, they are submitting to his or her will also. In a meeting of the Grand Council, Blake offers an egalitarian and ecumenical vision of religion that suits their purposes. He points out the diverse religious backgrounds of those involved in the struggle: Baptist, Catholic, pagan, Methodist, Presbyterian, Episcopalian, Swedenborgian (258). But now "we have all agreed to know no sects, no denomination, and but one religion for the sake of our redemption from bondage. . . . . No religion but that which brings us liberty will we know; no God but He who owns us as his children will we serve." They will create their own ceremonies, creeds, and practices. To reiterate their unity, each member of the council replies, "Amen," including Abyssa, the Methodist and former pagan, and Madame Cordora, the Catholic.[3] Human rights can be shared by all faiths.

Blake's dynamism is central to Delany's Pan-African ideal. Like the desire for human rights, the protagonist's journey into a new modern identity is natural. Throughout the novel, Blake blends in with many cultures, sees relationships, draws conclusions, and understands the bigger picture of the human rights struggle. Though much has been made of Delany's Black Nationalist leanings, I would suggest that Delany's Henry Blake hints at a kind of cosmopolitanism which recognizes our "obligations to others" as well as the value of our differences, to quote Kwame Anthony Appiah (xv). Blake is capable of seeing the value of involving both the Dismal Swamp conjurers and the United Nation of Chickasaw and Choctaw in this struggle (87). He recognizes the need for many individuals and many communities to contribute their talents. He needs Gondolier's fury, the intelligence of Mendi and Abyssa, the wealth of Cuban mulattoes, the words of Placido, and the deep history of the Chickasaw and Choctaw. This man of many names (Henry Blake, Henry Holland, Gilbert, Carolus Henrico Blacus) responds earnestly to the conditions of his time by becoming a broadly defined subject capable of seeing and supporting solidarity among many individuals, an identity able to hold many pieces of "humanness" together. Central to this identity is his recognition of the necessity of a collective and global network because national identities are fundamentally problematic. Even in Washington, D.C., Blake sees a slave prison among the other national monuments of the United States of America (117). This is, perhaps, where Douglass and Delany diverge. While Delany values the ideals of the founding fathers and links General Gabriel to the Revolutionary War, he does not necessarily see any hope in reasserting the values of a national document like the Constitution. Justice Taney had already had his say on that matter. The only promising identity is one that contrasts with white identities and white ideals. Blake concludes, "I am for war—war upon the whites. 'I come to bring deliverance to the captive and freedom to the bond.' Your destiny is my destiny; the end of one will be the end of all" (290).

This modern identity, I believe, rests on a platform of universal human rights, on the promotion of the equality of all humans, ideas brought to the forefront of human consciousness by the inhumane or *anti-human* conditions of chattel slavery. Slavery's horror, Delany writes, is a cancer, but not only for blacks:

SLAVE REBELS IN NINETEENTH-CENTURY FICTION

> *Few people in the world lead such a life as the white inhabitants of Cuba, and those of the South now comprising the "Southern Confederacy of America." A dreamy existence of the most fearful apprehensions, of dread, horror and dismay; suspicion and distrust, jealousy and envy continually pervade the community; and Havana, New Orleans, Charleston or Richmond may be thrown into consternation by an idle expression of the most trifling or ordinary ignorant black. A sleeping wake or waking sleep, a living death or tormented life is that of the Cuban and American slaveholder. For them there is no safety. A criminal in the midst of a powder bin with a red-hot pigot of iron in his hand, which he is compelled to hold and char the living flesh to save his life, or let it fall to relieve him from torture, and thereby incur instantaneous destruction, nor the inhabitants of a house on the brow of a volcano could not exist in greater torment than these most unhappy people. . . . . Of the two classes of these communities, the master and slave, the blacks have everything to hope for and nothing to fear, since let what may take place their redemption from bondage is inevitable. They must and will be free; whilst the whites have everything to fear and nothing to hope for, "God is just, and his justice will not sleep forever." (305)*

Delany offers a radical counter-narrative, a correspondence with Jefferson and Taney. Things will fall apart for all parties and what will be left, what will be built upon the ashes of the burned plantation houses? Delany invites the reader to imagine a global identity based on universal human rights. The second half of the novel's title, *The Huts of America*, implies an alternative universe or community within the Americas—huts having an African connotation that is lost within the discourse of Harriet Beecher Stowe's quaint "cabins." *Blake* highlights this "hidden transcript," the narrative of many slaves who seek human rights scattered about and waiting for the moment to rebel. "*Blake* is meant to suggest . . . that every slave family concealed a Nat Turner—perhaps even a Toussaint—and that alienation would lead to violent resistance before it led to escape" (Sundquist, "Slavery" 23).

LOOKING FORWARD, GLANCING BACK

In 1936, Arna Bontemps committed a dangerous act by writing *Black Thunder*, a novel about a slave rebellion, amidst the charged atmosphere of Alabama at the time of the Scottsboro Boys' trial. It was a task at once foolhardy and courageous. The administration of the school where he taught was none too pleased with the company he kept in those days or with his research into the slave narratives kept in the Fisk University archives and demanded he burn some of his books—one of those books was Frederick Douglass's narrative. At roughly the same time, men and women working on behalf of the Federal Writer's Project had fanned out across the southern United States to record the oral histories of former slaves—including that of George Cato. In a similar fashion Arna Bontemps's novel is part of a singular effort to recover a suppressed history, and, like Stono, the story of Gabriel Prosser's 1800 insurrection conspiracy exists in spite of itself. Bontemps simply gives voice to the motivations, intelligence, and desires of those involved in Gabriel's plot and shares with readers a long-dormant collective memory.

When *Black Thunder* was republished in 1968, Bontemps wrote in an introduction, "Time is not a river. Time is a pendulum"; and, in a sense, this concept justifies his novel, based on the actual events of Gabriel's rebellion in 1800 (xxi). The narrative of *Black Thunder*—a tale of slaves determined to organize an insurrection, the decisions they must make in order to survive, the indignities they must endure, and their quest to be treated as humans—was as prescient in 1936, when the novel was first published, as it was in 1968. The issues were similar. The pendulum was still swinging. The murder of Martin Luther King Jr. was a "shattered dream" akin to that of Gabriel's—a dream of equality gained through struggle. In Bontemps's version Gabriel is an illiterate (the real Gabriel was literate) slave who helps organize a sophisticated rebellion that was supposed to begin on the outskirts of Richmond, Virginia. The slaves would attack a weapons storehouse that was poorly guarded, overpower the guards, and then attack the city—tactics which seem quite familiar. A strong rainstorm on the date they were going to rebel disrupts their plans, and slaves farther out in the countryside could not join those closer to the city. Shortly after this disruption, the conspiracy was revealed by two slaves named Ben and Pharaoh.

Throughout *Black Thunder* African Americans are active subjects, not passive minstrels. They are aware of the irony of their status as slaves in a nation built on the ideals of human freedom and equality. Early in the novel, Gabriel overhears a conversation about the inherent "equality of man" between Alexander Biddenhurst and M. Creuzot and thinks to himself, "Here were words for things that had been in his mind, things that he didn't know had names. Liberty, equality, frater—it was a strange music, a strange music" (21). But it was a music that he understood. When fellow slave Ben is unsure about whether to join the rebellion, Gabriel asks, "What's the matter, nigger, don't you want to be free?" (56). Eric Sundquist claims that through these situations Bontemps counters the popular idea that blacks could not think in sophisticated terms nor could they imagine freedom and liberty in the ways that whites could (*Hammers* 96). Even the French residents of Richmond cannot imagine that slaves understand they have human rights. When a freedman named Mingo borrows M. Creuzot's musket to hunt, the Frenchman wonders, "Actually, *could* it be? Could these tamed things imagine, liberty, equality? .... The blacks were not discontented: they couldn't be. They were without the necessary faculties" (Bontemps 63). And yet, Bontemps shows that a desire for freedom is natural even to Criddle, the youngest rebel, who imagines, "Everything what's equal to a groundhog want to be free" (77). Later, Ben repeats this exact phrase (93). When Gabriel is put on trial, his white accusers cannot imagine that he could have come to such ideas on his own and insist he reveal which "foreign agitators" were involved in the plot. He replies, "I tell you. I been studying about freedom a heap, me. I heard plenty of folks talk and I listened a heap. And everything I heard made me feel like I wanted to be free. It was on my mind hard, and it's right there the same way yet. On'erstand? That's all. Something keep telling me that anything what's equal to a gray squirrel wants to be free. That's how it all come about" (210).

Gabriel's desire to be free, while inspired by another slave's reading of the Bible on at least one occasion, does not come about because of literacy. Gabriel, we learn, is "innocent of letters" and is only attracted to the "oral" tradition (20). James Sidbury writes, "Nature's language, not man's, compels the struggle for freedom"—as we see in *Blake* (271). He claims that Bontemps presents "a revision of natural rights that works both to radicalize the concept by separating the struggle for freedom from philosophical traditions open only to people educated in Western traditions and to point to alternate sources for movements like Gabriel's in the 'organic' development of local communities." Human rights, as John Locke notes, begin with the individual. Through his own searching and through the exchanges of stories and ideas within his oral culture, Gabriel has developed a passion for freedom and a sense of justice.

This slave leader exists within the context of the Age of Revolutions; indeed, Bontemps depicts the French American community in Richmond that was rumored to have been involved in the actual plot and to have colluded with abolitionists. The slaves have ideals similar to the Jacobins in France, but the paths of the slaves and the Richmond "Jacobins" never cross in any significant way. The slaves have their own idea of equality, of human rights—what Sundquist refers to as a "vernacular" interpretation of the Rights of Man (*Hammers* 100). Bontemps also connects the rights discourse of these slaves to that of the Haitian rebels directly. In one scene, a letter from Toussaint L'Overture is read to the conspirators; and when Gabriel is captured in Norfolk, a Haitian sailor outside of the jailhouse wonders if this slave rebel is "as tall as Christophe, as broad as Dessalines? Was he as stern-faced as Toussaint, the tiger?" (196). Gabriel's execution itself serves as his final commentary on this vision of rights discourse. When asked if he wants to make a final statement, he says, "Let the rope talk, suh" (223). The rope that hangs this daring slave speaks of human rights in a way that the Richmond Jacobins or the abolitionists could not.

Despite these connections to eighteenth-century rights discourse and eighteenth-century revolutions, Gabriel is no Henry Blake. Gabriel has no grandiose desire to lead a global rebellion. His goals are local, immediate, and community bound. Gabriel wants to be free in his homeland of Virginia, and that, he tells the authorities, is why he did not simply run away from the Prosser plantation: "I ain't got no head for flying away. A man is got a right to have his freedom in the place where he's born. He is got cause to want all his kinfolks free like hisself" (210). The theme of connection and community, the desire to be free, but only if everyone else is free too, is Bontemps's most significant contribution to developing a fictional narrative of slave rebellion. Blake recognizes the necessity of the efforts of others to the success of his rebellion, and yet he remains the central focus of the novel. Bontemps relies on free indirect discourse to *demonstrate* rather than discuss the absolute necessity of a collective effort for success, a formal choice that asserts the collective and an almost Rousseauian rights discourse. This narrative technique allows for frequent shifts in narrative voice from an indirect narrator to what an individual character is thinking and gives the reader a "cinematic" view into the interior monologues of many (Rampersad xix). The revolt is, perhaps, fueled by Gabriel's initial passions, but it will require countless individuals to pull it off successfully. Arnold Rampersad notes that "Gabriel's revolt was not, finally, a one-man show, an example of the 'great man' theory of history in which a single individual, by imposing his will on others, alters the course of events" (xx). Only through collective effort, in other words, can anyone be free. Mingo underlines this concept, saying, "It ain't good 'thout all the rest goes free too. . . . You ain't free for ture till all yo' kin peoples is free with you. You ain't sure 'nough free till you gets treated like any other mens" (Bontemps 115). The slaves begin to coalesce after Old Bundy is severely beaten by "Marse Prosser," and they gather around the slave's deathbed. Old Bundy says, "I don't mind dying, but I hates to die not free. I wanted to see y'-all do something like Toussaint done. I always wanted to be free powerful bad," to which Gabriel replies, "That you did, and we going to do something too" (34). Just then a nameless mourner cries out,

> "When Marse beat you with a stick, how you feel, old man?"
> "Feel like I wants to be free, chile."
> ... "When the jug get low and you can't go to town, how you feel?"
> "Bound to be free, chillun, bound to be free."
> ... "When the preacher preach about Moses and the chillun, about David and the Philistines, how you feel, old man?
> "Amen, boy. Bound to be free. You hear me? Bound to be free."

The questions or "calls" in this passage come from a nameless mourner, and the answers or "responses" come from Old Bundy, who could be speaking for all of the slaves. It seems that the voices become one; they chant together and as individuals. As with Stono, the historical record singles out one great hero, but the reality is that many were involved. The "great man theory" discounts the reality that most slaves despised their condition and wished to rebel.

And yet, if there was such unity, why does Bontemps's fictional insurrection fail? And why did he choose to write about an insurrection that failed in the first place? Perhaps he wished to show the possibility of imagining liberty and also the possibilities of failure if one does not have a unified and connected community. The slaves who reveal the plot, Pharaoh and Ben, are roadblocks for any idealistic reading of this fictional slave struggle. Of the two, Pharaoh is the least complicated: his motives are clear. He feels jilted when not asked to lead a column of rebel slaves into Richmond. Where Pharaoh is flat, Ben is round. Ben suffers from a kind of double-consciousness that prevents him from buying into the plan "wholesale." He is much respected by others and, to an extent, by his owner, Moseley Sheppard—even though he refers to Ben condescendingly as "a good boy." But Ben is jolted by Bundy's brutal death: "Marse Prosser thunk it was cheaper to kill a old wo'-out mule than to feed him. But they's plenty of things Marse Prosser don't know. He don't even know a tree got a soul same as a man, and he don't know you aint in that there hole, Bundy" (53). For the first time, he considers the possibility of fighting for his freedom. Later Ben considers what might have been, "For some reason it *did* tickle him to see a might powerful black fellow acting right sassy, scampering and cutting up like a devilish pant'er or a lion. It did more good than a pint of rum" (135). But, ultimately, Ben saw the project as a "burden" pressed upon him. When it was all over, "it was like a new day for Ben." After they have revealed the plot, Ben and Pharaoh are pursued, or think they are being pursued, by other slaves. Pharaoh goes insane and vomits what he thinks is a snake or a lizard (216–217). The last we hear about him is that he is up a tree, barking like a dog. Such revenge comes from the spiritual world, from conjure, from the collective conscious of the community itself.

It appears that Gabriel's pompous denial of his African conjure roots causes the collapse of the conspiracy in the first place (Lane 9). The most egregious mistake occurs on the day of the rebellion. An intense storm sweeps across the land, but Gabriel wants to proceed. The rainstorm is taken as a sign that the slaves should not rebel, that they had not taken the proper folk religious steps, consulted conjure, and so on (103). Later, an old conjure woman says, "Gabriel done forgot to take something to protect hisself. The stars wasn't right. See? All that rain. Too much listening to Mingo read a white man's book. They ain't paid attention to the signs" (166). On the other hand, the Haitian rebels, like Delany's Blake, paid homage to both conjure and contemporary thought. Bontemps seems to say that Gabriel separated himself from the world of folk traditions, "a world that Gabriel could understand but from which he had detached himself intellectually" (Sundquist, *Hammers* 106). Gabriel was well aware that this world existed. When the slaves were "burying old Bundy in the low field by the swamp. They were throwing themselves on the ground and wailing savagely" (52). "The Negroes remembered Africa in 1800," writes Bontemps, reminding the reader that African carryovers were still common practice and could have been part of Gabriel's organizing efforts. Gabriel, though, denies these roots and before the rebellion puts on his coachman's uniform, a symbol of authority, he thinks, in the white community. He again distances himself from his community.

Ultimately, this is a novel about the radicalization of a community, about how a community can inspire itself through its own traditions and cultures and translate the traditions of other cultures to meet its own needs. Even though Bontemps is clearly not preferential to the *written* text, Sundquist writes that the novel is "permeated by a circulation of texts," political and natural voices of freedom, spoken and unspoken from humans and animals (*Hammers* 114). In this manner, Bontemps makes his own argument for human rights and for "nine young men, equally betrayed by the ideals of the nation, and on behalf of all African Americans who had had little voice in claiming their natural rights and writing their own public history" (129). Like Douglass and Delany, he writes fiction while also writing and rewriting American history. The long-dormant records of chattel slavery stored in the Fisk University library were simply the written texts of an ongoing and shared oral narrative. The power of this narrative of human rights will not sleep, nor will it allow those who oppress others to sleep. Bontemps writes that after "Mr. Moseley Sheppard produced his astonishing testimony in a Richmond court. How could any Virginian sleep? How could he be sure from now on the black slave who trimmed his lamps was not waiting to put a knife in his heart while he slept? .... This sickness called the desire for liberty, equality, was plainly among the pack" (134). And so it was in the wake of the Stono Rebellion: "On this occasion every breast was filled with concern.... With regret we bewailed our peculiar case, that we could not enjoy the benefits of peace like the rest of mankind and that our own industry should be the means of taking from us all the sweets of life and of rendering us liable to the loss of our lives and fortune" ("Report" 84). As long as the "sweets of life" come at the expense of the lives of others, masters like Mr. Mosely Sheppard or those in South Carolina will not sleep well. The persistence of heroic narratives of rebellions is enough to give such men and women nightmares.

As Bontemps and Delany suggest, it is not the success of the rebellion, it is the freedom demonstrated by the plan itself that is the most important indication of human dignity. The willingness to communicate freely, to construct narratives of liberty, these are the most crucial steps. White masters were well aware of this narrative, for it existed, however flawed, within their own historical narratives. And yet, this white narrative was all too limited for the world that it helped create. Slaves, as early as those who rebelled on September 9, 1739, recognized their own obligation to correct the European rights discourse. In the process, these slaves fostered a discourse of human rights rooted in a global, cosmopolitan communication network. This African American human rights discourse is a model for universal human rights discourse. Whether explicit or not, this discourse recognizes the complications of a fragmented modern identity and the necessity for an international rights regime. It constantly asks, Can identity be multiple? Can one belong to a nation as well as to the union of humanity? These questions were equally as challenging for eighteenth- and nineteenth-century abolitionists as they are for contemporary politicians, scholars, and citizens of the world.

Chapter 6

★ ★ ★ ★ ★ ★

PLANTATION TRADITIONS
Racism and the Transformation of the Stono Narrative

> South Carolinians knew that, as a rule, slaves were treated well.
> They resented the lies the Abolitionists told about abusing slaves and
> also disliked intensely having outsiders meddle in their affairs.
> —Mary C. Simms Oliphant, *The Simms History of South Carolina:
> For Use in Schools* (1932)

AT FIRST GLANCE, the business card appears somewhat innocuous. One side reads: "Stono Phosphate Co., Charleston, SC, Established 1869." But on the other side is a cartoon image right out of the blackface minstrelsy tradition or, perhaps, plantation myth literature: a happy "darky" with a wide grin on his face and a hoe in his hand chases after a smiling watermelon. In the background, one espies an "African" hut. Below the image is the following text:

> Stand back, Nigger, drop dat hoe.
> You can't ketch melon of de ole Stono.
> A little nonsense now and then,
> Is relished by the best of men.

The text implies that the image is simply a joke, not to be taken seriously. One could argue that this business card represents a particular cultural and historical moment and perspective. This perspective, closely associated with the plantation myth—the idea that slavery really was not that bad—emerged in the first half of the nineteenth century as a response, in part, to the rebellious narratives of Douglass and Delany, and even Harriet Beecher Stowe. It persisted into the twentieth century despite the human rights claims of writers like Bontemps.[1]

In this mythical plantation world blacks are not as human as whites. They are caricatures—savages, Sambos, happy darkies, mammies, and aunts. In some ways, these stereotypes persist today and continue their assault on the human rights claims of the Stono rebels. But how did it become appropriate for such racist discourse to appear on a business card? What cultural and social architecture was necessary for someone to print these cards and use them in hopes of soliciting customers? An examination of pro-slavery and plantation tradition literature would serve as a jumping-off point for understanding the origins of these racist stereotypes and assumptions. As indicated in previous chapters, racist stereotypes were a part of American culture and literature well before the nineteenth century. But in the lead up to the Civil War, these stereotypes assumed the added function of propping up the plantation regime as it breathed its last desperate gasps. The perpetuation of these stereotypes was surely an American, not merely a Southern phenomenon, but some of the "loudest yelps" to protect this regime sallied forth from a cabal of literati who called South Carolina home. Much of this literature seems plodding to contemporary readers, but a close reading of it is important to this analysis of the workings of discourse. To read this literature is to witness the formation of an imagined community. To read this literature is to understand why the Stono rebels called out "liberty" and to remind ourselves of the many hurdles, from the past and present, erected against the realization of an authentic and democratic human rights discourse.

ETHNOGENESIS

Antebellum Charleston was a hotbed for men of letters. The city began to break away from years of London-worship with many residents becoming "creators, not just consumers" of culture (Edgar 302). A few such creators, including novelist William Gilmore Simms and poets Henry Timrod, Paul Hamilton Hayne, and William Grayson, convened regularly in the back room of John Russell's bookstore on King Street to discuss literature and politics. Joining them were other gentleman scholars, members of the city's elite including Hugh Swinton Legaré, James L. Petigru, and Henry L. Pinckney. These backroom conversations were the catalyst for the publication of *Russell's Magazine* from 1857 to 1860. In general, work published in *Russell's* and by these members of the Charleston School, as the group was called, leaned heavily toward the lyrical and sentimental and showed a strong interest in contrasting the South and its culture with that of the industrial North. These writers "turned their backs on what they viewed as an increasingly hostile contemporary world," reveling in an imaginary and glorious colonial history (303). Stowe's *Uncle Tom's Cabin* typified this "hostile contemporary world" from which they wished to separate. When Stowe's novel emerged in March 1852, several Charleston School writers responded.

One response to Stowe was offered in 1856 by Beaufort native William J. Grayson in his poem "The Hireling and the Slave."[2] Grayson, a trained lawyer and former congressman and state legislator, was, in theory, opposed to secession, yet he authored a lengthy poem praising the virtues of slavery over the wage-labor practices of the North and of England. When it was first published, the poem was prefaced with a brief explanation of his intent, which chided abolitionists for complaining about an economic system which they did not understand while "wage slavery" existed in their own backyards. "Slavery is that system of labor which exchanges subsistence for work," he claims, "which secures a life-maintenance from the master to the slave, and gives a life-labor from the slave to the master..... Slavery is the Negro system of labor. He is lazy and improvident. Slavery makes all work, and it ensures homes, food and clothing for all. It permits no idleness, and it provides for sickness, infancy and old age. It allows no tramping or skulking, and it knows no pauperism" (vii). Unlike the economic system supporting the hireling, slavery, Grayson argues, is humane and paternalistic. Masters serve as "commissioner[s] of the poor" and as the police; they protect and serve their workers and are loyal to them in youth and old age (ix). What's more, slavery brought savage Africans to a Christian land and transformed them. Perhaps they endured "a rude mode of emigration," but one no worse than that of other immigrants (xi). Grayson suggests that abolitionists concerned about slaves should buy as many as they can and give them jobs elsewhere. He admits that slavery has its imperfections but believes it is significantly better than the systems of labor provided by industrial capital.

It would be difficult to argue with Grayson's claim that the Industrial Revolution fostered deplorable labor conditions in the United States and in England, but that is not the argument I attend to here. Grayson adds to the trope of the happy slave and doting, paternalist master, problematic at its core because it rests on a dehumanizing discourse that privileges whites over blacks. He introduces these arguments in the public sphere in an effort to counter those presented by Stowe and the many authors of slave narratives. He writes that before contact with their master, via voice and whip, African slaves know very little. But in the benevolent Southern slave society they learn: "... in the only school / Barbarians ever know—a master's rule, / The Negro learns each civilizing art / That softens and subdues the savage heart / ... And slowly learns, but surely, while a slave, / The lessons that his country never gave" (34). It is shameful, according to Grayson, that Northern abolitionists do not respect these transformations: "Not such with Stowe, the wish or power to please, / She finds no joys in gentle deeds like these" (42).

But Grayson was not the only poet from South Carolina to paint chattel slavery with such positive strokes. This re-imagining project—a political project, really—is also found in the work of Henry Timrod, aptly dubbed the poet laureate of the Confederacy.[3] Although only one volume of his poems was published during his lifetime, his poems, essays, and editorials were widely published in literary journals like the *Southern Literary Messenger* and *Russell's* as well as in numerous newspapers. He received his greatest public accolades for his poem "Ethnogenesis," a commemorative ode penned in honor of the meeting of the first Confederate Congress in Montgomery, Alabama, on February 8, 1861. It was first read at an upper-crust Charleston dinner party and published shortly thereafter in the Charleston *Daily Courier* on February 23, 1861 (Parks 92). The poem revels in the first steps of what Timrod imagines to be a new nation. He proclaims, "At last, we are / A nation among nations; and the world / Shall soon behold in many a distant port / Another flag unfurled" (150). All nature is aligned with the South, and "the very sun / Takes part with us" in preparation for battle with the North (150–151). And the North has sided with Satan, letting him "set up his evil throne." If the North chooses to attack, the South will respond, "marshaled by the Lord of Hosts, / And overshadowed by the mighty ghosts" of Revolutionary South Carolinians. And the natural world will side with the South. How can we lose, he writes, when "in our stiffened sinews we shall blend / The strength of pine and palm!" (152). Timrod concludes by noting the philanthropic potential of the Confederate States of America:

> Not only for the glories which the years
> Shall bring us; not for lands from sea to sea,

> And wealth, and power, and peace, though these shall be;
> But for the distant peoples we shall bless,
> And the hushed murmurs of a world's distress:
> For, to give labor to the poor,
> The whole sad planet o'er,
> And save from want and crime the humblest door,
> Is one among the many ends for which
> God makes us great and rich!

This new nation, Timrod asserts, will take care of the poor and calm the "world's distress." The genteel South with its honorable women and gallant men will ease the troubles of the poor in ways Northerners never could.

But how can this be? What undergirds this romantic, idealistic vision? Timrod's 1861 poem, "The Cotton Boll," gives one clue. In this Pindaric ode, Timrod meditates on the lowly cotton boll, and through his meditation whole worlds are revealed. The poem presents cotton as an economic solution, a "small sphere" capable of uniting "the sea-divided lands" (6). Through this globalizing product the poet reveals the pastoral landscape of the South.[4] This is obviously a poem with roots in British romanticism; floating birds, "endless fields" of lily-white cotton, and abundant exclamation points are dead giveaways. The South is plentiful, "with all the common gifts of God, / For temperate airs and torrid sheen / Weave Edens of the sod" (8). But Timrod remembers that there have been other poets, namely William Gilmore Simms, who exclaimed the glories of the Southern land. Thus, Timrod desires to be the first poet to write of "the source wherefrom doth spring / That mighty commerce" that links the South to the world through peaceful exchange (9–10). That peace, of course, had been broken on April 12, 1861.

Despite the enemies at the gates, there remains hope that the South, with the help of cotton, can "revive the half-dead dream of universal peace!" (10). The poet then compares himself to the coal miners of Cornwall, who keep on working despite storms brewing above. He, too, will continue to "calmly, weave my woof / Of song, chanting the days to come, / Unsilenced" (11). This despite "the bruit of battles" and "many gathering armies" that ruin the tranquility of his pastoral meditation. But he knows the South will be victorious and calls on God to join with them in battle, to help "save / These sacred fields of peace." He writes, "Oh, help us, Lord!" to send the Goths, the Northerners, back home to New York City, "where some rotting ships and crumbling quays / Shall one day mark the Port which ruled the Western seas."

In the first lines of this poem Timrod alludes, ever so briefly, to the human labor producing this cotton. He is given a cotton boll to examine, "by dusky fingers . . . / And shown with boastful smiles" (6). Those "dusky fingers," of course, belong to a slave, or, as Timrod would have us believe, a "happy darky" grinning as he dances up to the poet relaxing in the shade of a Carolina pine. The presence of the pastoral in this poem underscores the presence and absence of slavery—the real economic engine behind Timrod's bombastic rhetoric. How is it that he can hang out and "recline / At ease beneath / This immemorial pine"? What provides Timrod with that leisure?

Timrod was initially opposed to secession and would eventually grow tired of the war (Parks 91). And yet, many of his best-known poems are hardly ambiguous as to which team he is on in this conflict. Louis D. Rubin Jr. notes that through poems like "Ethnogenesis" Timrod became a "public poet, and he link[ed] his own personal hopes with the political objectives of his fellow Southerners" (196). Embracing the mantle of poet of the people, Timrod wrote verse with a broad Southern audience in mind. In his 1862 poem "Carolina" Timrod writes that South Carolinians must "hold up the glories of the dead" for inspiration; he is referring to soldiers who died during the Revolutionary War battle at Eutaw Springs (142). The poem serves as a Confederate battle cry—a reminder that this is not the first time a "despot" has infiltrated the "sacred sands" of South Carolina (141). But now Carolinians must stand up against the oppressing North with the strength of their heroic ancestors. He writes:

> I hear a murmur as of waves
> That grope their way through sunless caves,
> Like bodies struggling in their graves,
> Carolina!
> And now it deepens; slow and grand
> It swells, as, rolling to the land,
> An ocean broke upon thy strand,
> Carolina!
> Shout! Let it reach the startled Huns!
> And road with all thy festal guns!
> It is the answer of thy sons,
> Carolina!

The poem revels in an historical narrative that claims the accomplishments of Revolutionary-era South Carolinians were pivotal to the establishment of the nation. Timrod asserts that as that war was righteous and just, so too is the current conflagration with the North. Here, states' rights supersede human rights; slavery is not even mentioned in the poem. The enemy is described as an invading horde of "Huns," an implication that Northerners are a rootless, wandering people who lack the connection to place that South Carolinians have. Thus, Southern soldiers who die in battle are fighting for a worthy cause and will forever be revered. They will not have died in vain; their legacy will live on. These fallen soldiers "shall be safe beneath thy sod, / Carolina!" (144). Timrod's "Carolina" and, in turn, the poem's sentiments live on. In 1911, some of its lines were stitched together to form South Carolina's official state song.

While Timrod provided the poetry, William Gilmore Simms provided the narrative. His novels are *the* sourcebook for South Carolina's contribution to the historical imagination that spawned the plantation myth tradition. Simms "did as much as any single Southern writer or editor before the Civil War to make the South what it has been since: a commodity as well as a place, a creation as well as a birthright, and a global fascination as well as domestic preoccupation" (Moltke-Hansen 4). He was part and parcel to the plantation machine. Editor, novelist, poet, and one-term member of the South Carolina House of Representatives, Simms was born in Charleston on April 17, 1806, to rather modest circumstances. Throughout his lifetime, he was a prodigious writer and published eighty-two works. Simms made the most of his native land and married a planter's daughter later in life; this gave him the opportunity to live on a real plantation called "The Woodlands." But the war destroyed his wealth, his library, and his home, and he was struggling to support himself and his family when he died on June 11, 1870.

Simms's 1852 novel, *The Sword and the Distaff*, later published as *Woodcraft*, is often referred to as one of the first "anti-Tom" novels.[5] Appearing shortly after *Uncle Tom's Cabin*, it offers a sharp rebuttal to Stowe's view of slavery. Simms presents a blessed South—a paternalist society whose gentlemen and gentlewomen protect their slaves. These slaves honor their masters and are grateful for having been rescued from the horrors of the African jungle, from ignorance and paganism. In this novel, the last of his seven Revolutionary War romances, the protagonist Captain Porgy struggles to reorganize his life in the wake of the withdrawal of British troops from Charleston in 1782. The novel's subject is, in essence, the re-assertion of social and political order in post-colonial South Carolina. This order includes making sure slaves know their proper social role. When Porgy offers the slave Tom his freedom, Tom replies, "No! no! maussa. . . . I kain't t'ink ob letting you off dis way. . . . I's well off whar' I is I tell you; and I much rudder [rather] b'long to good maussa, wha' I lub, dan be my own massa and quarrel wid mese'f ebbry day" (509). Once order is achieved, Simms muses, "the days glided by as if all were winged with sunshine" and "peace reigned in the household" (509).

Even though most critics view *Woodcraft* as Simms's most important pro-slavery novel, his 1835 work, *The Yemassee: A Romance of Carolina*, speaks more to the realization of Locke and Shaftesbury's grand plan for South Carolina—an aristocratic, agriculture-based society resting on perceived racial differences. It imagines the birth of a nation, a world organized by a racist hierarchy and not human rights. Simms's novel returns to settlement, to the colonial days of South Carolina; it offers an ethnogenesis, of sorts, of the very regime that Jemmy and company contested. And Simms writes this ethnogenesis with the spirit of the mythmaker. In a preface to the book Simms acknowledges that this work is "a romance, and not a novel" (22). The romance, he claims, "is the substitute which the people of the present day offer for the ancient epic" (23). It "is of loftier origin than the Novel. It approximates the poem" (24). In other words, he intends this to be a moving tale, but one rooted in a kind of historical truth. His fiction, his artistry, is quite purposeful. As tensions grew between the North and the South, fiction proved another vehicle for "persuad[ing] young Southerners to remain in and defend their native region" (Wakelyn 59). And the myth he constructs in *The Yemassee* links the Southern hierarchy and culture to the final battle with the last holdout among coastal Native American groups. Vincent King writes, "Simms creates a myth of the past (the subjugation of the Indian) that not only validates the present (the enslavement of blacks) but also suggests a future—an America based, not on the notion that all men are created equal . . . but on the idea that there is a natural hierarchy among individuals which must be recognized if American society is to flourish" (6). In this way, Simms links race and hierarchy and thus touches his torch to the plantation tradition fire.

This novel, or romance, depicts the colony on the brink of the bloody Yemassee War of 1715, a moment in which, Simms claims, the civilization of South Carolina was threatened by hostile outside forces. And we learn from Simms's own footnote that this civilization was based on a model proposed by John Locke (169). The hero who has come to save the day is Lord Charles Craven, South Carolina's newly appointed governor, who travels throughout the colony under the pseudonym "Gabriel Harrison." Accompanying him is his trusty sidekick, a slave named Hector. Harrison, we learn, is a noble and dapper Cavalier, and yet, when the colonists are prepping for battle, he rolls up his sleeves like everyone else. He has got it all: he is "Gabriel Harrison, a man singularly compounded of daring, bravery, cool reflection, and good-humored vivacity" (141). His "good-humored vivacity" contrasts with lower-class turncoat Chorley and the dour Puritan father of the beautiful Bess Matthews, his love interest. Harrison boldly asserts his intentions to the Reverend early on, claiming, "Gabriel Harrison, with your leave, sir, and the future husband of Bess Matthews" (81). But this love story is an adjunct to Harrison's true purpose in the novel, which is to save the white colony of South Carolina, in danger of being destroyed by the pesky Spanish and the bitter Yemassee, native to the territory claimed by the white colonists. The Yemassee, in Simms's world, could not have come up with the idea to fight back on their own, so he plays up the role of the Spanish in these hostilities and refers to St. Augustine "as another Sallee" (295). This sounds familiar. Reference to this Moroccan port echoes the language of the South Carolina government post-Stono: "With indignation we looked at St. Augustine (like another Sallee) that den of thieves and ruffians! Receptacle of debtors, servants, and slaves! Bane of industry and society!" ("Report" 84).

But the Yemassee are problematic in their own right and have become restless. According to the narrator, they no longer know their place in the developing colonial hierarchy, and the two cultures are beginning to clash. The Yemassee are not like the white colonists; they are lazy and do not clear land (377). They are wild and partake in savage ceremonies full of "wild distortions—their hell-kindled eyes—their barbarous sports and weapons—the sudden and demoniac shrieks of the women" (278). It is virtually impossible that whites and native peoples will learn to live with each other. Harrison claims, "Until they shall adopt our pursuits, or we theirs, we can never form the one community for which your prayer is sent up; and so long as the hunting lands are abundant, the seduction of that mode of life will always baffle the approach of civilization among the Indians" (152). But fellow South Carolinian Hugh Grayson is even more direct. He claims that "it is utterly impossible that the whites and Indians should ever live together and agree. The nature of things is against it, and the very difference between the two, that of colour ... must always constitute them an inferior caste in our minds. Apart from this an obvious superiority in arts and education must soon force upon them the consciousness of their inferiority" (302–303). Having different cultures is one thing, but racial difference is something else entirely.

Simms takes this fear of a corrupt social order to its logical (or illogical) conclusion when the Yemassee go on the attack. In one scene the Matthews family home is surrounded by a band of Yemassee. Ishiagaska, the Yemassee who went to St. Augustine and has the closest relationship with the Spanish, slithers through the window of sleeping Bess Matthews's bedroom. She sleeps peacefully: "Her long tresses hung about her neck, relieving but not concealing, its snowy whiteness. One arm fell over the side of the couch, nerveless, but soft and snowy as the frostwreath lifted by the capricious wind. The other lay pressed upon her bosom above her heart, as if restraining those trying apprehensions which had formed so large a portion of her prayers when she laid herself down to sleep. It was a picture for any eye but the savage" (325).[6] Bess is the fair damsel in distress, the delicate representative of all Southern women who need protection; she is the "motherland," so to speak, and for her, for all white women, white men must band together to fight off the Yemassee. And they do. The rough and ready "foresters" are prepared to fight; "for one condition of security in border life was the willingness to volunteer in defense of one another" (346). As the novel progresses, Simms increasingly refers to all the whites as "Carolinians," identifying these people as a nation of valiant men born on the frontier and through this war. These Carolinians are almost superhuman and are clearly superior to all others, especially non-whites. While colonist Teddy Macnamara undergoes a Yemassee pre-battle torture ritual, which he withstands in a noble fashion, he calls the Native Americans "red naggers" (270). This racial epithet reveals the true meaning of Simms's narrative: King notes that "Simms is not really interested in Indians at all; they simply serve as a reminder ... of what will happen to African-Americans if they fail to accept their status as slaves" (2).

Racial distinctions are clear in Simms's novel and are best understood through Harrison's sidekick, Hector, who is a happy darky (the same type portrayed on the Stono Phosphate business card) with "his full white array of big teeth, stretching away like those of a shark, from ear to ear" (63). On one occasion when Harrison calls him, Hector shows up "as if hurried away from a grateful employ, with a mouth greased from ear to ear, and huge mass of fat bacon still clutched tenaciously between his fingers" (240). Hector is always "obedient to his orders" and a "faithful slave" (320). And yet Harrison treats Hector poorly, referring to him on separate occasions as a "dull beast," "my property," and "snow ball," a derogatory appellation (125, 150, 144). After Hector volunteers for a mission to rescue Bess Matthews from the "pirate" Chorley, he sings "a stanza of negro minstrelsy, common, even now, to the slaves of Carolina" (393). Hector belts out, "He come rain—he come shine, / Hab a good maussa, who da care / De black is de white and de white is de black, / Hab a gaad maussa, who da care?" (394). Harrison tells him to shut up, but eloquently, saying, "Be still, sirrah, or you shall feed on hickory." But because Hector is so happy, he looks beyond the harsh comments and poor treatment he receives from his master, and even saves Harrison's life.

But despite this apparent loyalty, Simms asserts that black slaves must be kept in check; they are savages on par with the Yemassee. In one scene we learn that Hector cannot use a gun very well—only knives and hatchets—implying that guns are too sophisticated (382). Barbarians are better off using clubs, and, according to Simms, they do. Indeed, slaves are the most ferocious soldiers the whites have. After decisive victories, they are assigned "clean up" duty in charge of "clear[ing] the woods with their clubs, beating out the brains of" their enemies (383). And after the novel's final battle they set to work "scouring the field of battle with their huge clubs and hatchets, knocking upon the heads all of the Indians who yet exhibited any signs of life. As wild almost as the savages ... sparing none, whether they fought or pleaded, and frequently inflicting the most unnecessary blows, even upon the dying and the dead" (414).

Simms's "negro slaves" take on this role because they are forever loyal to their white masters. But the ultimate expression of the loyalty of slaves to their master is Hector's refusal of freedom, which he is offered by Harrison as reward for saving his life. When Harrison gives him the news, Hector is most upset: "I d—n to h—ll, maussa, ef I guine be free! ... De ting aint right: and enty I know wha' kind of ting freedom is wid black man? Ha! You make Hector free, he turn wuss more nor poor buckrah—he tief out of de shop—he git drunk and lie in de ditch—den, if sick come, he roll, he toss in de wet grass od de stable. You come in de morning, Hector dead" (400). Simms writes, "The negro's objections to the boon of liberty, with which he so little knew what to do, were not to be overcome" (400). J. V. Ridgely writes that Hector's refusal of freedom, "allows Simms an opening for the earliest direct defense of slavery in his fiction" (58). Ridgely reminds that "by 1835 the abolitionist movement was afoot, and Simms had his eye on the coming challenge. He was not as yet a violent Southern nationalist but rather a committed sectionalist; and in *The Yemassee* he discovered his method of defending the South by positive statement about its virtues instead of direct retort to Northern agitators" (59). In the end, the social order is tied up with a nice ribbon when Hector informs Bess Matthews, now betrothed to Harrison/Craven, that she can also call him her servant (403). Thus, according to Simms, whites have nothing to fear as long as they remain honorable and treat their slaves well. He even claims that it is because of good treatment that so many slaves joined South Carolina's army during the Yemassee War. Of course, he leaves out the fact that most slaves fought because their owners forced them to and because their owners were paid to send them.

Of his fiction, rooted as it was in the history of the state, Simms once commented that it was his desire to rewrite South Carolina history (Edgar 303). But Simms did not have to *rewrite* South Carolina history. In many ways, he "wrote" it. His *History of South Carolina* was the basis for textbooks read by many young South Carolinians in the twentieth century. Simms wrote this history after embarking on an effort to teach his thirteen-year-old daughter about her home state. He felt that none of the available books were suitable for young people and decided to write his own. This textbook, written as it was almost on a whim, might be his most well-read and influential work.

One glance though this book, with its simple prose and review questions at the bottom of each page, and there is no doubt of Simms's pedagogical intentions. Sean R. Busick explains, "The two main lessons of the book are that South Carolinians ought always to depend on native leadership and that they ought also to present a united front against external foes" (51). Of course, this was also the lesson of *The Yemassee*. The Stono Rebellion was yet another example of white South Carolinians uniting against external forces, and Simms's rendering of the Stono narrative in the 1860 edition of *The History of South Carolina* is quite instructive. He views the Spanish offer of freedom to slaves as the primary motive for the rebellion. Simms writes, "The Negro can not long resist temptations which appeal to appetite; his passions are too strong; his intellect too mean and feeble, to suffer him to reason, even from his own experience; and the cunning enemy soon used the semi-barbarians at his pleasure" (106). He incorrectly cites 1740 as the date for the rebellion and calls the leader Cato. Simms notes that the slaves marched "with drums and colors" and that this "massacre was urged without remorse and without discrimination. They slaughtered the whites, mercilessly, without regard to sex or age; and compelled the negroes, however reluctant, to fall into their ranks, at all the plantations in their way" (106). The slaves are eventually discovered "carousing over the liquors which they had found by the way. They had halted in an open field, singing and dancing in all the barbarous exultation of success" (107). Like slaves in *The Yemassee*, the Stono rebels are bestial and must be destroyed before they corrupt the social order.

Busick notes that Simms was of a generation of historians that was not necessarily interested in producing historical works that exuded a "supposed dispassionate objectivity" (2). From Simms's description of the Stono Rebellion, one can clearly decipher the racist narrative, one intended for a large audience, that Simms's *passionate* approach produced. He hoped that his history would be adopted by the South Carolina legislature as a public school textbook, but it never was. However, "in 1917, long after his death, his granddaughter Mrs. Mary C. Simms Oliphant heavily revised the book and, in this form, won its adoption for use in public schools. *The Simms History of South Carolina* went through multiple printings and editions and remained in use by schools into the latter twentieth century" (62). Oliphant removed the Stono Rebellion from her narrative altogether while asserting that slavery was really not all that bad. She offered an apology, of sorts, for her ancestors, writing, "You must understand that, in those days, no one thought it wrong to own slaves. It was the custom of the time. . . . It was to the interest of the master to treat his slaves well and keep them in good condition, otherwise they would not be able to work for him" (75). Thus, William Gilmore Simms's approach to history set the tone for decades of South Carolina history.

EDMUND QUINCY, STONO, AND OTHER PLANTATION TRADITIONS

There were other South Carolinians raising their voices over slavery in the nineteenth century—and some of them were ardent abolitionists. One of the most well-known Palmetto State anti-slavery advocates was Charleston-born Angelina Grimké. As a child, Grimké was entrenched in the city's aristocratic culture, and her father, John Faucheraud Grimké, an important judge, owned slaves. She experienced slavery in a way most Northern abolitionists had not. As a teenager, Angelina moved to Philadelphia to live with her sister Sarah and became both a Quaker and abolitionist, a horrifying turn of events for the folks back home. When her 1836 essay, "An Appeal to the Christian Women of the South," reached South Carolina, it was apparently burned in the streets; and she was informed that if she returned, she would be arrested. Like Ann Tuke Alexander's "An Address to the Inhabitants of Charleston, South Carolina," Grimké's appeal targets slave owners and those linked with slavery in order to shame and blame them out of the practice. Her Southern roots give her argument more authenticity and, perhaps, make her female readers more receptive. She admits that she, too, was at first leery of abolitionists when she moved to the North (52). But they do know what they are talking about, she asserts; they have done their research. True knowledge of slavery is spreading far and wide: "This monster of iniquity has been unveiled to the world, her frightful features unmasked, and soon, very soon will she be regarded with nor more complacency by the American republic that is the idol of Juggernaut, rolling its bloody wheels over the crushed bodies of its prostrate victims" (52). Grimké's goal is to stop this idol in its tracks, and she appeals to "Christian Women of the South" to help. In due time, she hopes that those who are "virtuous" will know "that in principle it is as sinful to hold a human being in bondage who was born in Carolina, as one who was born in Africa" (4).

Like the arguments of many white anti-slavery advocates of the eighteenth century, Grimké's human rights discourse is rooted in her Christian faith while nodding in the direction "of our forefathers who declared to the world" the inalienable rights of all humans (4). But her exegesis tends to emphasize the role of slavery and ownership in the Old and New Testaments. She claims that God's promises to Adam and Noah are in fact the "first charter[s] of human rights" (5). Despite the existence of slavery among the patriarchs of her faith, slaves were never treated as "chattels personal" subject to the ultimate will of their owners. God was and is the ultimate arbiter of justice, according to Grimké. She cites as evidence the existence of the liberation of slaves during Jubilee years as well as God's disdain for the actions of Joseph's brothers (10). After listing a number of Southern slave laws, many with roots in South Carolina's Negro Act, she writes, "The laws of Moses protected servants in their rights as men and women, guarded them from oppression and defended them from wrong. The Code Noir of the South robs the slave of all his rights as a man, reduces him to a chattel personal, and defends the master, in the exercise of the most unnatural and unwarrantable power over his slave" (23). She concludes that slavery in the Old Testament was quite different from slavery in the American South. Therefore, the Bible should not be cited as evidence of God's approval of the institution.

Grimké asks women to examine their social roles, claiming that they must leave the private domestic sphere and speak in the public sphere. She urges women to "read," "pray," "speak," and, ultimately, to "act" for the end of slavery (30). "Above all," she writes, "try to persuade your husband, father, brothers, and sons, that slavery is a crime against God and man, and that it is a great sin to keep human beings in such abject ignorance; to deny them the privilege of learning to read and write" (33). As a first step toward activism, she suggests that women teach slaves to read and write. In part, she wants slaves to be better Christians, but she also wishes that they not be deprived of knowledge of their rights as human beings. The slave owners fear educated slaves because they know that "an enlightened population never can be a slave population" (55). Grimké acknowledges that teaching a slave to read or write is against the law but adds that it is a sinful law that should be broken (35). And women can break this law; women can do this work. There are many examples of women leaders in the Bible and in their time, and she notes the powerful activism of women abolitionists in England (43). "The women of the South can overthrow this horrible system of oppression and cruelty, licentiousness and wrong" (48). Women must be the first movers.

Not only does she make the radical assertion that white women are human beings who have the right to communicate in the public sphere, but Grimké asserts that black people are also whole human beings endowed with human rights. There is much work to be done, though, because slave owners have effectively turned blacks into "chattels personal" through law and practice. It was a "wise" decision on their part, she writes, "for before they could be robbed of wages, wives, children, and friends, it was absolutely necessary to deny they were human beings" (23). Humans must become "thing[s]" before they can be controlled and broken. And yet, this horrid fence is in the process of being dismantled. Proof of this "is manifest by the insurrections that so often disturb the peace and security of slaveholding countries. Who ever heard of a rebellion of the beasts of the field; and why not?" (25). When human beings are robbed of their human rights, they will rebel; they will seek to speak freely in the public sphere. She says to these Southern women that, in effect, slaves have been fighting for their human rights for some time—you must join them. Grimké's recognition of the actions of slaves themselves in this freedom struggle is quite significant. She depicts African Americans as human beings, in literary terminology, round characters. In doing so, Grimké undermines the often paternalist and racist discourse of abolitionism.

Because she was born and raised in South Carolina, perhaps Grimké is referring to Stono when she notes the many incidents of slave rebellions. For the most part, though, this narrative is largely absent from the written record of the nineteenth century save for its essential presence in the laws of South Carolina. One notable exception is a short story published in the 1847 issue of the *Liberty Bell* by Boston abolitionist Edmund Quincy (1808–1877) entitled "Mt. Verney: Or, an Incident of Insurrection," a fictionalized account of the rebellion.[7] Quincy was the son of former Boston mayor, U.S. congressman, and Harvard president Josiah Quincy. After the murder of Elijah Lovejoy and bearing witness to a mob attack on the office of William Lloyd Garrison's *Liberator*, Quincy became an abolitionist (Greenspan 134). He worked closely with Garrison and Wendell Phillips and was a prominent member of the Massachusetts, New England, and American Anti-Slavery Societies (M. Howe 377). He wrote numerous essays for abolitionist and mainstream publications and edited others, including the *Liberator* itself.[8]

"Mt. Verney" details the experiences of a Northern traveler who visits a Southern plantation and learns of the Stono rebellion from an old planter still mourning his losses from that day. The use of a frame narrative and the depiction of a close relationship between master and slave invite comparisons to the plantation tradition of post-bellum American fiction. Yet this story's protagonist, Arnold, is an intelligent, educated liberator reminiscent of Frederick Douglass's Madison Washington in *The Heroic Slave* or Martin Delany's rebellion organizer Henry Blake. Quincy's story, like Douglass's and Delany's, represents *the other* plantation tradition—one in which slaves are not content, but are actively pursuing the destruction of the slave regime. Quincy turns the plantation myth on its head (or, at the very least, on its side); this story offers another perspective, not only on the transformation of the Stono narrative, but on the black subject's desire for human rights.

Told in third person, "Mt. Verney" opens with a Northern gentleman named Mr. Langdon riding to Mt. Verney, a plantation located in the South Carolina midlands in April 1773.[9] A native of New England, Langdon is escaping his work and ever-growing tensions with Great Britain. The plantation is apparently far removed from that world, located as it is deep in a verdant landscape already overgrown in April. The proprietor, who lives on the plantation with no company other than his slaves, welcomes his guest with open arms and offers plenty of food and punch. As Langdon and Verney imbibe, they discuss the impending war with the British. The South Carolinian acknowledges his fear that if the colony is occupied, slaves will revolt; Langdon counters that they will not because of their deep-seated loyalty to their masters. Verney laughs, "My dear sir, had you lived your life among slaves, as I have done, you would know what reliance to put on that head!" (39). But Langdon refuses to accept this and declares that if slaves were prepared for freedom through education, they would not attack their masters: "A wolf may be tamed,—a negro may be civilized" (39). Verney concludes that his Northern visitor is essentially clueless.

The following day, the two men take up the previous night's conversation. Langdon expresses his abhorrence of slavery and Verney basically agrees: "What you say, my friend, is all unquestionably true. But, here we are, and there are the slaves, and what are we to do?" (42). Such a reply is reminiscent of Jefferson's in *Notes on the State of Virginia*. Verney continues, "We find ourselves bound up with the blacks in this infernal spell, and how to break it passes my art." Langdon again suggests educating the slaves in preparation for their freedom. Verney replies, "If I have reason to know anything on earth, it surely is the fallacy of your proposition." Verney then launches into a narrative, the back story, the events that brought on the Stono Rebellion.

He begins by explaining the history of his family, noting that the patriarch of the Verney clan in South Carolina was drawn to the Carolina colonial project, directed as it was by the "spirit of Shaftesbury" and the pen of John Locke (43–44). He then notes that when his father, Colonel Verney (and I'll refer to him hereafter as the Colonel to avoid confusion), was a young man, he was sent to England to be educated. He was assigned a body servant named Arnold to accompany him on his adventure. Arnold was well received as he traveled with Verney's father, "from Eton to Oxford and from Oxford to the Inns of Court" (45). The slave took advantage of his situation and sought to educate himself: "He availed himself to such snatches of instruction as he could seize by the way, with such success, that it was a common saying ... that Arnold knew more than his master. ... In his zeal for knowledge he was encouraged and assisted by his young master, who seemed to feel as if all the intelligence of his sable satellite was but the reflected radiance of his own." But Arnold's freedom to learn and the Colonel's freedom to feel proud of his slave's education came to an end around 1720 when both returned to the colonies. The change was drastic for Arnold, who was again treated as a slave. His stint in England had "made him forget" his status. The Colonel's father encouraged him to beat Arnold into renewed submission, but he refused. But as time passed, Arnold *seemed* to be cured of his lust for freedom.

On the contrary, in the midst of his depression Arnold had an epiphany: "'Why,' thought he, 'are my people and myself slaves? Why do we remain slaves? Is there, indeed, no remedy? .... [I]s it a necessity that we remain slaves forever?'" (46). Arnold realized the potential of the slaves to rebel, as well as the probable help they would receive from Spain. "He felt that a mind only was wanting to watch and guide events, in order to conduct such a revolution to a triumphant issue.... He looked upon the advantages of education he had enjoyed, as something providential, and designed for a mighty end." Arnold was ready to accept this responsibility, but above all, "he was willing to wait!" As the years passed, Arnold had the opportunity to travel throughout the state with his master—now in charge of his father's possessions and a man of prominence—and used this freedom to find others to support his plan. The moment finally came when it seemed that war with Spain "was inevitable" (47). The narrator tells us that the Spanish had made connections with Arnold through a Jewish spy "of Portuguese extraction" named Da Costa, a "pawn broker and dealer in small wares," a vocation which allowed for unsuspected mobility throughout the state. The two hatched a plan for an insurrection that would be supported by Spanish troops. Eventually, the freed slaves would control the colony as a "dependency of Spain" (48). However, Arnold "had no faith in the abstract zeal of the Spaniards for human rights, and he believed that their real purpose was only to substitute Spanish for English masters." He did not want endless war and struggle and after long consideration realized that the only solution "was the utter extermination of the whites!" (49). Arnold realized this would require the murder of his master and his master's family and was horrified: "He had neither wife nor child. All his affections centered, with passionate intenseness, in his master and his children. They were all he had to love." But his thoughts were interrupted by the cries of a woman being punished, which "sounded like the 'exceeding bitter cry' of his race, whose wrongs he had forgotten, reproaching him for his weakness." His determination to rebel was, thus, renewed.

And so the revolt began in the slave quarters one Sunday, where Arnold riled up the slaves and urged them to take part in the rebellion. The plantation overseer went to quell the disturbance and was immediately killed. Arnold then dispatched messengers to other plantations and rode on the dead overseer's horse to the plantation house. His master, Colonel Verney, was shocked and asked, "Why Arnold ... what means this disturbance?" Arnold replied, "It means liberty to slaves and death to tyrants!" (50). Colonel Verney moved to attack him and Arnold planted a sword "deep in the heart he loved most on earth." Arnold's boldness apparently motivated the rebels to act boldly as well. He ordered the slaves to Stono, "a small settlement above five miles off, where there was a warehouse full of arms and ammunition," while another group went after the rest of the family. As the rebels marched, their size increased until it was "four or five hundred strong" (51). They destroyed Stono and the surrounding plantations, including Verney's—though he was saved by his nurse—and, in the process, armed themselves for battle. Here the narrative echoes the historical record: "A quantity of white cloth furnished them with banners. Drums and fifes were also in the warehouse. ... So they took up their march towards Jacksonburgh, with drums beating and banners flying, in some show of military order."

The slaves continued marching and killed all those in their path but eventually found alcohol and became intoxicated. This was when they encountered "Governor Bull" and company. According to the narrator, "The Governor saw the whole truth in a moment and, wheeling about, galloped off with his companions in the opposite direction" (52). Arnold and several others chased after the men but were unsuccessful. Bull stopped at the church at Wiltown, where Archibald Stobo was preaching. The men in the church "sprung to their arms, which they were required by law to carry with them to church"; these men, led by a Captain Bee, found the rebels just as Arnold was beginning to lose control over them (52). Chaos spread as the white men began to fire upon them. The rebels held their ground until Bull arrived with reinforcements, but at that point it was a lost cause. Arnold and the rebels were defeated.

Quincy's version of the Stono story dramatizes the aftermath. He writes that when Arnold was finally knocked down, "a dozen sabers were uplifted to make his fate certain" (53). Bull saved him, crying out, "He knows things, which we must know, first!" He was tossed into a slave prison and the next day was interrogated: "He acknowledged, and justified, his own part in this rising; but he utterly refused to implicate any others, or to give information as to the extent of his conspiracy. He was tied and flogged (for the first time in his life) until he fainted from loss of blood; but no syllable of information, or cry of pain, could be extorted from him" (53). This went on for three days, and yet he said nothing. They offered forgiveness and he laughed. Finally, "they dragged him to the public square and hanged him like a dog. . . . He died, but his memory, spectre-like, long haunted the province" (53). We learn that "at the very next session of the Colonial Legislature, (1740,) the insurrection of slaves was made a highly penal offence. The alarm was universal. Every man feared lest he might have an Arnold on his estate" (53). According to the narrator, "the spirit of Arnold seemed to walk in the province" in the many attempted rebellions that followed (53).

When the story ends, Verney asks, "Was I not right in saying that I had had an experience that refuted your theory of educating slaves for freedom?" (53). Quincy writes that the Northerner was dumbfounded: "Mr. Langdon could make no reply to such a question, after such a story. He wrung his friend's hand in silence. He had nothing to say, for Philosophy had not as yet taught men by examples, that the safe, sufficient, and only possible preparation for freedom is EMANCIPATION" (53–54). Langdon left, but "while his heart bled for the blight which it had shed upon the life of Verney, he could not disguise from himself . . . that his deepest sympathies were with Arnold" (54).

At the end of an introduction to this story, historian Mark M. Smith reminds the reader to "keep in mind that this is a story used, quite openly and unapologetically, for political purposes" (*Stono* 36). Indeed, it "repeats in formulaic, scripted fashion the tropes of the educated slave, the tragedy of bondage, and the righteousness of slave insurrection" (35). And yet he stops short of calling this story "propaganda," which could imply that this story is undeserving of being grouped under the heading "Literature." As a historian, Smith notes that despite its flaws, "heavy romanticism, clumsy didacticism, and moral high-handedness, it is accurate on many details." Given a variety of specific details included, he says that Quincy appears to have relied heavily on Alexander Hewatt's account of the Stono Rebellion.

It is absolutely significant that Quincy resurrects the Stono narrative for his "political purposes"—to end gross human rights abuses—but its significance does not end there. Despite its clear intention to manipulate the sentiments of the reader, this text presents black subjects who shape their own historical narrative. Arnold endures the indignity of being presented with freedoms, with having access to information, and then having those freedoms taken from him. He realizes the power of his subaltern group and the necessity for collective action. And as black subject within a racist regime Arnold recognizes, not without reason, that as long as whites exist in the same communities as blacks, there will be struggle. He rebels; he counters the plantation myth and, for a moment, overturns white control. Quincy's version of Stono is romantic, but so are the founding myths of the United States. The kernel of truth he acknowledges is that the desire for freedom is also buried within the hearts of slaves and that they also have the inalienable human right to transform their social and political circumstances just as the founding fathers did. Langdon seems to speak to those foundational myths of the right to revolt when he claims, "If ever blood was spilt righteously for the vindication of rights or the redress of wrongs, that which has flowed in servile insurrection is the most hallowed of all" (50). Quincy's political literature counters and re-imagines the revolutionary and plantation traditions. In this sense it is in conversation with George Cato's narrative. This is the narrative the Charleston School wished to suppress.

My reading of "Mt. Verney" suggests that Langdon believes Arnold's actions are justified—despite evidence that he finds those actions alarming. Perhaps Edmund Quincy himself wishes the reader to identify with Arnold and, thus, the violent overthrow of slavery. Of course, there are other examples of abolitionists who began to offer radical, even violent, solutions for the problem of slavery. Thoreau publicly declared his support for John Brown's violent deeds, and Harriet Beecher Stowe, responding to critiques of her characterization of submissive Uncle Tom, wrote a novel about a slave insurrectionist called *Dred*. One could argue that the use of violence as a method for resistance was a lesson that abolitionists learned from slaves themselves; indeed, John Brown cited the maroons of Jamaica as his model (Reynolds 107–109). These examples occurred years after Quincy wrote his story. And yet, "Mt. Verney" shows Quincy toying with the idea that violence may be a just response to gross violations of human rights. The title, "Mt. Verney," seems to be a play on "Mt. Vernon," the founding father's home, built and sustained by slaves—much like the plantation of the story. That plantation—like all the other Southern plantations, like the United

States itself—is haunted by slavery and by the violence that slavery produced and produces. Does Quincy suggest a literal or figurative overturning of the founding father's house? Does he suggest that Arnold and his rebels represent a just revolution? Langdon/Quincy's parting thoughts lean in that direction: "But while his heart bled for the blight which it had shed upon the life of Verney, he could not disguise from himself, standing as he did on the brink of civil war, that his deepest sympathies were with Arnold" (54). Such sentiments held true with some Boston abolitionists. One of the most ardent abolitionists in this circle, Wendell Phillips, was a close friend of Quincy's, and the two worked side by side as activists. Is it possible that Phillips's occasional militancy rubbed off on Quincy? For the most part Phillips was a pacifist, but he would later become enamored with the actions of John Brown; again, this was many years after Quincy wrote "Mt. Verney."

And why would he choose the Stono Rebellion as source material for his short story? There were other more recent examples of slave rebellions or plots that ended with little bloodshed, Madison Washington's mutiny on the *Creole* (1841) or Cinque's, a.k.a. Sengbe Pieh, aboard the *Amistad* (1839), for example. Why Stono? Why a rebellion that resulted in the deaths of over sixty people—white and black? More importantly, why did he, as Smith notes, use Alexander Hewatt's 1779 account of the rebellion? David Ramsay's 1809 *History of South Carolina* would, perhaps, have been more readily available.

The choice of Hewatt makes sense because his history is critical of slavery in South Carolina. As noted above, Hewatt wrote that "slavery, in general, like several other enormities, ought to be ascribed to the corruption and avarice of men, rather than to any principle of nature and humanity, which evidently testify against it" (92). He writes that slavery violates the human rights of slaves (94). Reclaiming those rights is Arnold's goal. Edmund Quincy, though, did not belong to the militant wing of abolitionism. His only biographer notes that he "espoused the causes of women's suffrage, temperance, and nonresistance in a form which would now be held the extreme of pacifism" (M. Howe 378). Quincy once proclaimed that to the abolitionists "warfare was to be no wild crusade, but a holy war, a sacred strife, waged not with arms forged by human hands or tempered in earthly fire, 'but with weapons fresh from the armory of God . . . Prayer . . . Faith . . . and the word of God'" (qtd. in Sherwin 100). Elsewhere he is described as a "zealous nonresistant" (Stewart 126). Thus, we could read

"Mt. Verney" as simply a cautionary tale exploring the possible ramifications of God's justice.

And there is ample evidence that Quincy, like many of his abolitionist comrades, was quite the racist.[10] This is not surprising given "Mt. Verney's" obsession with the transformative nature of Western culture. The story assumes that the roots of human rights discourse are within Western culture and that Arnold's English education alone is the catalyst for his transformation. And the Northern abolitionist Langdon (does he speak for Quincy?) cannot imagine a solution to slavery coming from blacks themselves until he hears Verney's story. He privileges white paradigms, believing that blacks must be educated prior to liberation. Langdon perceives the Stono narrative to be a cautionary tale addressing what could happen if slaves are not freed, or if they encounter Western ideas and education while still enslaved. Contact with new ideas can be invigorating, but, as Arna Bontemps's Gabriel reminds us, "Anything what's equal to a gray squirrel wants to be free" (210). Liberty as an idea and the human right to communicate and claim it do not appear to have originated with Locke alone. Ultimately, Quincy's characterization of Arnold reveals that his sympathies lie with the slaves in a way that Northern abolitionists can digest. Arnold is a well-educated, literate, and methodical man. Would this story have been different if Arnold had been depicted as an illiterate field hand?

PALATABLE MINSTRELSY IN POST-BELLUM AMERICA

The idea that slavery engendered a more peaceful and civilized society did not disappear when the smoke cleared from Fort Sumter. When the war and Reconstruction were ostensibly over, and much blood had been spilled on both sides of the Mason-Dixon Line, a literature of reconciliation began to enter the public sphere. This literature was less polemical—to some extent—than the pro-slavery literature of the Charleston School before the Civil War, and yet it was clearly cut from the same cloth. This plantation tradition literature became immensely popular in the North by the end of the nineteenth century. Like Charleston School writers, the leading figures of this genre—Thomas Nelson Page, Joel Chandler Harris, James Lane Allen—told stories of a glorious and paternalistic South, though this time that South had fallen; it was not just about to do so. This New South wished to regain connections with the rest of the nation as well as reconsolidate power within the hands of white elites, the patriarchy of yesteryear, in an effort to stabilize (read "segregate") the South.

Plantation tradition literature of the late nineteenth century presents a literary opposition to human rights and is a close cousin to antebellum pro-slavery or anti-Tom literature. It is an attempt to contradict and silence African American narratives—for these writers, human rights are a non-issue. The damage done by the image of the lazy darky can be traced through this literature and its live-entertainment corollary—black face minstrelsy—to *Birth of a Nation* (1915), *Gone with the Wind* (1936),[11] and historian U. B. Phillips's *American Negro Slavery* (1918), which postulated that slavery was a benign institution and slaves were relatively content. The message promoted by these works is that there were no Madison Washingtons, Henry Blakes, Nats, Gabriels, or Jemmys. The good "Negro" is a pliant, ignorant, and non-communicative "Negro," dependent on the praise and progress of his white keepers. He is, most of all, content with his place, with his world, and remains, for the most part, unquestioning.

In *Orientalism* Edward Said famously investigates the ways in which Western academics were complicit in the colonization of the "Orient." He suggests that the Orient "was almost a European invention . . . a place of romance, exotic beings, haunting memories and landscapes, remarkable experiences" (1). It "was *essentially* an idea, or a creation with no corresponding reality" with "supporting institutions, vocabulary, scholarship, imagery, doctrines" (5, 2). What makes Orientalism all the more powerful is the interconnectedness of "ideas" about the places and people of the Orient to the schools and institutions of the West—a perpetuation of Antonio Gramsci's notion of cultural hegemony (7). Said is particularly interested in the manifestations of Orientalism in texts and instances in which people take for truth what they read and attempt to apply this "truth" to a reality which takes on a "textual attitude" (93). He claims that "people, places, and experiences can always be described by a book, so much so that the book (or text) acquires a greater authority and use, even than the actuality it describes" (93). The plantation tradition is also supportive of a "textual attitude," a counter-rights discourse wrapped up with other popular depictions of African Americans in nineteenth- and early twentieth-century America. We must not forget that "Jump Jim Crow" was first a minstrel song before Jim Crow became social and legal practice.

Ultimately, plantation tradition literature and culture leaves us wanting the slave's voice or, at the very least, the appearance of the slave's voice.

Both Simms and Quincy do not allow the slave to speak. Quincy privileges whiteness while Simms's Hector is rendered happily submissive. Both offer very different representations of history, but both *represent*. The forms of these plantation narratives mimic the limiting conditions established by physical plantations themselves. For example, on those plantations governed by the task system, slaves did, perhaps, have some freedom of movement when they completed their tasks. But as the Negro Act established, at the end of the day, when the back-breaking work of that task was done, slaves were still chattel, property, trapped in a netherworld, both human and thing. These white-produced plantation narratives demonstrate the ability of one discourse to bury another when one group has more complete access to privileged communication technologies. The central dilemma of a democratic-leaning society, then, is how to allow everyone to narrate their own lived experiences and to promote circumstances that provide them with the developmental freedoms to do so.[12] These developmental freedoms are further hindered by the cultural work of some historians and artists who shape and mold certain kinds of human subjects in the public sphere.

PRESERVATION SOCIETIES

On a warm Friday morning in May, I walked in front of the State House building in Columbia, South Carolina. A solemn ceremony was taking place on the steps of the immense Greek revival building, its majestic bronze dome catching the morning rays.[13] Women in black hoop mourning dresses stood about as the names of Confederate soldiers who died in the Civil War were read aloud by members of the South Carolina Order of the Confederate Rose. The names were read one by one, and a ringing bell accompanied each. Close by, the flag of the Confederacy fluttered in front of the Confederate war memorial. I paused, waiting to see where they were in the list of over eighteen thousand South Carolinians who died in that war; it would be a long time before they got to my ancestors.

This history is still alive for many in the United States—white and black. In generational terms, the war was not so long ago. These "preservation" societies, though not truly mainstream, hang on with a dogged persistence. The plantation narrative persists, too, in *Gone with the Wind*, Stono Phosphate business cards purchased on eBay, and resorts and housing developments called "plantations." The images produced by these byproducts of a bygone era perpetuate stereotypes that linger. We would do ourselves and our country a great service to begin to examine why this is so. One way to begin such an interrogation would be to examine the stories we tell about ourselves—the stories that construct our historical and cultural identities. Narratives that bury the freedom struggles of slaves have only recently been rejected. Generations of South Carolinians learned about the state's history as schoolchildren from various versions of William Gilmore Simms's "history" book. How the story is told, who is doing the telling, and whether or not the story is told at all *matters*.[14]

After leaving the women of the South Carolina Order of the Confederate Rose to do their thing, I encountered a group of third graders looking at the African American memorial located some fifty feet away from the Confederate one. This memorial incorporates Clarkson's famous image of the slave ship *Brooks*, which lies flat on the ground like a gravestone. As I marveled at the image—indeed, I'm stunned by the image each time I see it—a student asked his teacher, "What's that drawing of?"

The teacher responded, "I'm not exactly sure, honey. Looks like a slave ship."

I chimed in, saying, "That's a picture of a slave ship called the *Brooks*. Ships like that brought slaves to South Carolina."

The student responded, "Oh. But they didn't make them sit so close together like that, did they?"

"They did," I replied, "They really did." Behind me I could hear the name of another dead Confederate through the loudspeaker and then the ding of the bell. I walked on.

Chapter 7

★   ★   ★   ★   ★   ★   ★

DOIN' DE RIGHT
The Persistence of the Stono Narrative

Dum spiro spero or "While I breathe, I hope."
—South Carolina state motto

WE'RE STANDING ON A NARROW CAUSEWAY jutting into the marsh grass about one hundred yards to the west of Highway 17, the Savannah Highway, a stone's throw from where the rebellion supposedly began. It's a warm spring day, sun shining, fiddler crabs darting away as we walk along a narrow path. Centuries ago, rice would have been growing on either side of us. Here and there you can just make out the earthen banks that would have surrounded that rice. From the highway, all one can see is a strip of land strewn with oaks and cedars—in the midst of the causeway one encounters a motley assortment of bushes, weeds, wind-tamed trees, and the faint outline of a road.

"I was shocked when I realized that this old road was here. It shows up on USGS maps, and when you put those maps on top of eighteenth-century plats, they fit perfectly," explains Shawn Halifax, a public historian working for the Caw Caw Interpretive Center, an historical and natural learning center. The center is located just up the road on land that once belonged to Thomas Elliott and Thomas Rose, white planters intimately involved in the events of September 9, 1739.

"Now if they crossed at the Limehouse Boat Landing," he continues, "they would have come out to this road. This could have been the road they walked down to get to Hutchenson's Store, but we just don't know for sure."

"That's the thing," Halifax explains: there are a number of accounts of the Stono narrative floating around, both written and oral. Some oral accounts claim the rebellion started elsewhere and eventually reached

THE PERSISTENCE OF THE STONO NARRATIVE

Hutchenson's Store. According to Halifax, there are folks who believe the event started on John's Island, across the Stono River from where we are standing. Halifax isn't sure about this interpretation, and yet he's willing to suspend his disbelief. He points out that because there's so little documentation of the rebellion, one has to be open to different interpretations. That's why he's so fascinated by it, and that's why the event serves as an excellent educational tool for his work at the interpretive center.

"I did a program on September 9, 2007," Halifax explains, "and I was getting lots of questions from people wanting facts about the event. They wanted cut-and-dry, black-and-white answers about Stono. I had to stop and tell them that there aren't any answers, and if you come away from my presentation thinking that you've got the answers from spending a few hours with me, then I've failed."

Even though he has been researching and teaching about the rebellion for many years now, *he* still has many unanswered questions. Who were the rebels? How long had they been in South Carolina? How did they plan the rebellion? Where did it begin? What compelled some slaves, like July, to protect their masters? And what should the event be called?

"You know, I'm not comfortable with the term 'uprising' or 'rebellion.' I haven't been able to come to terms with a term. What I think comes the closest is that these people were looking for freedom. They were freedom seekers or freedom fighters. I see them more in those terms than as rebels. If we only think of them as rebels, then we're saying that what they did was wrong."

Ultimately, he says, this is a complex human story that we can all learn from, that we all can claim in some way. It's the story of a group of human beings seeking freedom, facing enormous obstacles, trying to make it. And it was a strenuous journey. His voice rising, he adds, "These guys they did a lot of walking! So by four o'clock in the afternoon, I can see why they would have wanted to take a break. From Hutchenson's Store to Battlefield Plantation it's almost seventeen or eighteen miles."

He wants to show me just how far they went, so we get back into his pickup truck and drive further down Highway 17, passing the site where Hutchenson's Store once stood. Eventually, we turn into a posh housing development called the Plantation at Stono Ferry, passing enormous suburban homes that seem somewhat out of place in the Lowcountry landscape. As we pull into a cul-de-sac capped by three large homes looking out over the Stono River, he says, "If they started on John's Island, they could have crossed right here where the river narrows considerably. This may not have been the exact spot, but you get the idea."

I was getting the idea. Indeed, where we go in the future depends on how we imagine this story, what it means, what it tells us about then and now. I imagine for a moment what it had been like that night—a group of slaves hopping out of a small skiff at this landing and then racing off in the direction of the storehouse. They are running in the direction of uncertainty, of another life, of freedom. What are they thinking? Are they scared? Assured? Angry? Is Jemmy among them? Is he already at the storehouse?

"You know," Halifax comments, "one of things that has always bugged me is that we don't know much about Jemmy or Cato. Do we? We don't even know which plantation he was associated with. We have no idea whatsoever. We're not even sure what to call him."

FINDING GEORGE CATO

George Cato's 1937 oral narrative, discussed in previous chapters, was part of the Federal Writers' Project (FWP), a program funded by Franklin D. Roosevelt's New Deal Works Progress Administration, the famous work program developed in 1935 to provide relief to the unemployed.[1] FWP was unique because it employed, for the most part, artists and writers, not laborers. At its peak, FWP provided jobs for about 6,500 people from offices in every state; these writers earned about twenty dollars a week, and among them were writers like Conrad Aiken, Saul Bellow, Arna Bontemps, Ralph Ellison, Zora Neale Hurston, and Richard Wright. The initial goal was to produce travel and historical guidebooks for each state,[2] but other ideas developed. One such idea was to record the narratives of former slaves before their stories disappeared. So between 1937 and 1938 approximately 2,300 narratives were compiled, only 2 percent of the former slaves living at the time. In South Carolina, writers conducted 284 interviews and produced about 1,200 manuscript pages—an incredible literature of witness.

But historians have long debated whether or not these oral history narratives can be useful historical evidence. They note that the pool of those interviewed was slim and not a random sample; that those interviewed were elderly; that the interviewers were not well trained; that the interviewers were overwhelmingly white; and, finally, that those interviewed may have lied in order to appease the interviewer out of fear that they might say the wrong thing. This was the 1930s. And this was the South, where power and race often combined in deadly ways.

So, is it possible to have a reliable narrator in such a situation? The racist views of some interviewers are obvious; use of the term "darky" was not uncommon, and over-zealous recording of dialect was the norm.[3] To combat these issues, African American poet Sterling Brown sent a memo to field offices in a number of states, including South Carolina, advising interviewers on the proper way to record the dialect of those interviewed in a less patronizing fashion—and to abstain from using racist epithets. Memo or not, race played an enormous role in the point of view expressed by the interviewee; the mere presence of a white body on the front porch of a black South Carolinian would have signaled a rather defined power structure. And in South Carolina 78 percent of the former slaves were interviewed by whites (Blassingame 90). It is not surprising, then, that former slaves interviewed in South Carolina paint a generally rosy picture of slavery. However, as John W. Blassingame points out, "former South Carolina slaves who were interviewed in Georgia had a far different view of bondage than those who were interviewed" in the Palmetto State (91).

Despite these problems, ex-slave narratives exist and, although often heavily mediated, they allow a subaltern people to speak publicly about their lived experiences. C. Vann Woodward makes a strong case for using the oral narratives to assist historical interpretation. He asks, "Shall historians discard the slave interviews as worthless? Not unless they are prepared to be consistent and discard most of the other sources they habitually use. Not while they use newspapers as sources, or, for that matter, diaries and letters and politicians' speeches and the Congressional Record and all those neatly printed official documents and the solemnly sworn testimony of high officials" (53). These texts are also complex and contradictory.

Reading the oral narratives, then, gives us a complicated view of slavery; but it is a view nonetheless. We must read these narratives with care, always alert to details, ambiguities, hidden meanings, or "hidden transcripts." Paul D. Escott writes, "The historian must start with the fact that these reports are not a direct representation of the slaves' views. They are not even a direct transcription of the interview itself" (41). Only a few were tape recorded. Most reports were based on notes taken down by the interviewer himself or herself. Interviewers were supposed to ask questions about marriage, work, and relations with their masters, and these themes run throughout the oral histories. But these questions were "often partially or totally ignored, and this resulted in rambling and trivia; when it was too closely followed, the result was stylized and superficial responses, devoid of spontaneity" (Yetman 552).

George Cato's narrative clearly does not fall into either of those categories. In some ways his narrative is unusual for this collection because of the topic discussed and because of the man interviewed. Cato was not a former slave. According to his interviewer, Stiles M. Scruggs, he was fifty years old at the time of the interview in 1937. Thus, he would have been born around 1887, many years after both slavery and the Civil War had ended. Locating George Cato, the man, is a bit of a mystery. Census data is inconclusive, not surprising in a decade of disruption, depression, poverty, and continued migration northward for many African Americans in South Carolina. On top of these obstacles, the pernicious practices of Jim Crow made life difficult for black South Carolinians. A glance through racially segregated Columbia city directories from the period will shed light on that reality. George Cato is listed with other "Colored Residents."[4] But what little we know about George Cato comes from these directories and from the introduction to the oral narrative itself. Cato was a "laborer," apparently married, and living at the rear of 1010 Lady Street in Columbia, South Carolina, a building that has long since been bulldozed. Today, a parking lot is there and a block away, over on Gervais Street, a bar called Liberty. Cato appears in at least six of the city directories and then disappears around 1939; he may have left Columbia, perhaps moving northward, lured by the promise of manufacturing jobs.

If we can't say much about the Cato of 1937, what about the Cato of 1739? Who was he? As noted in chapter 3, some historians have referred to the rebellion leader as Cato and not Jemmy. Are they talking about the same person? And where did he get that name? John C. Inscoe writes that some slave owners named their slaves after historic figures like Cato or Plato "for satiric or condescending reasons," but not always (543). Inscoe singles out George Cato as an instance in which one of these classical names was passed on generation after generation: "His father, grandfather, and great-grandfather had all been named Cato in honor of their rebellious ancestor, and, when emancipated, George made it his surname, which ensured its continuation within his family." Because of his ancestor's connection to the rebellion, his family reclaimed a name that may have initially been a joke. The surname Cato, like the narrative itself, became a badge of honor.

With this limited information, what else can we say about the narrative collected in 1937? First, of all, it's difficult to attest to its authenticity. Did George Cato really hear an oral account of the Stono Rebellion? Can we trust him? He mentions learning about the rebellion from his father and grandfather, both of whom could have been slaves. Would it have been possible for them to retain such specific details? And those details, where did they come from? The number of dead—twenty-one whites and forty-four blacks—are the same numbers Lieutenant Governor Bull mentions in his eyewitness account. But Bull doesn't mention the year of the event or the supposed name of the leader, as Cato does.

If Cato's narrative is based on some written account, then it may not have been passed down from generation to generation—taking the wind out of that sail. However, it *would* mean that George Cato is signifying on the historical record because he gives Cato/Jemmy a voice—something none of the white recorders of the rebellion do. Cato/Jemmy is spoken into humanity. As Frederick Douglass employs the pen and page to write himself into humanity, George Cato employs his voice and counts on the interviewer to reveal his truth.

And this truth is a testimony of resistance somewhat unique in the oral histories of ex-slaves in South Carolina. George Cato is proud of his family's history as he understands it. He says, "I sho' does come from dat old stock who had de misfortune to be slaves but who decided to be men, at one and de same time, and I's right proud of it" (98). He claims that his ancestor was treated well by his master, unlike some other slaves, and that it was from his master that he learned to read and write (99). This could be true, or it could be a case of the black interviewee telling the white interviewer what he wanted to hear. George Cato's comment begs the question, though: If his ancestor was treated so well, why did he rebel? Could George Cato be teasing the interviewer by claiming his ancestor was treated well?

We continue to read between the lines: George Cato is not sure how the rebellion started, how the slaves organized to bring so many together and get weapons from Hutchenson's Store on September 9, 1739. (He gives the exact date.) Cato continues, "They work fast, coverin' 15 miles, passin' many fine plantations, and in every single case, stop, and break in de house and kill men, women, and children. Then they take what they want" (99). When they finally and unfortunately run across Bull's path, the lieutenant governor "smell[s] a rat." When the militia returns, the rebels seem disorganized;

George Cato blames alcohol. "Cato and some of the de other leaders was cussin' at them sumpin awful. From dat day to dis, no Cato has tasted whiskey, 'less he go 'gainst his daddy's warnin'."

"This war last less than two days but it sho' was pow'ful hot while it last" (99). In the end, Cato claims that the forty-four who died were the ones that stood their ground while the so-called "drinkin' dancin' Negroes" fled (100). As they were taken captive, "Commander Cato speak for de crowd. He say: 'We don't lak slavery. We start to jine de Spanish in Florida. We surrender but we not whipped yet and we is not converted.' De other 43 say: 'Amen.' They was taken, unarmed, and hanged by de militia." He is, like Vesey, Turner, and Prosser, strong until the end. And the others who stand with him, they are also "not converted." They do not think that what they did was wrong. They believe they were trying to destroy a regime that perpetuated gross violations of human rights. George Cato understands his ancestor's speech and actions to signify a struggle for human rights (a counter to the plantation myth tradition) and concludes, "He die but he die doin' de right, as he see it."

Doing the right. Doing what was right. Doing what he needed to do in order to secure human rights for himself and for others. He wanted his liberty, or his death. This revolutionary human rights discourse resonates throughout the history of the United States—and I have given numerous examples throughout this book—and in many ways comes to a head in the twentieth century. If not in George Cato's oral narrative, the freedom struggle, the desire for human rights, can be found in the actions and words of a plethora of African Americans writers and activists. In a sense, they carry the torch, the spirit of the Stono rebels.

"THE HUMAN RIGHTS TREE KEEPS GROWING"

Americans must remember that our collective relationship to human rights has always been ambiguous and, as in the case of William Gilmore Simms, sometimes openly hostile. In the first half of the twentieth century the racist discourse of the plantation tradition won out, and millions of Americans existed in apartheid-like conditions. U. B. Phillips's interpretation of slavery was taught to countless schoolchildren. Woodrow Wilson screened D. W. Griffith's famous film in the White House. In 1925 the Ku Klux Klan marched on Washington, D.C. Forty years later policemen used dogs and teargas on African American protestors in Alabama. And on February 8, 1968, Samuel Hammond, Delano Middleton, and Henry Smith were killed by South Carolina patrolmen while protesting segregation in Orangeburg, South Carolina, my hometown.

The other side of this story is that many African Americans courageously picketed movie theaters that showed Griffith's film. A number of prominent black leaders played a crucial role in pushing the human rights agenda in the United States after World War Two. In fact, Mordecai W. Johnson, W. E. B. Du Bois, Walter White, Ralph Bunche, and Mary McLeod Bethune were accredited by the U.S. State Department to be observers at the United Nations conference in San Francisco in 1945.[5] On August 28, 1963, there was another march on Washington, this one in the name of civil rights. And who could have imagined that on November 4, 2008, the United States would elect Barack Obama, the nation's first black president? In many and important ways his election is a continuation of the universal human rights struggles of countless artists and activists before him.

But the public struggles of African Americans in the late 1950s and throughout the 1960s were also struggles for *human* rights. Many activists and writers made universal connections, claiming that first on the agenda was to obtain treatment befitting a human being, then that of a citizen. The call for liberty and human rights can also be found in the words and actions of many twentieth-century South Carolinians from Septima Clark to Modjeska Simkins to Cleveland Sellers. In a 1936 speech, South Carolina native Mary McLeod Bethune asserts the civil rights of African Americans: "Beginning as the Negro did with the founding of the colonies, contributing as he has to every phase of American life, he should have the same rights, privileges, immunities, and emoluments that have been and are accorded the American citizen" ("Closed Doors" 18). At times, though, she makes broader claims. In the same speech, she employs the metaphor of "closed doors" to describe the lack of human rights. She claims that "the principle of justice is fundamental and must be exercised if the peoples of this country are to rise to the highest and best, for there can be neither freedom, peace, true democracy, or real development without justice. The closed door of economic inequalities, of educational limitation, of social restrictions comprise the greatest injustice possible" (19). In a later speech entitled "Clarifying Our Vision with Facts," published in 1938, Bethune expands the connection between education and economic potential, between communication and social possibilities. Central to this vision is the assertion of a positive narrative of African American history, of struggle and progress. "We must tell the story with continually accruing detail from the cradle to the grave," she claims, and we must distribute it "through newspaper, storybook and pictures" (12). Telling the story will improve how we think of ourselves and will improve how others imagine us (13). Here, the right to communicate one's narrative goes hand in hand with the achievement of human dignity.

When human rights claims were made by two of the most prominent leaders of this struggle, Martin Luther King Jr. and Malcolm X, they were murdered shortly thereafter. Malcolm X, in particular, noted the distinction between civil and human rights and felt that achieving the latter should be the first goal of African Americans. In "The Ballot or the Bullet," he asserts human rights as "God-given" and "recognized by all nations of the earth" (35). Speaking directly to African Americans in this crucial moment, he says, "They keep you wrapped up in civil rights. And you spend so much time barking up the civil-rights tree, you don't even know there's a human-rights tree on the same floor" (34). His focus on human rights discourse intensified after completing the Hajj to Mecca in April 1964. This intensely spiritual experience that he shared with other humans who had white skin and yet shared a core belief in justice pushed him to promote a human rights agenda. Like Bethune, Malcolm X links education—especially the ability to communicate history—with achieving human rights. In the Organization of Afro-American Unity charter he promotes the notion that "education is an important element in the struggle for human rights. It is the means to help our children and our people rediscover their identity and thereby increase their self-respect" (*By Any Means* 43). In a speech from June 28, 1964, he is more specific, claiming that in the United States, "every little child going to school thinks his grandfather was a cotton picker. Why, your grandfather was Nat Turner; your grandfather was Toussaint L'Overture" (*By Any Means* 43). We could insert Jemmy into this list.

In drips and drabs, young people were and are learning about this history, a history that dismantles the architecture of the plantation tradition. At the end of the nineteenth century and into the twentieth century, some historians and schoolteachers were rewriting this false history. The Stono Rebellion was one event that needed to be retold, reframed. In

1890, Edward A. Johnson published *A School History of the Negro Race in America* in order to counter white-produced narratives of African American history. Johnson tellingly couches his discussion of Stono within a discussion of the hypocrisy of the American Revolution, writing that the rebellion was an obvious response to a deplorable situation. Johnson claims that Stono "followed the continued cruel treatment of slaves under the runaway code" (41). However, Johnson does not go much further than this reference. By 1922, with Carter G. Woodson's *The Negro in Our History*, the presence and significance of slave rebellions in eighteenth-century South Carolina was beginning to be, at the very least, acknowledged. About twenty years later Herbert Aptheker's *American Negro Slave Revolts* (1943) would situate the Stono Rebellion within the broader context of slave rebellions in a concerted effort to dispel once and for all the myth of the content slave.

But getting the narrative straight in textbooks has been a long time coming, according to Obi Kalu, a third-grade South Carolina history teacher at Mellichamp Elementary in Orangeburg, South Carolina. She says, "Initially when I taught South Carolina history it was about symbols and places and they very seldom mentioned slavery, but now they are talking about slavery more. And it wasn't until we adopted a book printed in 2000[6] that we had a good description of the Stono Rebellion. When I teach about Stono my students usually say, 'If I lived then, I'd run away, too, and they'd never catch me!'"[7] She shows me a creative letter written by one of her students. The student imagines taking part in a rebellion or escape and writes: "One night all the men were sleeping, and I told all of the men and women to put on everything black. Even though they had an alarm on the door, but we had a plan. We went out the window.... Then we escaped! I'm coming home!"

Kalu was born in Nigeria and has been in the United States for thirty-one years. I asked her how her own background has shaped her perspective of South Carolina's history.

"It's still eye-opening to learn about slavery and some of the things that happened," she answered. "You look in the book and sometimes see lies or half-truths. I think if we face it, maybe things will be a whole lot better."

"Do your third graders know a lot about slavery beforehand?" I wondered.

"They usually have no understanding about what slavery was. I don't think their parents talk to them about slavery. They'll go, 'Really? Did that happen?' And then as time goes on they'll say, 'Well, they're not supposed to do that!' But it's still vague to them because they've never been slaves before. So then we talk about how all of that's over with now and that everyone has the same rights and how it's up to them not to enslave themselves by going to school and doing a good job."

The Stono narrative has also shaped the way the history of slavery and resistance is taught in universities. Marvin Dulaney, a history professor for fourteen years at the College of Charleston and former executive director of the Avery Research Center for African American History and Culture, claims that knowledge of the rebellion shaped his teaching of American history from the moment he started teaching in 1975, shortly after Peter Wood's influential book on Stono, *Black Majority*, was released.

He notes that the rebellion "was a refutation of the Sambo thesis, which basically says that slaves didn't want to be free and could not exist in any other state, that they were passive Uncle Toms who loved their masters and mistresses."

Dulaney adds that things have changed in Charleston—especially the ways in which history is explained to the general public. "When I first got here there was little or no interpretation of slavery for the public. You could take a tour of the city and not hear anything about people who were enslaved. You could go to historic homes and plantations, believe it or not, and not hear anything about slavery. You'd get this interpretation that they were servants—like they'd been hired! Or they'd talk about the magnificent architecture or gardens and not address who was responsible for making all those things possible."

But in recent years, he claims, there has been a considerable shift in Charleston, and presentations on slavery have become the norm at plantations like Drayton Hall, Middleton Place, and Boone Hall. He says, "There's been a conscious effort across the board. But you can still get the Daughters of the Confederacy, Sons of Confederate Veterans, and the Neo-Confederates, those who maintain that the Civil War was not about slavery, that it was the War of Northern Aggression. But, honestly, I think those ideas no longer hold sway."

And, yet, old habits die hard.

"When they buried the remains of the crew of the *Hunley* a few years back—you know, that Confederate submarine—nearly ten thousand Confederate re-enactors were on hand. It was like we were under siege!"

THE PERSISTENCE OF THE STONO NARRATIVE

THE STONO REVOLUTION

On the South side of the bridge crossing Wallace's Creek[8] is the spot where Hutchenson's Store once stood, the site of the rebels' first bold move. Today, a roadside historical marker is the only indication of what happened here:

> *The Stono Rebellion, the largest slave rebellion in British North America, began nearby on September 9, 1739. About 20 Africans raided a store near Wallace Creek, a branch of the Stono River. Taking guns and other weapons, they killed two shop-keepers. The rebels marched south toward promised freedom in Spanish Florida, waving flags, beating drums, and shouting "Liberty!" The rebels were joined by 40 to 60 more during the 15 mile march. They killed at least 20 whites but spared others. The rebellion ended late that afternoon when the militia caught the rebels, killing at least 34 of them. Most who escaped were captured and executed; any forced to join the rebels were released. The S.C. Assembly soon enacted a harsh slave code, enforced until 1865.*

The marker sits on about twenty-two acres of land now owned by the Sea Island Farmer's Cooperative. Curtis Inabinett, one prominent member of the co-op and a Charleston County councilman, worked for some time to make that sign a reality.

We are sitting across from each other inside the co-op's meeting room, located on the site. I ask him how he first learned about the rebellion, and he admits that he first heard the story after he finished college. "When I was in college, blacks just didn't talk about our history. The history that I took in college focused mainly on whites—what they had done, their contributions. After being out, I made a personal effort to learn about slavery, and that's when I learned about the Stono slave rebellion."

It's mid-morning on an unusually cool June day. The steady sound of the trucks on the nearby highway makes it hard to imagine what this area used to be. "But when you first heard about Stono," I ask, "did you hear it or did you read about it?"

"Blacks around here passed on stories about slavery to their children and their children's children," he says, "and something of that significance was hard for people to forget. In general, though, it has been hard for blacks to get information about family and about significant events that happened during slavery."

Inabinett pauses, as if letting this enormous fact settle into the small size of the room we're sitting in. He tells me that it has always been hard, from his experience, for African Americans to trace their background. The reason, he imagines, is that whites wished to remove the unsightliness of slavery from history. But the presence of the Stono narrative in this community changes some of this negative history. It gives him hope and opens a new window into slavery.

Inabinett says, "It's extremely important because I don't think whites gave blacks enough credit for being smart during that era. There had been some other uprisings, but Stono was a total surprise. And this one, I've heard, involved organizing slaves from several different plantations. There were a number of ways that slaves communicated to organize. Before they were brought here they used drums—certain sounds or beats or what have you—and they were still able to do that in ways that most planters didn't understand."

Some of these communication technologies weren't allowed after Stono. And yet, some slaves figured out ways to get around the rules. Inabinett mentions the messages spread by the beats made by blacksmiths or by special patches on quilts. "After that rebellion South Carolina enacted strict laws. I'm seventy-six years old and old enough to remember and relate some of those old Southern traditions, so to speak. I've been able to live and experience treatment that was far better than what the slaves went through, but it was still very degrading. I went through things that in my heart I knew weren't right, but I didn't always have the means to rebel."

I ask him if he still feels connected to those events and to slavery. He says that, in a way, he does feel connected to his enslaved ancestors through the stories he has heard about slavery as well as through the treatment he received by whites as he was growing up. "The little that I know about slavery and about my ancestry, I can still feel their pain when I'm talking about it. Sometimes it's hard for people to understand how you feel because there's no measurement for feelings. Well, I don't know of any instrument that can do so."

The trucks and cars continue to roll by, and as the day heats up the sound of cicadas joins this din. I ask Inabinett if he thinks much has changed, and he notes that twenty-five or thirty years ago we might not even be talking to each other about these issues. "So to me a lot of progress has been made," he adds, "but there's a whole lot that we don't understand about those feelings." Learning about the Stono Rebellion helps, though, because it goes further to complete the picture of slavery in South Carolina—it demonstrates that slaves did feel the injustice, that they did fight back. Inabinett adds, "If young people today seriously studied the Stono slave rebellion, they would learn that slaves were never satisfied being slaves, that they always wanted to be free."

DAYCLEAN

What began at that storehouse in 1739 has been called at one time or another an insurrection, an uprising, a revolt, and a rebellion. One reference in a Charleston newspaper shortly after the Vesey incident refers to the Stono Rebellion as the "Gullah War,"[9] and yet another calls it the "Angola War." Once while teaching about Stono, a student asked me why it's called the Stono Rebellion and not the Stono Revolution. Rebellion implies disorder and chaos, a straying from a set and ordered society or community; it implies, too, that those naming the event are a part of a dominant group that, perhaps, does not look kindly upon the "rebellion." A revolution, on the other hand, means a turning over, a turn of the wheel, a change of perspective. The United States was founded through a revolution. Calling what took place outside of Charleston on September 9, 1739, a revolution recognizes that the event represents a turning over, an evolution of a discourse into something else; it serves as a starting point for our collective imagination, a starting point for a narrative that is new and different. "Liberty" is a word that slaves own, not John Locke. Through historical and discursive reassessment, the rebellion *becomes* a revolution.

The Negro Act limited the freedom of slaves but did not completely silence them. The act's laws did, however, restrict the ways in which slaves could achieve, the ways in which they could participate in the public sphere and represent themselves. The kinds of laws enacted in the wake of the Stono Rebellion—pass laws, literacy laws—would have a negative effect on African Americans for years to come. Obviously, slaves found ways to get around these laws, but at the end of the day the laws were on the books. As Roland Barthes writes, "All domination begins by prohibiting language"; in this light, Jim Crow laws served a similar function of limiting the communication potentials of African Americans (78). Despite these restrictions, the Stono narrative persisted. Whites tried to squelch the narrative, to rewrite it, to make themselves the victims and the heroic victors over a threatening outsider, to disguise the story for what it really was—a struggle for human rights.

Throughout this book I have discussed the significance of communication to the dissemination of ideas about human rights and to the relative control one group has had over human rights discourse. If this is so, the right to communicate the narrative of one's lived experience is crucial and is certainly the most fundamental of all fundamental human rights. How can we speak for ourselves and of ourselves if we do not have this right? How can we achieve an existence that respects our dignity as human brings? This is what the Stono rebels sought. In order to outline and emphasize the significance of the right to communicate, William F. Birdsall has proposed a "cultural-rhetorical" model as opposed to a "philosophical-legal" one, suggesting that the right to communicate be conceived of as an "'open work' that is sensitive to local diversity and interpretation" (1). Ultimately, it is a right that not only promotes a cultural narrative but is a cultural narrative itself. Birdsall bases this concept on Umberto Eco's notion of the literary text as "open work," a concept, Birdsall claims, that "values ambiguity and open-endedness" (4). A human right, then, is established by the public through debate in the public sphere. The public must make the claim that it values the right and that it values the narrative that the right represents. Clearly, the Stono narrative, one of humans breaking away from bondage, is one that all humans can understand, despite its bloody consequences. The rebels were saying something in 1739, and, I believe, the rebels are *still* saying something now.

Today, the right to communicate is a significant human right because in our media-saturated information society, formative narratives like Stono are often lost. But these narratives make us human, and we need to hold onto them, recognizing the powerful feelings that they engender and reclaim. This reclamation happens in many ways. Perhaps the most spectacular example of this began in the late 1960s, according to oral histories. For years the site where the Stono Rebellion began was used by the Ku Klux Klan for meetings and rallies. (That is, of course, until an upstart farmers' cooperative bought the land out from under them.)

"The Klan was leasing this site," Curtis Inabinett explains, "and we decided we wanted to buy it. So we got an attorney who agreed to work with us and buy it from the owner without letting the owner know that a group of black farmers wanted to buy it. Like the rebels, we had to communicate secretly! We purchased the property and came out here on a Saturday morning. The Klan's charred cross was still standing. So about fifteen of us started tearing it down, and as we were doing that a group of whites were gathering out there on the highway and started to come on the land. So we approached them and said, 'You need to know whose land you're on. We're asking *you* to leave immediately.' And we turned and finished tearing down the cross."

The process of establishing the right to communicate was a struggle for African Americans—one that is not complete. But that struggle was aided, throughout, by stories, by narratives of freedom—the purchase of this plot of land along Highway 17 is a story we can add to that mix.

A September 9, 2006, article in the *Charleston Post and Courier* noted the unveiling of the historical marker and claimed that it is located at the site of the beginning of the "bloody and unsuccessful Stono Rebellion" (Fennell). And yet, there is evidence that this claim that the rebellion was unsuccessful is false. The fact of the persistence of the story—a narrative of action, of boldness, of engagement by an abused people—is indicative of its success. Story is life. Story is existence. It is how we make sense of our world. The narrative of David and Goliath, of underdog and oppressor—this is not new. That Stono remains as a narrative in the collective history of some South Carolinians reveals much about African American culture and history as well as the intrinsic and human desire to communicate, to tell stories, and, ultimately, to craft one's own narrative of history.

The narrative that Stono represents has always existed in the hearts and minds of many Americans. For a moment, the Stono rebels sliced open—literally and figuratively—the public sphere in South Carolina, speaking directly to the philosophical concerns of many Enlightenment figures: What does it mean to be human? What does it mean to be free? The rebels responded to both questions. Their revolt was multicultural, multilingual, creative, organized, and effective—they made their point clear. Literary acts like Stono are, I believe, important for those interested in salvaging the human rights conversation. For human rights to work, we have to re-imagine who speaks of human rights, who claims them, how they claim them, and what requirements are "imposed" on the claims. Most importantly, we must re-imagine who enforces them. To do all of this, we must re-imagine the history of human rights and recognize that there were and are many architects of human rights. And we must place ourselves within that history—we must recognize it, understand it, and communicate it.

THE PERSISTENCE OF THE STONO NARRATIVE

Shawn Halifax and I are driving on the route of the rebellion, approaching the place near the Edisto River where it all ended that Sunday afternoon. "The first time I drove this route, I was getting chills," he says. "I would see some large live oak trees and think that they may have been witnesses to this thing. It was pretty powerful."

"Yes," I reply, "something amazing happened here and here we are going about our daily business, in a way."

"Right. And there's so many things that you can draw from it, so many unanswered questions. There's just enough information there for you to put yourself in someone's shoes for a little while, and get it. And there's not so much information that you have to be bombarded with accuracy, with historical facts and figures. You can get that way with any number of events that are over-documented. But that's missing the point."

The point is the story. We drive by the spot, Battlefield Plantation, where one plot line in the narrative came to an end. Historians are unsure if the place was called "Battlefield" before Stono or after Stono, or perhaps after the American Revolution. Nevertheless, the freedom struggle of sixty to a hundred slaves ended here many years ago. Most of them met painful deaths, their heads put on public display. Others got away. One wonders what might have happened if they'd all made it, if they'd all escaped. But in a way, they did make it—their narrative lives on in the many struggles for human rights that followed in their wake and the many struggles that continue.

The Gullah word for morning, dawn, a new day, is "dayclean." Looking southward, in the same direction the Stono Rebels were headed, I imagine what might have been if they had escaped, kept marching onward to freedom. They, calling out "liberty," march onward in the dayclean, the dawning of a day that we have yet to reach.

NOTES

INTRODUCTION

1. Throughout I use the terms "natural rights" and "human rights" interchangeably. This may seem contentious and, perhaps, anachronous. The term "natural rights" was in vogue in the eighteenth century and was used to describe those rights one has because one is a human being. However, some writers were using the term "human rights" at the tail end of the American Enlightenment.
2. Where appropriate, I have chosen to modernize language (spelling, italicization, and capitalization) in primary source quotations. In other places, especially when quoting from the narratives of former slaves, I retain what was recorded.

CHAPTER I. CAROLINA'S COLONIAL ARCHITECTURE AND THE AGE OF RIGHTS

1. Harold Nicholson writes, "Locke is the true originator of our modern conceptions of liberty"—religious, political, and intellectual (274).
2. I use Locke's traditional section numbers throughout rather than page numbers for ease of reference.
3. John Dunn believes that Locke's toleration and the social contract rest on religious convictions—these are duties one owes to God (264).
4. The version cited here was signed on March 1, 1669, and published in London in 1670. There were several versions made over the course of the project, and a few in 1669 and 1670. However, the changes made early on were mostly for clarification (Goldie 160).
5. Today, Locke Island is called Edisto Island.
6. Kenneth M. Stampp's *The Peculiar Institution* claims that "in 1669, Carolina's Lords Proprietors promulgated John Locke's 'Fundamental Constitutions' which gave every freeman 'absolute power and authority over his negro slaves'" (18). In his oft-cited history *From Slavery to Freedom*, John Hope Franklin attributes the writing of the Fundamental Constitutions to John Locke. And because of this document, he writes, "Not only was slavery sanctioned, but its existence was protected against any presumed jeopardy to which conversion might expose it. In no other colony did slavery begin more auspiciously, nor was there

NOTES

anywhere any greater prospect for its success" (78). Howard Zinn in 1980 writes: "the Fundamental Constitutions were written in the 1660s by John Locke, who is often considered the philosophical father of the Founding Fathers and the American system" (47). In his 1998 National Book Award–winning *Slaves in the Family*, Edward Ball claims, "When the English arrived, they carried with them a social contract, the Fundamental Constitutions, written in London by the philosopher John Locke" (30). And in 2000, David Robertson in *Denmark Vesey* acknowledges that Locke, "the philosopher, secretary to one of the proprietors, devised an elaborate constitution for the new colonists, a copy of which one of the Barbadian Adventurers carried with them" (14). Robertson places much emphasis on Locke's view of religious tolerance: "And in delayed fulfillment of John Locke's insistence that the Barbadian founders practice religious tolerance, Charles Town became a sanctuary from the late 1600s for Sephardim and other Jewish refugees from Europe" (16). Again, later on, he gives Locke credit for breeding religious tolerance in South Carolina for generations to come (20, 46).

7. It is quite clear that the colony was primarily a financial venture. See John Locke, "Carolina Notebook," MS. Locke c.30, Bodleian Library, University of Oxford, SCDAH. Thank you to Fred Porcheddu for helping me to decipher this text.

8. Peter Gay paints Johnson as a sort of abolitionist (421–423).

9. In "A Declaration from the Poor Oppressed People of England" Winstanley writes that the Diggers intend "to observe the Law of righteous action, endeavoring to shut out of the creation the cursed thing, called *Particular Propriety*, which is the cause of all wars, blood-shed, theft, and enslaving Laws, that hold the people under misery" (276). This insistence on communal human rights stands in sharp contrast to the self-interest-fueled program of the mercantilists. For a thorough discussion of this concept and its relationship to colonialism, see J. E. Crowley, *This Sheba, Self* (Baltimore: The Johns Hopkins UP, 1974).

10. See Hill, *The World Turned Upside Down*.

11. Giles Calvert "printed translations of Henry Niclaes and Jacob Boehme, the works of Saltmarsh, Dell, some Levellers, most of Winstanley, the Wellingborough broadsheet, many Ranters and very many Quakers, as well as the last speeches of the regicides in 1660" (Hill, *World* 373).

12. Parliament was serious about these new laws. In 1663, John Twynn, a printer, was drawn and quartered for printing a text that supposedly called for an overthrow of the government.

CHAPTER 2. DISSENSION IN THE RANKS: REGARDING, EVALUATING, AND REVEALING SLAVERY IN EIGHTEENTH-CENTURY AMERICA

1. Robert Ferguson notes, "No revolutionary culture has ever had a higher literacy rate than [did] some of the politically volatile areas of the thirteen colonies" (86).

2. "The equivalent sales today would be fifteen million, making it, proportionally, the nation's greatest best-seller ever.... [C]opies were shared, and those who

could not read it hear it read aloud in homes, taverns, workshops, and fields" (Kaye 43).

3. Despite his rhetoric, Brackenridge advocated that slaves should colonize the western edges of the colonies rather than be liberated among currently settled areas.

4. "On African Slavery" was composed the same year (1775) Paine joined the first anti-slavery society established in the North American colonies.

5. When this pamphlet was first published there was some controversy as to its authorship. This is evidenced on the title page of the copy currently housed in the New York Public Library's Rare Books collection. The first author penciled in is "Ben Rush, a Physician of Philadelphia." Below that someone has written Anthony Benezet. David Cooper's name is nowhere to be found except in the library's catalogue.

6. This pamphlet is entitled *A Serious Address to the Rulers of America on the Inconsistency of their Conduct respecting Slavery: Forming a Contrast Between the Encroachments of England on American Liberty, and American Injustice in tolerating Slavery.*

7. African American scientist Benjamin Bannaker had already written to Jefferson a number of times before he penned these lines.

8. For an introduction to religious anti-slavery arguments in early America, see Turner's "The Anti-Slavery Movement Prior to the Abolition of the African Slave-Trade." Another useful source is Rosalie Murphy Baum's "Early-American Literature: Reassessing the Black Contribution," *Eighteenth-Century Studies* 27.4 (summer 1994): 533–549. The most thorough volumes on the subject are, of course, David Brion Davis's Pulitzer Prize–winning *The Problem of Slavery in Western Culture* as well as his *The Problem of Slavery in the Age of Revolution.*

9. See Coppe's *Fiery Flying Roll* and Winstanley's "Fire in the Bush."

10. Sandiford's dedication and preface do not have page numbers. Pagination begins with the main text. This citation appears on the second page of the dedication.

11. Sandiford, though, has his prejudices and reveals certain intolerances. Slavery, he notes, is more apropos the "Religion of Mahomet" (28).

12. Sandiford's vociferous condemnations are somewhat curious in light of his possible connections to servitude. Roberts Vaux notes that in his will Sandiford gave a life estate to his female servant (70). In addition, Library Company of Philadelphia librarian Phillip Lapsansky and I discovered an advertisement from the *Pennsylvania Gazette* (September 26, 1732) in which a "Ralph Sandiford" seeks a runaway servant by the name of "John King." Servitude, of course, is not the same as slavery, but it still implies serious restrictions on human liberty.

13. "Sons of Thunder" refers to brothers James and John, apostles in the New Testament. See Mark 3:17.

14. Benjamin Rush and Roberts Vaux recount several stories about Lay that demonstrate the passion of this anti-slavery advocate. He was often literally tossed out of meeting. On one such occasion he remained sprawled across the

NOTES

meeting house threshold, forcing attendees to walk over him as they left. Once Lay took his boot off in the midst of winter and buried his bare foot in a snow bank. When told to stop by some Friends, he asked why they were showing concern for him when they make their slaves work in the winter barely clothed.

15. The title is *All Slave-Keepers that Keep the Innocent in Bondage, Apostates Pretending to lay Claim to the Pure & Holy Christian Religion; of what Congregation so ever; but especially in their Ministers, by whole example the filthy Leprosy and Apostacy is spread far and near; it is a notorious Sin, which many of the true Friends of Christ, and his pure Truth called Quakers, has been for many Years, and still are concern'd to write and bear Testimony against; as a Practice so gross and hurtful to Religion, and destructive to Government, beyond what Words can set forth, or can be declared of by Men or Angels, and yet lived in by Ministers and Magistrates in America.*

16. South Carolina banned the slave trade in 1787, but re-opened it in 1803. Because the slave trade continued despite the ban, it was deemed unenforceable.

CHAPTER 3. CLAIMING RIGHTS: THE STONO REBELS STRIKE FOR LIBERTY

1. Peter Wood's *Black Majority* provides a thorough account of South Carolina's slave population prior to the Stono Rebellion as well as one of the most important discussions of the rebellion itself. I am personally indebted to Professor Wood; his research opened up a page in my home state's history that had been hidden from me. Gratitude is also due to Mark M. Smith, who has, as of late, recovered several "forgotten" sources of the Stono Rebellion.
2. I have chosen to retain the recorded "dialects" of those interviewed by WPA interviewers. For a more thorough discussion of this project, see chapter 7.
3. "Whereas it hath been represented . . ." *South Carolina Gazette* (80), July 21–28, 1733.
4. The slave culture developing in South Carolina was quite different from that which was developing in the Chesapeake region of Virginia, where slaves were less dispersed and plantations more developed. See Gerald Mullin.
5. William Bull became lieutenant governor, in effect, "acting governor," in 1737. The appointed governor was James Glen, who did not come to the colony until 1743.
6. There were approximately thirty-nine thousand blacks and twenty thousand whites (Wood 131–166).
7. There is some confusion about the name of the leader of the slave rebellion. David Ramsay refers to the slave leader as Cato, and this is repeated elsewhere in written (most famously by William Gilmore Simms) and oral accounts (63). In his *American Negro Slavery*, U. B. Phillips calls him "Jonny" (473). The general consensus is that his name was Jemmy. I will discuss this controversy further in chapter 7. See also Wood 315, n. 26.
8. Robert Olwell places the slaves' rendezvous on Saturday night, September 8, 1739 (51–52).

9. Today, this is off of Highway 17, the Savannah Highway, about twenty miles outside of Charleston, near the bridge at Wallace Creek. A historical marker erected by the Sea Island Farmer's Cooperative marks the spot.
10. In a description of the colony in 1770, William Bull cites what he believes to be the cause of the Stono Rebellion: "that indeed took rise from the wantonness, and not oppression of our slaves, for too great a number had been very indiscreetly assembled and encamped together for several nights, to do a large work on the public road; with a slack inspection; but such indiscretion is now provided against the law" (260).
11. Displaying heads was a common practice in England and in the South Carolina colony. The *South Carolina Gazette* (January 22–29, 1731) provides one example of the practice: "One day last week, Mr. Charles Jones pursuing a runaway Negro, who had robbed him, and coming up with the Negro, he refused and fought him, and he struck the lock of his musket into the Negro's skull and kill'd him. He went and told a justice what he had done, who ordered him to cut his head off, fix it on a pole, and set it up in a cross road, which was done accordingly near Ashley Ferry." See also Wood 282–284. Decapitation was a common post-rebellion punishment well into the nineteenth century. And, yet, there is no certainty as to any specific symbolic significance of decapitation for the Stono Rebels. I have not yet discovered any specific symbolic meaning attached to decapitation in Kongolese culture. Therefore, we can speculate that this moment served as a warning, a declaration of intent, or as some sort of retributive act.
12. Today, the former site of these plantations is home to the Caw Caw Interpretive Center. Shawn Halifax, an historian employed by the center, helped me put the pieces of the actual rebellion puzzle together, and I am indebted to his advice and observations.
13. David Ramsay writes that Bull "crossed over to Johns island thence came to Charlestown with the first intelligence" (111). According to Ramsay, a Mr. Golightly informed the church at Wiltown. This version of events appears only in Ramsay's account, which incorrectly dates the event as having occurred in 1740 rather than 1739. Edward McCrady provides a similar account though his dates are correct (185).
14. Bullock or Bulloch was apparently married to Jean Stobo, daughter of Rev. Archibald Stobo.
15. Oral history accounts claim that a large oak tree marked the center of the field where the final engagement of the Stono Rebellion occurred. This tree was called "Battlefield Oak"; however, there is no evidence that the tree is still alive. See Beulah Glover's *Vanished Towns around Colleton County* (Walterboro Book Club, 1947).
16. See Le Jau 55, 108, 121, 130.
17. I borrow this term, "uncanny networks," from Geert Lovink's analysis of contemporary media studies, *Uncanny Networks: Dialogues with the Virtual Intelligentsia* (Cambridge: MIT Press, 2002).

18. Networks are sets of nodes linked by some particular relationship. "Nodes may consist of individuals, organizations, and eventually—if more rarely—other entities such as neighborhoods or states. They may also consist of events linked by persons, or as in some recent application, even of elements of speech" (Diani 6–7).
19. Aptheker provides perhaps the best summary of slave revolts in the Americas.
20. See Linebaugh and Rediker 194. Le Jau mentions a plot in Goose Creek around Christmas in 1713.
21. See Mellville J. Herskovits, Sidney W. Mintz and Richard Price, and Sterling Stuckey, for example.
22. Mark M. Smith's "Remembering Mary, Shaping Revolt: Reconsidering the Stono Rebellion" and John K. Thornton's "African Dimensions of the Stono Rebellion."
23. Thornton claims, "At that time, Brazil was the only region that had a greater percentage of Kongolese among its people" (*Kongolese* 211).
24. Both Alexander Hewatt (73) and Edward Pearson (22) attribute this dancing to a premature celebration.
25. See Landers 34.
26. Víctor Andrés Belaúnde asserts rather glowingly that the principles of human rights and of individual human dignity were in the air throughout the Spanish colonial era. He notes, "To be sure colonial policy often contradicted the principles which follow the concept of human personality" (Belaúnde and Crawford 82). While this is clear, he claims that we cannot discount the efforts of many to legislate rights on behalf of slaves and indigenous populations and that the ideology undergirding those efforts had roots in the Catholic belief in the human personality.
27. Alexander Hewatt writes as though the law was in place at the time of the rebellion and, thus, the white men at Stobo's church in Wiltown had their guns on them when Bull and company arrived to warn them of the rebellion. However, this assertion cannot be corroborated though other sources (Hewatt 73). One could assume that some men were in the habit of carrying their guns to church, but the record shows that the *requirement* to carry arms to church went into effect on September 29.
28. For more on this phenomenon see Richards.
29. In most cases Le Jau cites instances where masters opposed having their slaves baptized. Becoming literate, though, often went along with being baptized. For more on this, see Le Jau 50–51, 55, 60.
30. A letter from Andrew Leslie of St. Paul's Parish, site of the Stono Rebellion, dated December 29, 1736, was also read at this same meeting. Leslie mentions the rural nature of the parish, as many of his flock lived quite far apart and had trouble attending services.
31. For a thorough account of Hugh Bryan, see Jackson. Also of interest is a letter Bryan wrote to the *South Carolina Gazette*, published in the January 1, 1741, issue.

32. This liberation theology reminds one of Winstanley, Sandiford, and Lay, among others discussed above.
33. See Thomas J. Davis.
34. From the *Boston News Letter*, September 25, 1729. Elizabeth Donnan notes, "There is nothing unusual about this disaster to the *Clare* save the wide publicity which it seems to have received" (274). News of the event was printed in the *Country Journal, Weekly Journal or British Gazette, Fog's Weekly Journal*, and the *Gloucester Journal*.
35. Some historians have placed greater emphasis on the relationship of work to rebellion than I do here. For example, Eugene D. Genovese's argument in *Roll, Jordan, Roll* that slave rebellions were an "ultimate manifestation of class war" (588) or Edward Pearson's argument that Stono was the result of changing work relations for men and women.
36. The passage Stampp cites is from Benjamin Drew's *The Refugee: or the Narratives of Fugitive Slaves in Canada* (Boston, 1856), 27.
37. George Cato claims, "From dat day to dis, no Cato has tasted whiskey" (99).
38. Peter Wood in *Slavery and the Making of America: The Downward Spiral* (Thirteen/WNET, video recording; New York: Ambrose Video, 2005).
39. There are many examples of humans using cultural practices and artistic expression in order to assert their humanity. One that comes to mind is Rafael Schachter's interpretation of Verdi's *Requiem* at Terezin concentration camp. This performance was an act of defiance and an expression of human dignity amidst traumatic circumstances. His project was disrupted more than once when members of the chorus were shipped off to be murdered.

CHAPTER 4. NEGRO ACTS: COMMUNICATION AND AFRICAN AMERICAN DECLARATIONS OF INDEPENDENCE

1. Perhaps the South Carolina media response to Stono may be considered the norm. Winthrop Jordan notes, "Most striking of all reactions to the Gabriel plot was the virtually complete silence in the Charleston press, a silence not attributable to lack of interest" (395).
2. See the *Pennsylvania Gazette*, November 8, 1739. British periodicals that contain references to the rebellion include the *London Daily Post*, the *Daily Gazetteer of London*, the *Gentleman's Magazine, London and Country Journal, London Evening Post, London Magazine*, and the *Scots Magazine*.
3. In 1740 George Whitefield writes, "One of my friends inferred, that these Negroes might be some of those who lately had made an insurrection in the province, and had run away from their masters" (380).
4. South Carolinians had been unnerved by public gatherings of slaves before. See *South Carolina Gazette*, March 23–30, 1733.
5. In their introduction to *The Slave's Narrative*, Charles T. Davis and Henry Louis Gates Jr. refer to the Negro Act, citing it as evidence of the "correlation of political rights and literacy" (xxiv).

6. Article 11 of the French Declaration of the Rights of Man and of the Citizen: "La libre communication des pensées et des opinions est un des droits les plus précieux de l'homme ; tout citoyen peut donc parler, écrire, imprimer librement" or "Free communication of ideas and opinions is one of the most precious of the rights of man. Consequently, every citizen may speak, write, and print freely." This is, perhaps, the first clear articulation of the human right to communicate freely in a broad sense. See "The French Declaration of the Rights of Man and Citizen (1789)." *The Human Rights Reader.* Ed. Micheline Ishay. New York: Routledge, 1997. Also see http://www.hrcr.org/docs/frenchdec.html.
7. It is a "potential" right because it, in fact, does not exist as a legal right, even though it has manifested in a variety of policy papers and international covenants, most recently in the 2005 UNESCO Convention on the Protection and Promotion of the Diversity of Cultural Expression, Article 2.1.
8. Some of these rights are defined by Articles 18 (belief/religion), 20 (assembly), and even 26 (education) and 27 (participate in cultural life). Education is particularly important in an age where access to information and the ability to exchange it influence one's economic stability. "United Nations Universal Declaration of Human Rights." *The Human Rights Reader.* Ed. Micheline Ishay. New York: Routledge, 1997.
9. Brent Staples makes the connection between access to literacy in the nineteenth century and how that relates to the success of present-day African Americans. He writes, "In the 1940's . . . the sociologist E. Horace Fitchett surveyed students at Howard University, then the seat of the black elite. Half of his respondents claim to be descended from that small part of the black population that was free before Emancipation, which typically had greater access to education." These students came from literate families capable of avoiding "swindlers who regularly stripped illiterate people of land and other assets. For these families, literacy was a form of social capital that could be passed from one generation to the next." See Staples.
10. See chapter 3, note 2.
11. Prohibitions on teaching slaves to read and write seem to have been reasserted often South Carolina. One such reassertion came in December 1834 and suggested penalties for whites and blacks teaching slaves to read or write.
12. Benjamin Quarles writes about the effect of another American Revolution on blacks in the United States: "Black Americans, not unexpectedly, gave an entirely different reading to these war-spawned concepts. To them freedom was everyone's birthright; everyone had certain inalienable rights. . . . To black Americans the theory of natural rights did not lose its relevance with the departure of the British troops. Blacks were left no choice other than to oppose all efforts to de-revolutionize the Revolution" (293).
13. An appropriate and relevant analysis is Henry Louis Gates Jr.'s assertion of intertextuality among the "signifying monkey" stories (60–61).

NOTES

14. This declaration was entitled "To the Honorable Council and House of Representatives of the State of Massachusetts-Bay in General Court assembled January 13th 1777: The Petition of a great number of Negroes who are detained in a state of Slavery in the Bowels of a free and Christian Country Humbly Shewing" (see Hall).
15. Prince Hall (1735?–1807) was either freeborn or was manumitted later in life. Hall organized a society that later became a Masonic lodge, African Lodge No. 459, on May 6, 1787.
16. The poem's complete title is, "To the Right Honourable William, Earl of Dartmouth, His Majesty's Principal Secretary of state for North-America, &c."
17. Omar ibn Said, also called Uncle Moreau or Moro, was Fullah and was born near the Senegal and Bounon rivers, captured, and brought to Charleston in 1807. During his life in Africa he made the hajj to Mecca. Said died in North Carolina in 1863 or 1864
18. See Scott.

CHAPTER 5. THE HEIRS OF JEMMY: SLAVE REBELS IN NINETEENTH-CENTURY AFRICAN AMERICAN FICTION

1. I borrow this concept of "manipulating sentiments" as a method for exposing the public to human rights abuses from Richard Rorty (263).
2. Martin Delany (born May 6, 1812; died January 24, 1885) spent much time in South Carolina serving in the Freedman's Bureau at Hilton Head. He was involved in politics and made an unsuccessful run for lieutenant governor.
3. A similar ecumenicalism was necessary to create a unified public during the American Revolution. See chapter 2.

CHAPTER 6. PLANTATION TRADITIONS: RACISM AND THE TRANSFORMATION OF THE STONO NARRATIVE

1. Related terms include "Confederate romance" or literature of the "lost cause."
2. Grayson was born in Beaufort, South Carolina, on November 10, 1788, and died in Newberry, October 4, 1863.
3. Timrod was born on December 8, 1828, in Charleston and died October 7, 1867, in Columbia after suffering from tuberculosis and intense poverty in the wake of the war. Timrod's supposed mixed-race ancestry is rather interesting given the company he kept. His mother was supposedly a quadroon, and court records indicate that his great-grandmother was once prohibited from testifying in a court cause because she was a free black. For another perspective on this, see Taylor.
4. For a thorough discussion of the pastoral in Southern poetry, see Barge.
5. Caroline Lee Hentz's *The Planter's Northern Bride* (1854) also falls within this genre. There are earlier examples of defenses of slavery in fiction, for example, John Pendleton Kennedy's *Swallow Barn* (1832).
6. This situation—damsel in distress amidst an attack on a "cabin in the pines"—is replayed in the cabin attack scene in D. W. Griffith's *Birth of a Nation* when a

- 192 -

rabble of carpetbaggers and black soldiers breaks into a cabin serving as the last refuge for a white family.
7. Thank you to Mark M. Smith for "recovering" this story and bringing it to my attention. Another exception to the rule is Joshua Coffin's mention of Stono in his *Account of Some of the Principal Slave Insurrections* (1860).
8. Quincy also wrote a short novel called *Wensley* that was first published in *Putnam's Journal* in 1853.
9. This despite the fact that the actual rebellion took place in the section of the South Carolina known as the Lowcountry—specifically, fifteen miles south of Charleston.
10. In an essay exploring the connections between Quincy, Frederick Douglass, Herman Melville, and Lemuel Shaw, Robert K. Wallace presents several unsavory phrases from Quincy's pen that reveal Quincy's racist side. See Stewart (103–104) and Wallace.
11. *Gone with the Wind* was published in 1936 and the movie based on the book premiered in 1939.
12. I borrow this concept from Amartya Sen's *Development as Freedom* (New York: Knopf, 1999).
13. "South Carolina Roll of Dead," May 27, 2008 http://www.scor.org/Events/RollofDead.htm.
14. One interesting example of this is John J. Dargan's *School History of South Carolina* (1906). In a chapter entitled "Negro Insurrections," he claims that slaves were generally content. "History has recorded only two uprisings of slaves in South Carolina" (129). One "was led by the negro Cato, and is known as the Stono Insurrection, or the 'Gullah War.' It resulted in the butchering of a few white men, women, and children, and in the robbery and burning of some homes. A company of whites was soon formed under Captain Bee. They overtook the negroes, drunk on the liquors that they had taken from the homes of the whites and carousing in the nosiest manner." They were caught off guard and easily defeated. Cato was executed. In the end, "the whites showed great moderation and self-control after the capture. The most prominent and vicious rioters were brought to regular trial by the courts, and, after legal sentence, were hanged; but most of the captives were pardoned" (130).

CHAPTER 7. DOIN' DE RIGHT: THE PERSISTENCE OF THE STONO NARRATIVE

1. Norman Yetman offers an introduction to this project. See also Donna J. Spindel, "Assessing Memory: Twentieth-Century Slave Narratives Reconsidered," *Journal of Interdisciplinary History* 27.2 (autumn 1996): 247–261.
2. South Carolina's WPA guidebook includes a discussion of slavery and of the Stono Rebellion. Its authors note, "Until the Revolutionary War the number of slaves rose consistently. Although the fears of possible revolt increased, desire for more wealth and more slaves outweighed them. Opposition to the formal education of Negroes came early in the eighteenth century, after it was noted

that the slave insurrections were usually led by Negroes of some learning" (46). A discussion of Stono follows directly afterward and includes the text of Bull's eyewitness account (46–47). See *South Carolina: A Guide to the Palmetto State*, WPA (New York: Oxford, 1941).

3. For examples of this see chapters 3 and 4.
4. See *Hill's Columbia City Directory* (Richmond: Hill Directory, Inc., 1937). George Cato is listed in directories from 1934 to 1939.
5. For a more thorough discussion, see Carol Anderson's *Eyes off the Prize: The United Nations and the African American Struggle for Human Rights, 1944–1955* (New York: Cambridge UP, 2003).
6. Patricia H. Kline and Paul A. Horne Jr., *South Carolina: Its History and Geography* (Selma: Clairmont Press, 2000).
7. Another more recent textbook that mentions Stono is Joel Walker and Donald O. Stewart's *The South Carolina Adventure* (Salt Lake City: Gibbs Smith, 2005). Also published in 2005 is Scott Foresman's *Social Studies: South Carolina* (New York: Pearson, 2005). Foresman's account of Stono refers to the rebel leader as Cato. He writes, "The Stono Rebllion occurred near the Stono River in 1739. Led by Cato, the group broke into a store, stole guns, and killed the owners. When this rebellion ended, about 75 people had died" (134).
8. Wallace's Creek is now officially known as Wallace's River.
9. Benjamin Elliot, "To Our Northern Brethren," *Charleston City Gazette and Commercial Advertiser*, September 27, 1822. This letter was reprinted for the perusal of those "Northern Brethren" in the *Providence Patriot*, November 23, 1822.

BIBLIOGRAPHY

SPECIAL COLLECTIONS

Library Company of Philadelphia. Philadelphia, Pennsylvania.
New York City Public Library Rare Books. New York, New York. (NYPL)
South Carolina Department of Archives and History. Columbia, South Carolina. (SCDAH)
South Carolina Historical Society. Charleston, South Carolina.
South Caroliniana Library. Columbia, South Carolina. (SCL)

PRIMARY SOURCES

"Advice from Charles-Town." *London and Country Journal*, November 20, 1739.

American Papers of the Society for the Propagation of the Gospel in Foreign Parts: Meeting Minutes. MS vol. bd. Microfilm, reel 3 (R742) and 4 (R743). SCL.

An Account of the Late Intended Insurrection among a Portion of the Blacks of This City: Published by the Authority of the Corporation of Charleston. Charleston: A. E. Miller, 1822. This will be cited in the text as *Account 1822*.

"An Account of the Negroe Insurrection in South Carolina." *The Colonial Records of the State of Georgia*. Ed. Allen D. Candler, William L. Northern, and Lucian L. Knight. Vol. 22.2. Atlanta: Byrd, 1913. 232–236. This will be cited in the text as "Account."

"An Account of the Negro Insurrection in South-Carolina." *London Magazine and Monthly Chronologer* 9 (March 1740): 151–152. This will be cited in the text as "Account, London."

"An Act for the Better Ordering and Governing Negroes and Other Slaves in this Province." *The Statutes at Large of South Carolina*. Ed. Thomas Cooper and David J. McCord. Columbia: Johnston, 1840.

"An Act for the better Security of the Inhabitants of this Province against the Insurrections and other wicked Attempts of Negroes and other Slaves." *South Carolina Gazette*, August 11–August 18, 1739. SCDAH.

Adams, Samuel. *The Rights of the Colonists: The Report of the Committee of Correspondence to the Boston Town Meeting, Nov. 20, 1772.* Old South Leaflets no. 173. Boston: Directors of the Old South Work, 1906. 7: 417–428.

Alexander, Ann Tuke. "An Address to the Inhabitants of Charleston, South Carolina." Philadelphia: Kimber, Conrad, and Company, 1805. Repr. in *Early American Abolitionists: A Collection of Anti-Slavery Writings, 1760–1820.* Ed. James G. Basker. New York: Gilder Lehrman Institute of American History, 2005.

Benezet, Anthony, and John Wesley. *Views of American Slavery.* New York: Arno Press, 1969.

Bethune, Mary McLeod. "Clarifying Our Vision with the Facts." *Journal of Negro History* 23.1 (January 1938): 10–15.

———. "Closed Doors." *Sisters in the Struggle: African American Women in the Civil Rights–Black Power Movement.* Ed. Bettye Collier-Thomas and V. P. Franklin. New York: New York UP, 2001.

Bontemps, Arna. *Black Thunder: Gabriel's Revolt, Virginia, 1800.* Boston: Beacon Press, 1992.

Boswell, James. *Life of Johnson.* London: Oxford UP, 1970.

Brackenridge, Hugh Henry. *A Hugh Henry Brackenridge Reader.* Ed. Daniel Marder. Pittsburgh, Penn.: U of Pittsburgh P, 1970.

Bull, William. "Governor William Bull's Representation of the Colony, 1770." *Colonial South Carolina Scene: Contemporary Views, 1697–1774.* Ed. H. Roy Merrens. Columbia: U of South Carolina P, 1977.

Cato, George. "The Stono Insurrection Described by a Descendant of the Leader." *The American Slave: A Composite Autobiography*, Supplement, ser. 1. Vol. 11: *North Carolina and South Carolina Narratives.* Ed. George P. Rawick. Westport, Conn.: Greenwood, 1977. 98–100.

Cooper, David. *A Mite Cast into the Treasury: or, Observations on Slave-Keeping.* Philadelphia, 1772. Repr. in *Early American Abolitionists: A Collection of Anti-Slavery Writings, 1760–1820.* Ed. James G. Basker. New York: Gilder Lehrman Institute of American History, 2005.

———. *A Serious Address . . .* Trenton, 1783. Repr. in *Early American Abolitionists: A Collection of Anti-Slavery Writings, 1760–1820.* Ed. James G. Basker. New York: Gilder Lehrman Institute of American History, 2005.

Crèvecoeur, J. Hector St. John de. *Letters from an American Farmer.* Gloucester, Mass: Peter Smith, 1968.

"La Déclaration des Droits de l'homme et du citoyen, 1789." *Conseil Constititutionnel.* September 24, 2008. http://www.conseil-constitutionnel.fr/textes/d1789.htm.

Declaration of the Rights of Man and of the Citizen, 1789. Accessed July 4, 2008 http://www.hrcr.org/docs/frenchdec.html.

Delany, Martin R. *Blake; or, The Huts of America.* Boston: Beacon Press, 1970.

"Diary entry, Friday, Sept 28, 1739." *Detailed Reports on the Salzberger Emigrants Who Settled in America . . . Edited by Samuel Urlsperger.* Vol. 6. 1739. Repr. Trans. and

Ed. George Fenwick Jones and Renate Wilson. Athens: U of Georgia P, 1981. 226.

Douglass, Frederick. *The Heroic Slave. Three Classic African-American Novels.* Ed. William L. Andrews. New York: Mentor, 1990.

———. *Narrative of the Life of Frederick Douglass, An American Slave, Written By Himself.* Norton Critical Edition. Ed. William L. Andrews and William S. McFeely. New York: Norton, 1997.

———. "What to the Slave is the Fourth of July?" *Narrative of the Life of Frederick Douglass, An American Slave, Written By Himself.* Norton Critical Edition. Ed. William L. Andrews and William S. McFeely. New York: Norton, 1997.

Du Bois, W. E. B. *The Souls of Black Folk.* New York: Norton, 1999.

Dulaney, Marvin. Personal interview. June 25, 2008.

Dwight, Timothy. *Greenfield Hill: A Poem in Seven Parts.* New York: Childs and Swaine, 1794.

Easterby, J. H., ed. *The Colonial Records of South Carolina: The Journal of the Commons House of Assembly.* Vol. 2, *Sept. 12, 1739–May 10, 1740.* Columbia: Historical Commission of South Carolina, 1953. 83–84.

Elliot, Benjamin. "To Our Northern Brethren." *Charleston City Gazette and Commercial Advertiser,* September 27, 1822.

Equiano, Olaudah. *The Interesting Life of Olaudah Equiano, or Gustavus Vassa, the African.* Leeds: James Nichols, 1814. Repr. in *The Classic Slave Narratives.* Ed. Henry Louis Gates Jr. New York: Mentor, 1987.

"Extract of a Letter from S. Carolina." *Scots Magazine* 2 (March 1740): 138–139.

"Extract of a Letter from South Carolina, Dated October 2." *Gentleman's Magazine* 10 (March 1740): 127–129.

"Extract of a Letter from South Carolina, Dated September 15, 1739." *Daily Gazetteer of London,* November 17, 1739.

Franklin, Benjamin. *The Autobiography of Benjamin Franklin.* New Haven: Yale UP, 2003.

Grayson, William. *Hireling and the Slave Chicora, and Other Poems.* Charleston: McCarter & Co., 1856. Repr. Miami, Fla.: Mnemosyne Pub. Co., 1969.

Grimké, Angelina. *Appeal to the Christian Women of the South.* New York: New York Anti-Slavery Society, 1836. Repr. Ed. Lloyd Benson and Ryan Burgess. Greenville, S.C.: Furman U, 2006. Accessed May 1, 2008 http://history.furman.edu/~benson/docs/grimke2.htm.

Gronniosaw, James Albert Ukawsaw. *A Narrative of the Most Remarkable Particulars in the Life of James Albert Ukawsaw Gronniosaw, an African Prince, Written by Himself.* Newport, R.I.: Solomon Southwick, 1774. Repr. Documentary Sources Database. American Multiculturalism Series. Unit One. Documenting the African American Experience. Accessed March 3, 2008 http://etext.virginia.edu/readex/13311.html.

Halifax, Shawn. Personal interview. March 10, 2008.

Hall, Prince. "A Charge Delivered to the African Lodge, June 24, 1797, at Menotomy." *Early Negro Writing, 1760–1837*. Ed. Dorothy Porter. Boston: Beacon Press, 1971.

———. "To the Honorable Council & House of Representatives for the State of Massachusetts-Bay in General Court assembled January 13th 1777." *Massachusetts Historical Collections*. 5th series, no. 3. Ed. Jeremy Belknap. Boston, 1788. Repr. *The Heath Anthology of American Literature*. 5th ed. Ed. Paul Lauter. Boston: Houghton Mifflin Company, 2006.

Haynes, Lemuel. "Liberty Further Extended: Or Free Thoughts on the Illegality of Slave-Keeping." *Black Preacher to White America*. Ed. Richard Newman. Brooklyn: Carlson Publishing, 1990.

Henry, Patrick. "Patrick Henry to Robert Pleasants, January 18, 1773." Repr. *The Spirit of Seventy-Six*. Ed. Henry Steele Commager and Richard B. Morris. Edison, N.J.: Castle Books, 2002.

Hewatt, Alexander. *An Historical Account of the Rise and Progress of the Colonies of South Carolina and Georgia*. 2 vols. London: Alexander Donaldson, 1779. NYPL.

Higginson, Thomas Wentworth. *Army Life in a Black Regiment*. New York: Longmans, Green, and Co., 1896.

Hinrichs, Johann. "Diary of Captain Johann Hinrichs: Feb. 4, 1780." Trans. Bernard A. Uhlendorf. *The Siege of Charleston*. Ann Arbor: U of Michigan P, 1938.

Holy Bible: King James Version Authorized in 1611. Nashville: Holman Bible Publishers, 1973.

Hurmence, Belinda, ed. *Before Freedom When I Just Can Remember: Twenty Seven Oral Histories of Former South Carolina Slaves*. Winston-Salem: John F. Blair, 1989.

Inabinett, Curtis. Personal interview. June 18, 2008.

Jacobs, Harriet A. *Incidents in the Life of a Slave Girl Written by Herself*. Ed. Jean Fagin Yellin. Cambridge: Harvard UP, 1987.

Jefferson, Thomas. *Notes on the State of Virginia*. New York: Penguin Books, 1999.

———. *Writings*. New York: Library of America, 1984.

Johnson, Samuel. *Political Writings*. Ed. Donald J. Greene. New Haven: Yale UP, 1977.

Kalu, Obi. Personal interview. June 19, 2008.

Ladd, Joseph Brown. *The Literary Remains of Joseph Brown Ladd*. Ed. Elizabeth Haskins. New York: Garrett Press, 1970.

Laurens, Henry. "Henry Laurens to John Laurens." Repr. in *The Spirit of Seventy-Six*. Ed. Henry Steele Commager and Richard B. Morris. Edison, N.J.: Castle Books, 2002.

Lay, Benjamin. *All Slave-keepers that Keep the Innocent in Bondage, Apostates....* New York: Arno Press, 1969.

Le Jau, Francis. *The Carolina Chronicle of Dr. Francis Le Jau, 1706–1717*. Ed. Frank J. Klingberg. Berkeley and Los Angeles: U of California P, 1956.

Leslie, Andrew. "St. Paul Parish to the Society for the Propagation of the Gospel, January 7, 1739 [1740]." SPG Records. Microfilm, reel 5. SCDAH.

"A Letter from South Carolina [dated September 28, 1739]." *Boston Weekly News-Letter*, November 1–8, 1739.

"Letters from Carolina." *London Daily Post*, November 17, 1739.

"Letters from Carolina." *London Evening Post*, November 15, 1739.

"Letters from Charlestown in SC, of the 14th of September." *Boston Gazette*, October 29–November 5, 1739.

"Letters from South-Carolina." *London General Evening Post*, November 15, 1739.

Locke, John. *First Treatise on Civil Government. Two Treatises of Government and A Letter Concerning Toleration*. Ed. Ian Shapiro. New Haven: Yale UP, 2003.

———. "The Fundamental Constitutions of Carolina." London: 1670. Early English Books Online. Denison U Library, Granville, Ohio. Accessed May 20, 2008 http://-eebo.chadwyck.com.

———. "Letter Concerning Toleration." *The Works of Locke*. Vol. 5. London: Printed for Thomas Tegg, 1824.

———. *Political Essays*. Ed. Mark Goldie. Cambridge: Cambridge UP, 1997.

———. *Second Treatise on Civil Government. Social Contract: Essays by Locke, Hume, and Rousseau*. Ed. Sir Ernest Barker. New York: Oxford UP, 1960.

Martyn, Benjamin. "An Impartial Enquiry into the State and Utility of the Province of Georgia." *Voices of the Old South: Eyewitness Accounts*. Athens: U of Georgia P, 1994.

Milton, John. *The Complete Poems*. Ed. John Leonard. New York: Penguin, 1998.

Morton, Sarah Wentworth Apthorp. "The African Chief." *My Mind and Its Thoughts in Sketches, Fragments, and Essays*. Reproduction. Delmar, N.Y.: Scholars' Facsimiles and Reprints, 1975.

———. *Beacon Hill*. Repr. in *Early American Abolitionists: A Collection of Anti-Slavery Writings, 1760–1820*. Ed. James G. Basker. New York: Gilder Lehrman Institute of American History, 2005.

"Number IX. Darien." *The Colonial Records of the State of Georgia*. Ed. Allen D. Candler, William L. Northern, and Lucian L. Knight. Vol. 3. Atlanta: Byrd, 1913. Repr. New York: AMS Press, 1970. 427–428.

Oglethorpe, James. "Charlestown, South-Carolina, April 1, 1740." *New-York Weekly Journal*, no. 333, April 28, 1740. *America's Historical Newspapers: Early American Newspapers*. Series 1–5, *1690–1922*. Infoweb. Denison U Library, Granville, Ohio. Accessed March 3, 2008 http://o-infoweb.newsbank.com>.

Otis, James. "The Rights of the British Colonies Asserted and Proved." *Am I Not a Man and a Brother: The Antislavery Crusade of Revolutionary America*. Ed. Roger Bruns. New York: Chelsea House Publishers, 1977.

Paine, Thomas. *The Thomas Paine Reader*. Ed. Michael Foot and Isaac Kramnick. New York: Penguin Books, 1987.

———. *Rights of Man*. London: Wordsworth, 1996.

Pennsylvania Gazette. November 8, 1739.

Pinckney, Eliza Lucas. *The Letterbook of Eliza Lucas Pinckney, 1739–1762*. Ed. Elise Pinckney. Chapel Hill: U of North Carolina P, 1972.

Pinckney, Thomas (Achates). *Reflections, Occasioned by the Late Disturbances in Charleston*. Charleston: A. E. Miller, 1822. Repr. Westport, Conn.: Negro UP, 1970.

Pringle, Robert. "To John Richards." *The Letterbook of Robert Pringle*. Ed. Walter Edgar. Columbia: U of South Carolina P, 1972.

Purry, Peter. "Proposals by Mr. Peter Purry, of Newfchatel . . ." Charlestown, 1731. Repr. in *Historical Collections of South Carolina*. Vol. 2. Ed. B. R. Carroll. New York: Harper, 1836.

Quincy, Edmund. "Mother Coelia." *Liberty Bell* (Boston). 1839: 10–17.

———. "Mount Verney: Or, an Incident of Insurrection." *Liberty Bell* (Boston) 1847: 165–228. Repr. in *Stono: Documenting and Interpreting a Southern Slave Revolt*. Ed. Mark M. Smith. Columbia: U of South Carolina P, 2005.

The Qur'an: Translation. Trans. N. J. Dawood. New York: Penguin Books, 1990.

"A Ranger's Report of Travels with General Oglethorpe, 1739–42." *Travels in the American Colonies*. Ed. Newton D. Mereness. New York: Antiquarian Press, Ltd., 1916. 222–223.

Rawick, George P., ed. *South Carolina Narratives*. Westport, Conn.: Greenwood Publishing Company, 1972.

"Report of the Committee Appointed to Enquire into the Causes of the Disappointment of Success in the Late Expedition against St. Augustine—July 1, 1741." *The Colonial Records of South Carolina: The Journal of the Commons House of Assembly, May 18, 1741–July 10, 1742*. Ed. J. H. Easterby. Columbia: Historical Commission of South Carolina, 1953. 83–84.

Rousseau, Jean-Jacques. *Discourse on Inequality: Rousseau's Political Writings*. Ed. Alan Ritter and Julia Conway Bondanella. New York: W. W. Norton and Company, 1988.

———. "The Social Contract." *Social Contract: Essays by Locke, Hume, and Rousseau*. Ed. Ernest Barker. New York: Oxford UP, 1960.

Rush, Benjamin. *An Address on the Slavery of the Negroes in North America*. New York: Arno Press, 1969.

Said, Omar ibn. "Autobiography of Omar ibn Said, Slave in North Carolina, 1831." Ed. John Franklin Jameson. *American Historical Review* 30.4 (July 1925): 787–795.

Sandiford, Ralph. *A Brief Examination of the Practice of the Times*. New York: Arno Press, 1969.

Sewall, Samuel. "The Selling of Joseph." *Am I Not a Man and a Brother: The Antislavery Crusade of Revolutionary America*. Ed. Roger Bruns. New York: Chelsea House Publishers, 1977.

Simms, William Gilmore. *The History of South Carolina*. New York: Redfield, 1860.

———. *Views and Reviews in American Literature History and Fiction*. 1st series. Ed. C. Hugh Holman. Cambridge: Belknap P of Harvard UP, 1962.

———. *Woodcraft, or Hawks about the Dovecote.* New York: Norton, 1961.
———. *The Yemassee.* New York: Twayne, 1964.
"Sir Peter Colleton to Locke, [about October 1673]." *The Correspondence of John Locke.* Ed. E. S. De Beer. Oxford: Clarendon Press, 1976.
South Carolina Gazette. January 8, 1732–December 27, 1742. Microfilm, reel 1, SCL.
Stephens, William. "A Journal of the Proceedings in Georgia, Beginning October 24, 1737." *The Colonial Records of the State of Georgia.* Vol. 4. Ed. Allen D. Candler. Atlanta: Franklin, 1906. 412–413.
Timrod, Henry. *Poems of Henry Timrod.* Richmond: B. F. Johnson Publishing Company, 1901.
"To the Honorable David Ramsay Esquire President and to the rest of the Honorable New Members of the Senate of the State of South Carolina . . ." Repr. "Eighteenth Century Petition of South Carolina Negroes." Ed. Herbert Aptheker. *Journal of Negro History* 31:1 (January 1946): 98–99.
Voltaire. *Candide: The Portable Voltaire.* Ed. Ben Ray Redman. New York: Penguin, 1968.
Walker, David. *David Walker's Appeal.* Ed. Peter P. Hinks. University Park: Pennsylvania State UP, 2000.
Wheatley, Phillis. *The Poems of Phillis Wheatley.* Ed. Julian D. Mason Jr. Chapel Hill: U of North Carolina P, 1989.
Whitefield, George. *George Whitefield's Journals.* Ed. William V. Davis. Gainsville, Fla.: Scholars' Facsimiles & Reprints, 1969.
Winstanley, Gerrard. *The Works of Gerrard Winstanley.* Ed. George H. Sabine. New York: Russell and Russell, 1965.
Woolman, John. *The Journal of John Woolman and a Plea for the Poor.* The John Greenleaf Whittier Edition Text. New York: Citadel Press, 1961.
———. "Some Considerations on the Keeping of Negroes." *Am I Not a Man and a Brother: The Antislavery Crusade of Revolutionary America.* Ed. Roger Bruns. New York: Chelsea House Publishers, 1977.
Wright, Richard. *Twelve Million Black Voices.* New York: Viking, 1941.
X, Malcolm. "The Ballot or the Bullet." *Malcolm X Speaks: Selected Speeches and Statements.* Ed. George Breitman. New York: Grove Weidenfeld, 1990.
———. *By Any Means Necessary: Speeches, Interviews, and a Letter.* Ed. George Breitman. New York: Pathfinder, 1970.

SECONDARY SOURCES

Anderson, Benedict. *Imagined Communities.* New York: Verso, 1991.
Appiah, Kwame Anthony. *Cosmopolitanism: Ethics in a World of Strangers.* New York: W. W. Norton and Company, 2006.
Aptheker, Herbert. *American Negro Slave Revolts.* New York: International Publishers, 1993.
Armitage, David. *The Declaration of Independence: A Global History.* Cambridge: Harvard UP, 2007.

Arneil, Barbara. "Trade, Plantations, and Property: John Locke and the Economic Defense of Colonialism." *Journal of the History of Ideas* 5.4 (October 1994): 591–609.

Ashcraft, Richard. "John Locke's Library: Portrait of an Intellectual." *John Locke: Critical Assessments*. Ed. Richard Ashcraft. New York: Routledge, 1995.

Axelrad, Jacob. *Philip Freneau: Champion of Democracy*. Austin: U of Texas P, 1967.

Ball, Edward. *Slaves in the Family*. New York: Ballantine Books, 1998.

Barge, Laura. "Changing Forms of the Pastoral in Southern Poetry." *Southern Literary Journal* 26 (fall 1993): 30–41.

Barthes, Roland. *S/Z*. Trans. Richard Miller. New York: Hill and Wang, 1974.

Belaúnde, Víctor Andrés, and W. Rex Crawford. "Human Rights in the Cultural Tradition of Spanish America." *Annals of the American Academy of Political and Social Science* 243 (January 1946): 82–86. JSTOR. Denison U Library, Granville, Ohio. Accessed May 20, 2008 http://jstor.org.

Birdsall, W. F. "A Right to Communicate as an Open Work." *Media Development* 53.1 (2006): 41–46. Accessed January 15, 2007 http://www.wacc.org.uk/wacc/publications/media_development.

Blassingame, John W. "Using the Testimony of Ex-Slaves: Approaches and Problems." *The Slave's Narrative*. Ed. Charles T. Davis and Henry Louis Gates Jr. New York: Oxford UP, 1985.

Bove, Paul A. "Discourse." *Critical Terms for Literary Study*. Ed. Frank Lentricchia and Thomas McLaughlin. Chicago: U of Chicago P, 1995.

Bowden, Mary Weatherspoon. *Philip Freneau*. Boston: Twayne Publishers, 1976.

Brown, Ira V. "Pennsylvania's Antislavery Pioneers, 1688–1776." *Pennsylvania History* 55.2 (April 1988): 59–77.

Bullitt, John M. *Jonathan Swift and the Anatomy of Satire*. Cambridge: Harvard UP, 1966.

Busick, Sean R. *A Sober Desire for History: William Gilmore Simms as Historian*. Columbia: U of South Carolina P, 2005.

Butler, Judith. "Afterword: The Humanities in Human Rights—Critique, Language, Politics." *PMLA* 121.5 (October 2006): 1658–1661.

———. *Excitable Speech: A Politics of the Performative*. New York: Routledge, 1997.

Byerman, Keith. "Black Voices, White Stories: An Intertextual Analysis of Thomas Nelson Page and Charles Waddell Chesnutt." *North Carolina Literary Review* 8 (1999): 98–105.

Calhoun, Richard James. "William J. Grayson, Autobiographer." *Witness to Sorrow: The Antebellum Autobiography of William J. Grayson*. Ed. Richard James Calhoun. Columbia: U of South Carolina P, 1990.

Callcott, George H. "Omar Ibn Seid, a Slave Who Wrote an Autobiography in Arabic." *Journal of Negro History* 39.1 (January 1954): 58–63.

Campbell, Karlyn Kohrs. "The Power of Hegemony: Capitalism and Racism in the 'Nadir of Negro History.'" *Rhetoric and Community: Studies in Unity and Fragmentation*. Ed. J. Michael Hogan. Columbia: U of South Carolina P, 1998.

Césaire, Aimé. *Discourse on Colonialism*. Trans. Joan Pinkham. New York: Monthly Review Press, 2000.
Christmann, James. "Dialect's Double-Murder: Thomas Nelson Page's *In Ole Virginia*." *American Literary Realism* 32.3 (spring 2000): 269–274.
Coppe, Abiezer. *Fiery Flying Roll: A Collection of Ranter Writings of the Seventeenth Century*. Ed. Nigel Smith. London: Junction Books, 1983.
Cornelius, Janet. "'We Slipped and Learned to Read': Slave Accounts of the Literacy Process, 1830–1865." *Phylon: The Atlanta University Review of Race and Culture* 44.3 (1983): 171–186.
Cranston, Maurice. *John Locke: A Biography*. London: Lonmans, Green, and Co., 1957.
———. *What Are Human Rights?* London: Bodley Head, 1973.
Creel, Margaret Washington. *A Peculiar People: Slave Religion and Community-Culture Among the Gullahs*. New York: New York UP, 1988.
Curti, Merle. "The Great Mr. Locke: America's Philosopher, 1783–1861." *John Locke: Critical Assessments*. Vol. 1. Ed. Richard Ashcraft. New York: Routledge, 1991.
d'Arcy, Jean. "Direct Broadcast Satellites and Right to Communicate." *EBU Review* 118B (November 1969): 13–18.
Dargan, John J. *School History of South Carolina*. Columbia: State Company, 1906.
Davis, Charles T., and Henry Louis Gates Jr., eds. *The Slave's Narrative*. New York: Oxford UP, 1985.
Davis, David Brion. *The Problem of Slavery in the Age of Revolution, 1770–1823*. New York: Oxford UP, 1999.
———. *The Problem of Slavery in Western Culture*. New York: Oxford UP, 1966.
Davis, Natalie Zemon. "Printing and the People." *Re-Thinking Popular Culture: Contemporary Perspectives in Cultural Studies*. Ed. Chandra Mukerji and Michael Schudson. Berkeley: U of California P, 1991.
Davis, Thomas J. *A Rumor of Revolt: The "Great Negro Plot" in Colonial New York*. New York: Free Press, 1985.
De Beer, E. S., ed. *The Correspondence of John Locke*. Oxford: Clarendon Press, 1976.
Diani, Mario. *Social Movements and Networks*. New York: Oxford, 2003.
Diouf, Sylviane A. *Servants of Allah: African Muslims Enslaved in the Americas*. New York: New York UP, 1998.
Donnan, Elizabeth, ed. *Documents Illustrative of the History of the Slave Trade to America*. New York: Octagon Books, 1965.
Donnelly, Jack. *Universal Human Rights in Theory and Practice*. Ithaca, N.Y.: Cornell UP, 2003.
Drake, Thomas E. *Quakers and Slavery in America*. Gloucester, Mass.: Peter Smith, 1965.
Duncan, John Donald. "Servitude and Slavery in Colonial South Carolina, 1670–1776." Diss., Emory U, 1972.
Dunn, John. *The Political Thought of John Locke*. Cambridge: Cambridge UP, 1969.
Edgar, Walter. *South Carolina: A History*. Columbia: U of South Carolina P, 1998.

Elliot, Emory. *Revolutionary Writers: Literature and Authority in the New Republic, 1725–1810*. New York: Oxford UP, 1986.
Escott, Paul D. "The Art and Science of Reading WPA Slave Narratives." *The Slave's Narrative*. Ed. Charles T. Davis and Henry Louis Gates Jr. New York: Oxford UP, 1985.
Fanon, Frantz. *Black Skins, White Masks*. Trans. Charles L. Markmann. New York: Grove Press, 1967.
Farr, James. "'So Vile and Miserable an Estate': The Problem of Slavery in Locke's Political Thought." *Political Theory* 14. 2 (May 1986): 263–289.
Fennell, Edward C. "Marker Recognizes 1739 Slave Rebellion." *Charleston Post and Courier*. September 9, 2006.
Ferguson, Robert A. *The American Enlightenment: 1750–1820*. Cambridge: Harvard UP, 1997.
Foner, Eric. *Tom Paine and Revolutionary America*. New York: Oxford UP, 1976.
Foucault, Michel. *The Archaeology of Knowledge*. Trans. A. M. Sheridan Smith. New York: Pantheon Books, 1972.
———. *Discipline and Punish*. Trans. Alan Sheridan. New York: Pantheon, 1977.
———. "The Discourse on Language." Trans. Rupert Sawyer. *The Archaeology of Knowledge*. New York: Pantheon Books, 1972.
Franklin, John Hope. *From Slavery to Freedom*. New York: Vintage Books, 1947.
Fraser, Nancy. "Rethinking the Public Sphere: A Contribution to the Critique of Actually Existing Democracy." *Justice Interruptus: Critical Reflections on the "Postsocialist" Condition*. New York: Routledge, 1997.
Friedman, Lawrence J. *The White Savage: Racial Fantasies in the Postbellum South*. Englewood Cliffs, N.J.: Prentice Hall, 1970.
Gaston, Paul. *The New South Creed: A Study in Southern Mythmaking*. New York: Knopf, 1970.
Gates, Henry Louis, Jr. *Figures in Black*. New York: Oxford UP, 1987.
———. *The Signifying Monkey*. New York: Oxford UP, 1988.
Gates, Henry Louis, Jr., and Nellie Y. McKay. "From Phillis Wheatley to Toni Morrison: The Flowering of African-American Literature." *Journal of Blacks in Higher Education* 14 (winter 1996–97): 95–100.
Gay, Peter. *The Enlightenment: An Interpretation*. Vol. 2. New York: Norton, 1969.
Gebhard, Caroline. "Reconstructing Southern Manhood: Race, Sentimentality, and Camp in the Plantation Myth." *Haunted Bodies: Gender and Southern Texts*. Ed. Susan V. Donaldson and Anne Goodwyn Jones. Charlottesville: UP of Virginia, 1997. 132–155.
Genovese, Eugene. *From Rebellion to Revolution: Afro-American Slave Revolts in the Making of the Modern World*. Baton Rouge: Louisiana State UP, 1979.
———. *Roll, Jordan, Roll: The World the Slaves Made*. New York: Vintage Books, 1974.
Gilroy, Paul. *The Black Atlantic*. Cambridge: Harvard UP, 1993.
Glausser, Wayne. "Three Approaches to Locke and the Slave Trade." *Journal of the History of Ideas* 51.2 (April–June 1990): 199–216.

BIBLIOGRAPHY

Gobodo-Madikizela, Pumla. *A Human Being Died That Night: A South African Woman Confronts the Legacy of Apartheid.* Boston: Houghton Mifflin, 2003.
Goldie, Mark, ed. *Locke: Political Essays.* New York: Cambridge UP, 1997.
Greene, Donald. *The Age of Exuberance.* New York: Random House, 1970.
Greenspan, Ezra. "Addressing or Redressing the Magazine Audience: Edmund Quincy's *Wensley*." *Periodical Literature in Nineteenth-Century America.* Ed. Kenneth M. Price and Susan Belasco Smith. Charlottesville: UP of Virginia, 1995.
Gross, Theodore. *Thomas Nelson Page.* New York: Twayne, 1967.
Habermas, Jürgen. *The Structural Transformation of the Public Sphere.* Trans. Thomas Burger. Cambridge, Mass.: MIT Press, 1989.
Harding, Vincent. *The Other American Revolution.* Los Angeles: Center for Afro-American Studies, University of California–Los Angeles, 1980.
———. *There Is a River.* New York: Vintage, 1981.
Herskovits, Melville J. *The Myth of the Negro Past.* Boston: Beacon Press, 1990.
Hill, Christopher. *The Century of Revolution, 1603–1714.* New York: Norton, 1961.
———. *The World Turned Upside Down.* New York: Penguin, 1972.
Hirsch, Jerrold. *Portrait of America: A Cultural History of the Federal Writers' Project.* Chapel Hill: U of North Carolina P, 2003.
Hochschild, Adam. *Bury the Chains: Prophets and Rebels in the Fight to Free an Empire's Slaves.* Boston: Houghton Mifflin, 2005.
———. *King Leopold's Ghost.* New York: Houghton Mifflin Company, 1999.
Hoffer, Peter Charles. *Sensory Worlds in Early America.* Baltimore: Johns Hopkins UP, 2003.
Holstun, James. *Ehud's Dagger.* New York: Verso, 2000.
Howe, George. *History of the Presbyterian Church in South Carolina.* Columbia: Duffie and Chapman, 1870.
Howe, M. A. DeWolfe. "Biographer's Bait: A Reminder of Edmund Quincy." *Proceedings of the Massachusetts Historical Society* 68 *(1944–46)*. Boston: Massachusetts Historical Society, 1950.
Hubbell, Jay B. *The South in American Literature: 1607–1900.* Durham: Duke UP, 1954.
Hunt, Lynn. *Inventing Human Rights: A History.* New York: W. W. Norton, 2007.
Iannini, Christopher. "'The Itinerant Man': Crevecoeur's Caribbean, Raynal's Revolution, and the Fate of Atlantic Cosmopolitanism." *William and Mary Quarterly* 61.2 (April 2004): 201–234.
Inscoe, John C. "Carolina Slave Names: An Index of Acculturation." *Journal of Southern History* 49 (November 1983): 527–554.
Ishay, Micheline R. *The History of Human Rights.* Berkeley: U of California P, 2004.
Jackson, Harvey H. "Hugh Bryan and the Evangelical Movement in Colonial SC." *William and Mary Quarterly* 43.4 (October 1986): 594–614.
James, C.L.R. *The Black Jacobins.* New York: Random House, 1963.
Johnson, Edward A. *A School History of the Negro Race in America.* Raleigh: Edwards & Broughton Printers, 1890.

Jordan, Winthrop. *White over Black*. Chapel Hill: U of North Carolina P, 1968.
Joyce, James Avery. *The New Politics of Human Rights* New York: St. Martin's Press, 1978.
Kaye, Harvey J. *Thomas Paine and the Promise of America*. New York: Farrar, Straus, and Giroux, 2005.
King, Vincent. "'Foolish Talk 'bout Freedom': Simms's Vision of America in *The Yemassee*." *Studies in the Novel* 25.2 (summer 2003): 139–149. Literary Reference Center. EBSCOhost. Denison U Library, Granville, Ohio. Accessed May 20, 2008 http://web.ebscohost.com.
Lambert, Frank. "'I Saw the Book Talk': Slave Readings of the First Great Awakening." *Journal of African American History* 87 (winter 2002): 12–25.
Landers, Jane. *Black Society in Spanish Florida*. Urbana: U of Illinois P, 1999.
Lane, Suzanne. "Black Thunder's Call for a Conjure Response to American Negro Slavery." *African American Review* 37 (winter 2003): 295–309.
Laslett, Peter. "Introduction." *Two Treatises of Government*. Cambridge: Cambridge UP, 1988.
Lepore, Jill. *New York Burning: Liberty, Slavery, and Conspiracy in Eighteenth-Century Manhattan*. New York: Vintage Books, 2005.
Linebaugh, Peter, and Marcus Rediker. *The Many-Headed Hydra: Sailors, Slaves, Commoners, and the Hidden History of the Revolutionary Atlantic*. Boston: Beacon, 2000.
Logue, Cal M. "Transcending Coercion: The Communicative Strategies of Black Slaves on Antebellum Plantations." *Quarterly Journal of Speech* 67 (1981): 31–46.
Lovink, Geert. *Uncanny Networks*. Cambridge: MIT Press, 2002.
Martin, Matthew R. "The Two-Faced New South: The Plantation Tales of Thomas Nelson Page and Charles W. Chesnutt." *Southern Literary Journal* 30.2 (spring 1998): 17–36.
Marx, Leo. *The Machine in the Garden*. London: Oxford UP, 1964.
Mason, Julian D., Jr. "Introduction." *The Poems of Phyllis Wheatley*. Chapel Hill: U of North Carolina P, 1989.
May, Larry, Christine Sistare, and Jonathan Schonsheck. *Liberty, Equality, and Plurality*. Lawrence: UP of Kansas, 1997.
McCrady, Edward. *The History of South Carolina under the Royal Government, 1719–1776*. New York: Macmillan, 1899.
McHenry, Elizabeth. *Forgotten Readers: Recovering the Lost History of African American Literary Societies*. Durham: Duke UP, 2002.
Mintz, Sidney W., and Richard Price. *The Birth of African American Culture: An Anthropological Perspective*. Boston: Beacon Press, 1992.
Moltke-Hansen, David. "Between Plantation and Frontier: The South of William Gilmore Simms." *William Gilmore Simms and the American Frontier*. Ed. John Caldwell Guilds and Caroline Collins. Athens: U of Georgia P, 1997.
Morgan, Phillip D. *Slave Counterpoint: Black Culture in the Eighteenth-Century Chesapeake and Lowcountry*. Chapel Hill: U of North Carolina P, 1998.

Mullin, Gerald W. *Flight and Rebellion: Slave Resistance in Eighteenth-Century Virginia.* New York: Oxford UP, 1972.

Mullin, Michael. *Africa in America: Slave Acculturation and Resistance in the American South and the British Caribbean, 1736–1831.* Urbana: U of Illinois P, 1992.

Nash, Gary. *Red, White, and Black.* Englewood Cliffs, N.J.: Prentice Hall, 1974.

Nicholson, Harold. *The Age of Reason: The Eighteenth Century in Reason and Violence.* Garden City, N.Y.: Doubleday, 1960.

Oliphant, Mary C. Simms. *The Simms History of South Carolina: For Use in Schools.* Columbia: The State Company, 1932.

Olwell, Robert. *Masters, Slaves, and Subjects: The Culture of Power in the South Carolina Low Country, 1740–1790.* Ithaca, N.Y.: Cornell UP, 1998.

Parker, Mattie Erma Edwards. *North Carolina Charters and Constitutions, 1578–1698.* Raleigh: Carolina Charter Tercentenary Commission, 1963.

Parks, Edd Winfield. *Henry Timrod.* New York: Twayne, 1964.

Paulson, William. *Literary Culture in a World Transformed.* Ithaca, N.Y.: Cornell UP, 2001.

Pearson, Edward A. "'A Countryside Full of Flames': A Reconsideration of the Stono Rebellion and Slave Rebelliousness in the Early Eighteenth-Century South Carolina Lowcountry." *Slavery and Abolition* 17 (August 1996): 22–50.

Pendleton, Emily, and Milton Ellis. "Philenia: The Life and Works of Sarah Wentworth Morton, 1759–1846." *Maine Bulletin* 34.4 (December 1931).

Phillips, U. B. *American Negro Slavery.* Baton Rouge: Louisiana State UP, 1966.

Quarles, Benjamin. "The Revolutionary War as a Black Declaration of Independence." *Slavery and Freedom in the Age of the American Revolution.* Ed. Ira Berlin and Ronald Hoffman. Charlottesville: UP of Virginia, 1983.

Rampersad, Arnold, "Introduction to the 1992 Edition." *Black Thunder: Gabriel's Revolt, Virginia, 1800.* Arna Bontemps. Boston: Beacon Press, 1992.

Ramsay, David. *History of South Carolina: From its first Settlement in 1670 to the Year 1808.* Newberry, S.C.: W. J. Duffie, 1858. Repr. Spartanburg, S.C.: Reprint Co., 1959–60.

Rath, Richard Cullen. *How Early America Sounded.* Ithaca, N.Y.: Cornell UP, 2003.

Reid-Pharr, Robert. "Violent Ambiguity: Martin Delany, Bourgeois Sadomasochism, and the Production of a Black National Masculinity." *Representing Black Men.* Ed. Marcellus Blount and George P. Cunningham. New York: Routledge, 1996.

Reynolds, David. *John Brown, Abolitionist.* New York: Alfred A. Knopf, 2005.

Richards, Jeffery H. "Samuel Davies and the Trans-Atlantic Campaign for Slave Literacy in Virginia." *Virginia Magazine of History and Biography* 3.4 (2003): 333–378.

Ridgely, J. V. *William Gilmore Simms.* New York: Twayne, 1962.

Robertson, David. *Denmark Vesey.* New York: Alfred A. Knopf, 1999.

Rogers, George C. *Charleston in the Age of Pinckneys.* Norman: U of Oklahoma P, 1969.

Rorty, Richard. "Human Rights, Rationality, and Sentimentality." *On Human Rights: Oxford Amnesty Lectures.* Ed. Stephen Shute and Susan Hurley. New York: Basic Books, 1993. Repr. *The Human Rights Reader.* Ed. Micheline Ishay. New York: Routledge, 1997.

Rubin, Louis D., Jr. *The Edge of the Swamp: A Study in the Literature and Society of the Old South.* Baton Rouge: Louisiana State UP, 1989.

Rush, Benjamin. "Biographical Anecdotes of Benjamin Lay." *Essays, Literary, Moral, and Philosophical.* Philadelphia: Thomas and Samuel F. Bradford, 1798.

Said, Edward. *Orientalism.* New York: Vintage Books, 1978.

Sale, Maggie Montesinos. *The Slumbering Volcano: American Slave Ship Rebellions and the Production of Rebellious Masculinity.* Durham: Duke UP, 1997.

Scheuner, Ulrich. "Comparison of the Jurisprudence of National Courts with that of the Organs of the Convention as Regards Other Rights." *Human Rights in National and International Law.* Ed. A. H. Robertson. Dobbs Ferry, N.Y.: Oceana Publications, 1968.

Scott, James C. *Domination and the Arts of Resistance: Hidden Transcripts.* New Haven: Yale UP, 1990.

Sherwin, Oscar. *Prophet of Liberty: The Life and Times of Wendell Phillips.* New York: Bookman Associates, 1958.

Shuffleton, Frank. "Introduction to *Notes on the State of Virginia.*" *Notes on the State of Virginia.* New York: Penguin Books, 1999.

Sidbury, James. *Ploughshares into Swords: Race, Rebellion, and Identity in Gabriel's Virginia, 1730–1810.* New York: Cambridge UP, 1997.

Sirmans, Eugene M. *Colonial South Carolina: A Political History, 1663–1763.* Chapel Hill: U of North Carolina P, 1966.

———. "The Legal Status of the Slave in South Carolina." *Journal of Southern History* 28 (1962): 462–473.

Smith, Mark M. "Remembering Mary, Shaping Revolt: Reconsidering the Stono Rebellion." *Journal of Southern History* 68.3 (August 2001): 513–534.

———, ed. *Stono: Documenting and Interpreting a Southern Slave Revolt.* Columbia: U of South Carolina P, 2005.

Soderlund, Jean R. *Quakers and Slavery: A Divided Spirit.* Princeton: Princeton UP, 1985.

Stampp, Kenneth M. *The Peculiar Institution.* New York: Vintage Books, 1956.

Staples, Brent. "Why Slave-Era Barriers to Black Literacy Still Matter." *New York Times.* January 1, 2006.

Starr, Paul. *The Creation of the Media: Political Origins of Modern Communications.* New York: Basic Books, 2004.

Stepto, Robert B. "Storytelling in Early Afro-American Fiction: Frederick Douglass's 'The Heroic Slave.'" *Critical Essays on Frederick Douglass.* Ed. William L. Andrews. Boston: G. K. Hall and Company, 1991.

Stewart, James Brewer. *Holy Warriors: The Abolitionists and American Slavery.* New York: Hill and Wang, 1976.

Storey, John. *An Introduction to Cultural Theory*. 2nd ed. Athens: U of Georgia P, 1998.
Stuckey, Sterling. *Slave Culture: Nationalist Theory and the Foundations of Black America*. New York: Oxford UP, 1987.
Suggs, Jon-Christian. *Whispered Consolations: Law and Narrative in African American Life*. Ann Arbor: U of Michigan P, 2000.
Sundquist, Eric J. *The Hammers of Creation: Folk Culture in Modern African-American Fiction*. Athens: U of Georgia P, 1992.
———. "Slavery, Revolution, and the American Renaissance." *The American Renaissance Reconsidered*. Ed. Walter Benn Michaels and Donald E. Pease. Baltimore: The Johns Hopkins UP, 1985.
Suttles, William C., Jr. "African Religious Survivals as Factors in American Slave Revolts." *Journal of Negro History* 56 (April 1971): 97–104.
Taylor, Rupert. "Henry Timrod's Ancestress, Hannah Caeser. *American Literature* 9.4 (1938): 419–430.
Thomas, Laurence Mordekhai. *Vessels of Evil: American Slavery and the Holocaust*. Philadelphia: Temple UP, 1993.
Thornton, John K. *Africa and Africans in the Making of the Atlantic World, 1400–1800*. New York: Cambridge UP, 1998.
———. "African Dimensions of the Stono Rebellion." *American Historical Review* 96.4 (October 1991): 1101–1113.
———. *The Kingdom of Kongo: Civil War and Transition, 1641–1718*. Madison: U of Wisconsin P, 1983.
———. *The Kongolese Saint Anthony: Dona Beatriz Kimpa Vita and the Antonian Movement, 1684–1706*. Cambridge: Cambridge UP, 1998.
Topazio, Virgil W. *Voltaire: A Critical Study of His Works*. New York: Random House, 1967.
Tourgee, Albion W. "The South as a Field for Fiction." *Forum* 6 (December 1888): 404–413.
Tuckness, Alex. "Rethinking the Intolerant Locke." *American Journal of Political Science* 46.2 (April 2002): 288–298.
Turner, Lorenzo Dow. "The Anti-Slavery Movement Prior to the Abolition of the African Slave Trade." *Journal of Negro History* 14.4 (October 1929): 373–402.
Twelve Southerners. *I'll Take My Stand: The South and the Agrarian Tradition*. New York: Harper and Row, 1962.
Vaux, Roberts. *Memoirs of the Lives of Benjamin Lay and Ralph Sandiford; Two of the Earliest Public Advocates for the Emancipation of the Enslaved Africans*. Philadelphia: Solomon W. Conrad, 1815.
Wakelyn, Jon L. *The Politics of a Literary Man: William Gilmore Simms*. Westport, Conn.: Greenwood P, 1973.
Wallace, Robert K. "Douglass, Melville, Quincy, Shaw: Epistolary Convergences." *Leviathan: A Journal of Melville Studies* 6:2 (October 1, 2004): 63–71.
Walter, Krista. "Trappings of Nationalism in Frederick Douglass's *The Heroic Slave*." *African American Review* 34 (summer 2000): 233–247.

Warner, Michael. *The Letters of the Republic.* Cambridge, Mass.: Harvard UP, 1990.

———. *Publics and Counterpublics.* Cambridge: MIT Press, 2002.

Wax, Donald. "'The Great Risque We Run': The Aftermath of the Slave Rebellion at Stono, South Carolina, 1739–1745." *Journal of Negro History* 67.2 (summer 1982): 136–147.

Weinauer, Ellen. "Writing Revolt in the Wake of Nat Turner: Frederick Douglass and the Construction of Black Domesticity in 'The Heroic Slave.'" *Studies in American Fiction* 33 (autumn 2005): 193–202.

Weir, Robert M. *Colonial South Carolina: A History.* Columbia: U of South Carolina P, 1997.

Williams, Kathleen. *Jonathan Swift and the Age of Compromise.* Lawrence: U of Kansas P, 1967.

Wilson, Edmund. *Patriotic Gore: Studies in the Literature of the Civil War.* New York: Oxford UP, 1962.

Wood, Peter. *Black Majority: Negroes in Colonial South Carolina from 1670 through the Stono Rebellion.* New York: Alfred A. Knopf, 1974.

Woodson, Carter G. *The Negro in Our History.* Washington, D.C.: Associated Publishers, 1922.

Woodward, C. Vann. "History from Slave Sources." *The Slave's Narrative.* Ed. Charles T. Davis and Henry Louis Gates Jr. New York: Oxford UP, 1985.

Wroth, Lawrence C. *The Colonial Printer.* New York: Dover, 1994.

X, Malcolm. *By Any Means Necessary: Speeches, Interviews, and a Letter.* Ed. George Breitman. New York: Pathfinder Press, 1970.

———. *The Speeches of Malcolm X at Harvard.* Ed. Archie Epps. New York: William Morrow & Company, 1968.

Yetman, Norman. R. "The Background of the Slave Narrative Collection." *American Quarterly* 19.3 (autumn 1967): 534–553.

Ziff, Larzer. *Writing in the New Nation: Prose, Print, and Politics in the Early United States.* New Haven: Yale UP, 1991.

Zinn, Howard. *A People's History of the United States.* New York: Perennial Classics, 1999.

INDEX

abolition/abolitionists, 45, 57–58, 93, 112, 154–55, 161–62
"Account of the Negroe Insurrection in South Carolina, An," 72, 74, 78
Adams, John, 41
Adams, Samuel, 38
Africa, 75, 77
Agrippa, 91
Aiken, Conrad, 169
Akin, James, 91
Alabama, 133, 174
Alexander, Ann Tuke, 63–64, 154
Allen, James Lane, 163
All Slave-Keepers that Keep the Innocent in Bondage, Apostates (Lay), 61
American Negro Slave Revolts (Aptheker), 176
American Negro Slavery (Phillips), 164
Anderson, Benedict, 13, 14, 116
Angola, 75
Anthony, Saint, 80
Antigua, 74, 83
Appeal . . . to the Colored Citizens of the World (Walker), 118–19
Appiah, Kwame Anthony, 132
Aptheker, Herbert, 74, 89, 90, 94, 176
Arkansas, 129
Armitage, David, 43
Arneil, Barbara, 21
Ashley, Lord. *See* Cooper, Anthony Ashley

Bahamas, 74
Ball, Edward, 91, 185n6
Baltimore, Md., 126
Barbados, 55, 58, 62, 67, 68, 78, 83, 98
Barthes, Roland, 180
Bathurst, Robert, 70
Beccaria, Cesare, 6
Bee, Captain, 71
Belaúnde, Víctor Andrés, 189n26
Bellow, Saul, 169
Benezet, Anthony, 49, 58, 63
Bennett, Rolla, 106
Bethune, Mary McLeod, 174
Bible, 55, 57, 62, 64, 82, 83, 88, 106, 131, 135, 154–55; Acts, 88; Exodus, 88; Psalms, 114
Bill of Rights, 37
Birdsall, William F., 181
Birth of a Nation, 164
Black Majority (Wood), 73, 177
Black Thunder (Bontemps), 133–39
Blake; or, The Huts of America (Delany), 120, 125–32, 135
Blassingame, John W., 170
Boltzius, Johann Martin, 91
Bontemps, Arna, 133–39, 141, 163, 169
Boston, Mass., 96, 109, 111, 112, 119
Boston Gazette, 76
Boston Weekly News-Letter, 69, 71
Bove, Paul A., 7
Boyd, Nellie, 105

INDEX

Brackenridge, Hugh Henry, 45
Brief Examination of the Practice of Our Times, A (Sandiford), 58–59
Brown, John, 161, 162
Brown, Sterling, 170
Bryan, Hugh, 88
Bull, William, 3, 69, 70–71, 98, 172, 188n10
Bullock, James, 71
Bunche, Ralph, 174
Busick, Sean R., 152, 153
Butler, Judith, 43, 64, 84

Calvert, Giles, 32
Canada, 130
Candide (Voltaire), 27
Catholicism, 79, 80, 81
Cato, George, 93–94, 95, 120, 134, 161, 169, 171, 172, 173
Cato/Jemmy. *See* Jemmy/Cato
Césaire, Aimé, 101
Charles II, 66
Charleston, S.C., 69, 104, 111, 113, 118–19, 126, 142, 144, 148
Charleston Post and Courier, 182
Charleston School, 10, 142–43, 161, 163
Charles Town, S.C., 52, 53, 67, 70, 75–76, 88, 91, 99, 104
Cherokee, 100
Chickasaw, 132
Choctaw, 132
Christianity, 47, 57–58, 59, 89, 112, 114
Civil War, 163, 165, 177
Clare (slave ship), 92
Clark, Septima, 174
Clarkson, Laurence, 32
Cole, Thomas, 114
College of Charleston, 177
Colleton, Peter, 21, 24
Columbia, S.C., 165, 171
Common Sense (Paine), 38, 39–40
communication rights, 9, 34, 37, 181–82
Confederate States of America, 144
Congress, U.S., 52
Constitution, U.S., 37, 44, 45, 132

Cooper, David, 47–49
Cooper, Anthony Ashley, 20, 21, 22, 24
Coppe, Abiezer, 32, 58
Cornelius, Janet, 82, 83
Cornish, Samuel, 117
Cranston, Maurice, 22
Craven, Charles, 149
Creel, Margaret, 80
Crèvecoeur, J. Hector St. Jean de, 42, 52, 53–54, 105
Cuba, 126, 129, 131

Daily Courier (Charleston), 144
d'Arcy, Jean, 103
Dargan, John J., 193n14
Darien, Ga., 65
Daughters of the Confederacy, 177
Davis, Charles T., 190n5
Davis, David Brion, 25, 43, 56, 59, 60
Davis, Natalie Zemon, 13, 74
Declaration of Independence, 41, 42, 43–44, 45, 49, 107, 108, 109, 110, 117
Delany, Martin R., 10, 120, 125–33, 139, 141, 156
Diani, Mario, 73, 189n18
Diouf, Sylviane, 113
"Discourse of Language, The" (Foucault), 8
Discourse on Colonialism (Césaire), 101
Discourse on Inequality (Rousseau), 27
Dona Beatriz Kimpa Vita, 80, 87–88
Donnan, Elizabeth, 69, 93, 190n34
Donnelly, Jack, 33
Douglass, Frederick, 10, 117, 119–25, 132, 134, 141, 156, 273
Drake, Thomas, 60
Dred (Stowe), 161
Dred Scott case, 125
drums, 4, 77, 78, 101, 105
Du Bois, W. E. B., 107–8, 109, 127, 174
Dulaney, Marvin, 177
Duncan, John Donald, 92

Eco, Umberto, 181
Edgar, Walter, 21, 73, 142, 152
Edinburgh, 87

- 212 -

INDEX

education, 82. *See also* literacy
Elkins, Fairy, 105
Elliot, Thomas, 70, 99, 167
Ellison, Ralph, 169
England, 13, 30–31, 39, 45, 143, 155
English language, 81–83
Enlightenment, 5, 6, 27, 28, 37
Equiano, Olaudah, 10, 67–68, 110
Escott, Paul D., 170

Fanshawe, Charles, 72, 92
Farr, James, 25
Fayetteville, N.C., 113
Federal Writers' Project, 82, 93, 134, 169
Fennell, Edward C., 182
Ferguson, Robert A., 37, 40, 42, 43, 44, 51, 185n1
Filmer, Robert, 15, 16
First Treatise on Civil Government (Locke), 15
Fisk University, 134, 139
Fleming, George, 105
Florida, 69, 71, 78, 86, 96, 97
folk songs, African American, 108
Foner, Eric, 40, 41
Fortune, T. Thomas, 117
Foucault, Michel, 7–8, 44, 63
Fox, George, 61
France, 13, 18, 136
Franklin, Benjamin, 4, 35, 61, 63, 96
Franklin, John Hope, 38, 184n6
Fraser, Nancy, 29
Freedom's Journal, 117
"French Declaration of the Rights of Man and of the Citizen," 34, 102, 191n6
French Huguenots, 18
Fugitive Slave Law, 123
Fundamental Constitutions of Carolina, 20–24, 30, 66
Furly, Benjamin, 25

Garden, Alexander, 82
Garrison, William Lloyd, 156
Gates, Henry Louis, Jr., 102, 190n5
Gay, Peter, 28, 29
Genovese, Eugene D., 190n35

Gentleman's Magazine, 87
George III, 42, 43
Georgia, 98
Gibbs, Mr., 70
Gilroy, Paul, 93, 130
globalization, 12
Gobodo-Madikizela, Pumla, 117
Godbold, Hector, 105
Godfrey, Mr., 70
Godin, Benjamin, 69
Gone with the Wind, 164, 165
Gracia Real de Santa de Mose, 78
Gramsci, Antonio, 164
Grant, Charlie, 105
Grayson, Hugh, 149
Grayson, William J., 142, 143–44
Greene, Donald, 17
Greenspan, Ezra, 156
Griffith, D. W., 173, 174
Grimké, Angelina, 10, 154
Grimké, John Faucheraud, 154
Guadeloupe, 74
Guerard, John, 69
Gullah, 82
Gutenberg, Johann, 12

Habermas, Jürgen, 12, 29, 87
Haiti, 87, 89, 90, 110
Halifax, Shawn, 71, 167–69, 183
Hall, Prince, 10, 109–10, 114, 115
Hammond, Samuel, 174
Hampton, Va., 121
Harding, Vincent, 91, 92
Harris, Joel Chandler, 163
Hayne, Paul Hamilton, 142
Haynes, Lemuel, 110, 114
Henry, Patrick, 49, 122
Heroic Slave, The (Douglass), 120, 121–25, 156
Herskovits, Melville J., 74
Hewatt, Alexander, 24, 71, 76, 85–86, 104, 160, 162
Hext, Colonel Hugh, 71
Higginson, Thomas Wentworth, 108
Hill, Christopher, 32, 185n11

INDEX

Hill, Richard, 69
Hinrichs, Captain Johann, 24
Historical Account of the Rise and Progress of the Colonies of South Carolina and Georgia, A (Hewatt), 24
History of South Carolina (Ramsay), 162
History of South Carolina, The (Simms), 152
Hochschild, Adam, 28, 98
Hoffer, Peter Charles, 78
Holland, 13
Holstun, James, 31
Howe, George, 72
Howe, M. A. DeWolfe, 156, 162
Hughes, Langston, 117
human rights, 5–6, 7, 14, 27, 34, 93, 135, 173; in *Black Thunder*, 136; in *Blake*, 128, 132; and the Constitution, 44; discourse, 8, 20, 95, 107, 112, 114, 117, 124, 130, 139–40, 173; in the Revolution, 38, 39–40
Hunt, Lynn, 5–6
Hurmence, Belinda, 68, 109
Hurston, Zora Neale, 169

Iannini, Christopher, 53
Inabinett, Curtis, 178–80, 181
Industrial Revolution, 143
Inscoe, John C., 171
Inventing Human Rights: A History (Hunt), 5
Ishay, Michelle, 6

Jacobs, Harriet, 117, 118
Jamaica, 74, 78, 100, 161
James, C. L. R., 85
Jefferson, Thomas, 10, 41, 42, 49–52, 109, 110, 119, 122, 127, 133, 157; and slavery, 43, 50–51
Jemmy/Cato, 3, 70, 76, 93, 94, 169, 171, 172, 173
Johnson, Edward A., 176
Johnson, Mordecai W., 174
Johnson, Samuel, 27, 45
Johnson, William, 83
Jordan, Winthrop, 190n1

Kalu, Obi, 176
Kaye, Harvey J., 40, 186n2

Keith, George, 57
King, Martin Luther, Jr., 134, 175
King, Vincent, 148, 150
Kingdom of Angola, 75
Kingdom of Kongo, 75, 76, 77, 79, 88
Ku Klux Klan, 173, 181

Ladd, Joseph Brown, 53
Lambert, Frank, 89
Lane, Suzanne, 138
Laslett, Peter, 21, 24
Laurens, Henry, 56
Laurens, John, 56
Lay, Benjamin, 58, 60–63, 64
Legaré, Hugh Swinton, 142
Le Jau, Francis, 55–56, 79, 81–82, 88–89
Lemy, Mr., 70
Lepore, Jill, 90
Leslie, Andrew, 4, 72, 73
"Letter Concerning Toleration" (Locke), 18–20, 22, 32, 33
Letters from an American Farmer (Crèvecoeur), 42, 52
Liberator, 156
Liberty Bell, 23, 156
Linebaugh, Peter, 90
literacy, 4, 81, 82, 83, 94, 101, 105, 106, 116, 119, 135, 155
Locke, John, 6, 9, 15–26, 29, 30, 33, 41, 87, 135, 149; on government, 17; influence of, 38, 48; on revolution, 17; on separation of church and state, 18; and slavery, 20–21, 24–26, 46; and toleration, 19–20, 32
Logue, Cal M., 83
London Magazine, 87
Louisiana, 118
Louis XIV, 29
Lovejoy, Elijah, 156
Lovink, Geert, 188n17
Luther, Martin, 12

Macon, William, Jr., 83
Madison, James, 44
Malcolm X, 175

INDEX

Marshall, Milton, 68
Martyn, Benjamin, 97
Marx, Leo, 49
Mason, Julian D., Jr., 111
Mathews, Peter Bassnett, 115
May, Larry, 27
McHenry, Elizabeth, 116, 117
McKay, Nellie, 102
Middle Passage, 67, 74, 75, 92
Middleton, Delano, 174
Milton, John, 61, 62
minstrelsy, 164
Mississippi, 126
Mite Cast into the Treasury, A (Cooper, D.), 47
Molte-Hansen, David, 147
Montgomery, Ala., 144
More, Thomas, 28
Morgan, Philip D., 74
Morris, Gouverneur, 44
Morton, Sarah Wentworth Apthorp, 56–57
"Mt. Verney: Or, an Incident of Insurrection" (Quincy), 156–63
Mullin, Gerald, 75, 83, 86
Mullin, Michael, 82

Nash, Gary, 100
Nash, Mr., 71
Native Americans, 99–100
Negro Act, 4, 68, 98, 99, 100, 101, 103–4, 105, 115, 154, 165, 180
Negro in Our History, The (Woodson), 176
Neo-Confederates, 177
New Jersey, 91
New Orleans, La., 121, 128, 131
New York, 90, 91
New York City, 100, 145
New-York Weekly Journal, 90, 96
Nicholson, Harold, 184n1
North Carolina, 112, 113
North Carolina University Magazine, 114
Norton Anthology of African American Literature, 102
Notes on the State of Virginia (Jefferson), 49, 50, 127, 157

Obama, Barack, 174
Oglethorpe, James, 11, 86–87, 90, 91, 97
Oliphant, Mary C. Simms, 153
Olwell, Robert, 82, 86, 98
"On African Slavery" (Paine), 46
Orangeburg, S.C., 174, 176
Organization of Afro-American Unity, 175
Orientalism (Said), 7, 164
Otis, James, 46

Page, Thomas Nelson, 57, 163
Paine, Thomas, 10, 35, 38–41, 46–47
Pan-Africanism, 130
Paradise Lost (Milton), 62
Parker, Mattie Erma Edwards, 21
Parks, Edd Winfield, 144, 146
pass system, 4, 100, 101
Patrol Act, 98
Paulson, William, 107
Pearson, Edward, 6, 86, 94, 190n35
Penn, William, 61
Pennsylvania, 58, 60
Pennsylvania Gazette, 72, 96
Petigru, James L., 142
Philadelphia, Pa., 35, 41, 47, 60, 63, 154
Phillips, U. B., 164, 173
Phillips, Wendell, 156, 162
Pinckney, Charles Cotesworth, 111
Pinckney, Eliza Lucas, 83
Pinckney, Henry L., 142
Pinckney, Thomas, 106
plantation myth tradition, 141, 147, 156, 161, 163–65, 175
Pleasants, Robert, 49
Poems on Various Subjects, Religious and Moral (Wheatley), 111
Polite, Sam, 68, 109
Pope, Alexander, 111
Portuguese language, 79, 81
press, the, 116–17
Pringle, Robert, 4, 69, 72, 96
printing press, 13–14, 32
Prosser, Gabriel, 94, 118, 127, 134
publishing industry, 12, 13–14, 36–37

- 215 -

INDEX

Quakers, 58–59, 60–63
Quarles, Benjamin, 191n12
Quincy, Edmund, 10, 23, 156–63, 165
Quincy, Josiah, 156
Qur'an, 113

Rampersad, Arnold, 136
Ramsay, David, 162, 188n13
Randolph, Edmund, 44
Rath, Richard Cullen, 77, 105
Rediker, Marcus, 90
Reid-Pharr, Robert, 127
religion, 131; and slaves, 22–23. *See also* Bible; Christianity
Revolution, American, 37–43, 132, 146, 176
Reynolds, David, 161
rice cultivation, 67, 68, 69
Richards, John, 96
Richmond, Va., 123, 134, 135, 136, 137
Ridgely, J. V., 152
Rights of the Colonists, The (Adams), 38
Robertson, David, 94, 185n6
Rogers, George C., 69
Roosevelt, Franklin D., 169
Rorty, Richard, 192n1
Rose, Thomas, 70, 167
Rousseau, Jean-Jacques, 26–27, 30
Royal African Company, 20, 25, 76, 81
Rubin, Louis D., Jr., 146
Rush, Benjamin, 61
Russell, John, 142
Russell's Magazine, 142, 144
Russworm, John, 117
Rutledge, Edward, 111

Sacheverell, Thomas, 71
Said, Edward, 7, 164
Said, Omar ibn, 10, 112–14
Sale, Maggie Montesinos, 121
Sancho, Ignatius, 50
Sandiford, Ralph, 58–60, 63, 186n11
sangemento, 86
San Miguel de Guadeloupe, 89
Savage, Benjamin, 69

Savannah, Ga., 90, 97
Scheuner, Ulrich, 5
School History of the Negro Race in America, A (Johnson), 176
Scots Magazine, 87
Scott, James C., 113
Scottsboro Boys' trial, 133
Scruggs, Stiles M., 93, 171
Second Treatise on Civil Government (Locke), 16, 18, 20, 25, 33, 38, 41, 48
Security Act, 36, 80
Sellers, Cleveland, 174
Sewall, Samuel, 58, 61, 88
Sherwin, Oscar, 162
Shuffleton, Frank, 50
Sidbury, James, 135
Simkins, Modjeska, 174
Simms, William Gilmore, 10, 57, 142, 145, 147–53, 165, 166, 173
Simms History of South Carolina, The, 153
Sirmans, M. Eugene, 21, 23, 86, 99, 100
slave codes, 4
slave narratives, 119, 120, 134, 144
slave songs, 128
Smith, Adam, 28
Smith, Edward, 119
Smith, Henry, 174
Smith, Mark M., 6, 74, 79, 160, 162
Social Contract, The (Rousseau), 26
Society for Propagation of the Gospel in Foreign Parts (SPG), 55, 72, 73, 79, 82, 83
Society of Friends, 58, 60, 61, 63
Soderlund, Jean, 58
Sons of Confederate Veterans, 177
South Carolina Commons House of Assembly, 4, 84, 85, 97
South Carolina Gazette, 4, 36, 68, 80, 81, 89, 96, 102, 188n11
South Carolina Order of the Confederate Rose, 165, 166
Southern Literary Messenger, 144
Spain, 69, 73, 98, 158
Sprye, Royal, 71
Stamp Act, 36

Stampp, Kenneth, 93, 98, 184n6
Staples, Brent, 191n9
Starr, Paul, 36, 37
St. Augustine, Fla., 78, 86, 90, 96, 97, 98, 149
Stephens, William, 70, 72, 78, 97
Stepto, Robert B., 123
Stewart, James Brewer, 162
St. John, 74
St. Kitts, 78
Stobo, Archibald, 71
Stono Rebellion, as a literary act, 9
Storey, John, 7
Stowe, Harriet Beecher, 120, 121, 133, 141, 143, 144, 147, 161
Stuckey, Sterling, 74, 92
Suggs, Jon-Christian, 95
Sundquist, Eric, 133, 135, 136, 138, 139
Sword and the Distaff, The (*Woodcraft*) (Simms), 147–48

task system, 68
Thomas, Laurence Mordekhai, 6
Thoreau, Henry David, 161
Thornton, John K., 6, 14, 67, 74, 75, 76, 77, 79, 86, 87, 88
Timothy, Lewis, 35–36, 64
Timrod, Henry, 10, 142, 144–47
Toussaint L'Overture, 26, 87, 133, 136
Tuckness, Alex, 19
Turner, Nat, 89, 94, 118, 127, 133
Tuscaroras, 100

Uncle Tom's Cabin (Stowe), 120, 143, 147
United Nations, 5, 174; Covenant on Economic, Social, and Cultural Rights, 103; International Covenant on Civil and Political Rights, 103
United States Magazine, 45
Universal Declaration of Human Rights, 5, 9, 102

Vásquez de Ayllón, Lucas, 66, 89
Vaux, Roberts, 58, 63
Vesey, Denmark, 89, 94, 104, 105–6, 118, 180

Virginia, 43, 49, 136
Virginia Gazette, 83
Voltaire, 27–28, 29, 54

Wakelyn, Jon L., 148
Walker, David, 10, 117, 118–19
Wallace, Mr., 70
Walpole, Horace, 45
Walter, Krista, 122, 125
Warner, Michael, 13, 29, 44
Washington, D.C., 132, 174
Washington, Madison, 121–25
Wax, Donald, 6, 98, 104
Webb, Mathew, 115
Weir, Robert W., 21, 101
Wheatley, Phillis, 10, 50, 111–12, 114
White, Walter, 174
Whitefield, George, 88, 89, 96, 190n3
Whitemarsh, Thomas, 35
Wilson, James, 44
Wilson, Woodrow, 173
Winstanley, Gerrard, 29–30, 31–33, 59, 185n9
Wollstonecraft, Mary, 33
Wood, Peter, 6, 36, 67, 69, 73, 80, 177
Woodson, Carter G., 176
Woodward, C. Vann, 170
Woolman, John, 58, 59
Wragg, Joseph, 69
Wright, Richard, 169

Yeamans, John, 66
Yemassee, 100, 148–50
Yemassee, The (Simms), 148–52
Yemassee War, 148, 152
Yetman, Norman R., 171

Ziff, Larzer, 42, 52
Zinn, Howard, 43, 100, 185n6